# UNTIMELY SACRIFICES

# UNTIMELY SACRIFICES

Work and Death in Finland

**Daena Aki Funahashi**

CORNELL UNIVERSITY PRESS   ITHACA AND LONDON

First published 2023 by Cornell University Press

Library of Congress Cataloging-in-Publication Data

Names: Funahashi, Daena Aki, 1975– author.
Title: Untimely sacrifices : work and death in Finland / Daena Funahashi.
Description: Ithaca [New York] : Cornell University Press, 2023. | Includes
    bibliographical references and index.
Identifiers: LCCN 2022025622 (print) | LCCN 2022025623 (ebook) |
    ISBN 9781501768071 (hardcover) | ISBN 9781501768088 (paperback) |
    ISBN 9781501768095 (pdf) | ISBN 9781501768101 (epub)
Subjects: LCSH: Job stress—Finland. | Burn out (Psychology)—Finland. |
    Employees—Mental health—Finland. | Work environment—Finland—
    Psychological aspects. | Finland—Economic conditions—21st century.
Classification: LCC HF5548.85  (print) | LCC HF5548.85  (ebook) |
    DDC 331.25/6—dc23/eng/20220720
LC record available at https://lccn.loc.gov/2022025622
LC ebook record available at https://lccn.loc.gov/2022025623

To my teacher,
James Siegel

# Contents

# Acknowledgments

Every project demands a sacrifice. Alone in the field, I was haunted by the faces of family and friends whose presence I sorely missed; but it was also in the field that I had the good fortune of meeting the most amazing individuals.

I am indebted to Tarja Aurema and her daughter, Sallí Halén. Tarja introduced me to her wonderful colleagues at Mielenterveyden Keskusliitto. It was through them that I was able to put a face to the complex system of mental health and rehabilitation centers in Finland. Tarja also went out of her way to take me under her wing. She called herself my "*Suomen äiti*," my Finnish mom. Time with Tarja was a time of bliss. Time was no longer splintered in terms of time set apart from the telos of the project and all else besides it. Without this melting together of time, this project would have had no projected life beyond the confines of the project as project.

In Helsinki, Susanna Suckcharoen helped me navigate the city in ways only a Stadilainen could. Annie Chen is a citizen of the world. I thank her and Mikko Kivistö for hosting a wonderful dinner that brought me in touch with Antti Aro and Katariina Salmela-Aro who both generously gave their time to meet with me. I wish also to thank Petra for our conversations about history, burnout, and stress. Without her help in the data collecting process, this project would not be where it is now.

I am completely indebted to the entire staff at Pääskynpesä, especially Ulla Harain-Pehkonen, Marika Kastinen (then Kontturi), Heli Eklund, and the amazing activities leaders Esa and Marjaana for taking it upon themselves to welcome me to the rehabilitation center. Were it not for their generosity and patience, I would never have been able to experience the wonders of Ilomantsi or the significance of place in terms of rehabilitative space. My stay in Ilomantsi was also enhanced by the amazing hospitality of Ritva Korhonen, director of Iljala. Her take on silence as it relates to presence forced me to rethink the significance silence played in the everyday.

I would also like to thank the researchers, staff, and clients at Kaisankoti, Nyyti, the National Public Health Institute (KTL), the Social Insurance Institution of Finland (KELA), and the Finnish Institute of Occupational Health (FIOH) for taking the time to talk to me. Out of these institutions, Jouko Lönnqvist, Juha Lavikainen, Kirsi Ahola, and Jari Hakanen stand out as individuals whose support and insights have been indispensable to the development of my project.

There are those from these spaces I cannot mention by name: the clients. I refer to those receiving treatment, therapy, and rehabilitation using pseudonyms in the pages that follow but besides this anonymity, it is to them that I owe everything. I wish to acknowledge the risk they took by talking to me and sharing with me their stories and their frustrations. My book pales in comparison to the force of their lives. I only here wish to echo their spirit and to honor the time they spent with me.

From the University of Helsinki, I gained invaluable support from Jukka Tontti and Juha Siltala. Pertti Anttonen from the University of Eastern Finland gave me much needed guidance during a moment of self-doubt. Each of these individuals helped me to push the project in directions I could not have pushed by myself. Their exceptional openness and collegiality are qualities of that encounter I still cherish.

Mentors are important. At Cornell, I am extremely grateful for Andrew Willford who saw something in the project when I could not, and for that I cannot thank him enough. Dominic Boyer supported me throughout. His unflagging support for my scholarship pushed me through hard times. Magnus Fiskesjö is one of the most nurturing and generous thinkers I know. I am also thankful for Keith Hjortshoj who took the time to talk to me about the act of writing as more than a technique. His support is exceptional in that he did not have to give it. Exceptional also has been James Siegel. Without him I would not have been an anthropologist. He has been more than a teacher. He has been the inspiration for anything good that comes of this book.

Besides my immediate mentors, I am also inspired by Hoon Song. He is one of those special individuals who can teach without teaching. Reading and thinking with him have been the most rewarding moments in my intellectual development—and something I hope to continue to do. I thank him for keeping what fascinates me about anthropology alive. Peter Redfield has encouraged me throughout. Our conversations on the impact of technological developments on labor over lunches at "the Institute" have been one of the best experiences I have had in New Jersey. Danilyn Rutherford is someone I wish to thank for providing me with a model for how to be nurturing and generous in an increasingly competitive academic environment. I am always amazed by her energy and her willingness to give her time and energy to junior scholars such as myself. I cannot thank her enough for participating in my book workshop. I wish to thank Michael Herzfeld for his wisdom and his advice. Another person I wish to thank for their generosity is Erik Harms. Scholarship for me is never divorced from how you live. Erik exemplifies this spirit. He has reached out in ways that no one else has. I am in awe of someone who writes and lives with the politics and ethics as he does.

Learning is never complete without kindred spirits. A friend, but also someone I have always admired as a scholar to aspire to has been David Rojas. I can never repay the intellectual debt I owe him. Another inspirational friend has been Tarandeep Kang. I learn from him every time I talk to him. I know no one as wise as Claudine Ang. I wish to also thank Michael Bobick, Tania Kotik, Pamela Corey, Cuong Pham, Jennifer Erickson, Jane Ferguson, Nina Hien, Pittayawat "Joe" Pittayaporn, Beth Tamayose, and Chika Watanabe for each making Ithaca, NY, a memorable place. Andrew Alan Johnson has been with me throughout this journey. His belief in my scholarship has given me the strength necessary to keep writing. I cannot thank him enough.

At Aarhus University in Denmark, I wish to give special thanks to Jens Seeberg and Heather Swanson. My colleagues at University of California, Berkeley, continue to be sources of inspiration as well as my future. I am especially grateful to Lawrence Cohen, Ian Whitmarsh, and Charles Hirschkind for reading my book manuscript in its nascent stages. Their comments came at a crucial point in the development of the book manuscript, and I cannot thank them enough. Besides them, I wish to thank Charles Briggs, Mariane Ferme, Danny Fisher, Junko Habu, Cori Hayden, James Holston, Rosemary Joyce, Laura Nader, Karen Nakamura, Aihwa Ong, Stephania Pandolfo, Trude Renwick, William Stafford, Bill White, Laurie Wilkie, Alexei Yurchak, and Liu Xin for each taking the time to reach out in friendship and support. Last, but not least, I am especially indebted to Will Hanks for going over and beyond the task of a mentor to help me flourish.

This project has been funded by the dissertation fieldwork grants from the Wenner-Gren Foundation as well as by Fulbright-IIE. I am also grateful to the Institute for European Studies at Cornell University for awarding me the Michele Sicca Research Grant that has helped me go back to the field to collect additional material for this book. This project could not have taken shape as a book without the patience and support of my editors from Cornell University Press, James Lance and Clare Jones. I also wish to thank Stuart McLean and an anonymous reviewer for offering me encouragement and comments on the manuscript. It takes a lot of energy to review manuscripts, and to review them in the generous, thoughtful, and constructive ways in which they reviewed mine. Their care and effort are truly appreciated.

I wish to thank the American Anthropological Association for giving me permission to re-visit some ethnographic contexts and arguments I have made in an article published in 2013 as "Wrapped in Plastic: Transformation and Alienation in the New Finnish Economy," *Cultural Anthropology* 28 (1): 1–21. Portions of this article can be found in chapters 1 and 4.

Finally, I wish to thank my parents, Reiko Funahashi and Kimihiro Funahashi, for standing by me and giving me the time I needed to write and rewrite this book. Writing is an activity that feeds on the energy and support of those around us. Writing cannot be divorced from the immediacy of life that surrounds us. The book's completion I owe to C. August Ogarro. His enthusiasm for life fuels this book.

# UNTIMELY SACRIFICES

# INTRODUCTION

**"To dare is to lose one's footing momentarily. Not to dare is to lose oneself."**

—Søren Kierkegaard

Iiris showed up at our usual café in Helsinki two hours late. It was eight in the evening, and people around us were either finishing their dinner or were starting on a round of drinks. "I'm sorry I'm late," she said, as she eyed my empty cup of coffee. "Something came up. Everyone else had gone home, and I didn't *dare [en uskalla]* leave it undone."

As Iiris prepared to leave the office to see me, she found on her desk some paperwork with a memo that said, "URGENT." Yet, how urgent could the task have been when it was left in the office with a memo addressed to no one? Indeed, everyone ignored it—everyone except Iiris.

What she "didn't dare" leave undone was the kind of odd task that electrified the sacrificial mechanisms of the office community. As the memo addressed no one in particular, it was a task anyone from the office could have offered to do. But there is nothing given about this process whereby this one who is to sacrifice for the whole is called into being.

How does the memo reach an addressee? How does someone come from anyone? Moreover, why is it that Iiris "dares not" ignore the memo? What ethics, politics, and/or economics come to bear on the production of this one?

With increasing cases of death from overwork affecting workers around the world today (Schaufeli and Enzmann 1998; Li et al. 2020), the question of how individuals become this *one*, the one who takes it upon him- or herself to address the demands of the workplace finds timely relevance.

The category "death from overwork" references a broad spectrum of lethal conditions ranging from occupational sudden mortality to suicide, to drug and

1

alcohol abuse (Araki and Iwasaki 2005; Lane 2017). It results when individuals face what appears to be an insurmountable demand to work that despite efforts to keep up never relents. Contra Sisyphus who endures his fate with a certain lucidity and resignation, here, the enormity of work drives workers into the arms of death.

Under advanced capitalism, what has been extra to the labor contract has become what is constitutive of labor proper. As occupational health experts tell us, working long hours alone does not kill us. The morbidity of death from overwork stems from the stress and despair that come from societal demands for an unflagging positive attitude and a willingness to go the extra mile under flagging states of state welfare.

In a postindustrial economy driven by finance and technological innovation, capital has increasingly come to depend on the positive "can do" attitude of workers and their creative aptitude. Under such shifting conditions of production, the welfare of workers has come to play second fiddle to the well-being of workers.

As recent scholarship on well-being shows (e.g., Ahmed 2010; Davies 2011), it is with making a link between a happy worker and a self-driven worker that being well and feeling well come to matter under advanced capitalism. However, this unrelenting demand for an eagerness to work despite ever larger holes in the social safety net places workers under increasing amounts of pressure. Stress mounts with lethal effects. And it is with this significance placed on well-being that the morbidity of distress emerges as a limit to the further growth of capital.

The Finnish word for welfare, *hyvinvointi*, includes within it the psychic and physical notion of well-being. Along with other Nordic countries, welfare, however, focused on the control of living conditions through the management of resources. Under state welfare, each member of the national public was to have equal right and equal access to housing, health care, education, employment, and so forth—all the resources necessary to attain a degree of economic independence and personal well-being. Moreover, classic state welfare justified high public expenditure for the production of a citizenry capable of contributing to the common pool.

Under postindustrial conditions, however, the universalism of state welfare that once provided social security for the entire workforce shifted in favor of targeted public spending. Where greater cohesion between the workforce under industrialization and mass production shaped welfare policy to address the workforce as one unit to be governed, postindustrial conditions opened onto increasing sectoral differentiation and particularization in worker needs.

Political and economic projects once aimed at disciplining the workforce as a whole moved aside for projects that attempt to ignite the productive potentials of affective energies at the individual level. Under advanced capitalism, it became the responsibility of the workforce itself to maintain the force necessary to work.

Thus, from the proliferation of disciplinary techniques invested in reshaping the body, the concern with well-being attends to the psyche as a realm ripe for economic extraction.

As Byung-Chul Han (2017) puts it, rather than discipline, advanced capitalism seduces. Work under its regime becomes a seductive arena through which individuals are to find pleasure and fulfillment. This personalization of work transforms it into something one must compete and fight for. Work ceases to be a universal right owed by the state to its citizens as the means to economic independence. Rather, work, under advanced capitalism, becomes part of the workers' own enjoyment and vehicle for personal growth. Through work, individuals are to realize their potential, their value to society. According to Han, such a conception of work creates potentials for "self-exploitation" (30). What limitation there is becomes the limits of one's talents, one's skills, one's charisma to make happen. One turns aggression inward rather than against a system that turns oneself against oneself. Despair reigns.

Whither welfare and labor under a regime of well-being? What vital economy does this turn to positive thinking and self-management (and/or self-exploitation) activate? Why do we sacrifice to its call? How does it ignite us into action?

That night when Iiris found the paperwork on her desk at the customer service wing of a media company, her coworkers had long since evacuated their cubicles. Iiris had stayed late that day, having volunteered to help a colleague in the accounting office, but her desk in her absence became a convenient resting place for odd tasks cast off by her immediate colleagues. As Iiris had already given her time to the accounting department, she could have easily excused herself. With the office all to herself, she could have passed the paperwork on to someone else's desk. It was, after all, work that belonged to no one and thus to everyone. And yet, she dares not.

Of concern to me was that this was not the first time that Iiris took it upon herself to give her time and energy to the office. Concerning also was the fact that she complained about doing so afterward. Clearly, work here was not a path toward enjoyment. As a constant witness to her protestations, I came to wonder what manner of self-giving her actions constituted.

Unrecognized and unrewarded, Iiris's sacrificed time and energy at the office appear as mere senseless loss, the repetition of which begs the question of her sanity. What draws her to give? How are we to understand such an experience that withdraws from our comprehension just as we come to apprehend its mystery?

For example, that evening, Iiris expressed her "irritation" at coworkers who "never offered to do anything." It was an irritation that had a dangerously contagious effect. The solution seemed to be eminently accessible, and yet just beyond reach. Irritation ensues.

Iiris had given enough to the office; common sense seemed to dictate that she should not volunteer for anything more unless she gets the recognition that is her due. Yet, the expected resolution kept slipping out of reach every time Iiris volunteered herself for another task.

Why does Iiris expend herself in spite of herself? What is it that moves her? Irritation marks the limit of sense. It emerges when common sense would dictate there be an answer and we are instead frustrated. What irritates, what limits the production of sense not only challenges the givenness of what we call common sense, but also what is "common" about common sense.

Irritation, here, also speaks to a kind of dehiscence. Iiris complains about all the things she does and have done for the office, and yet she dares not ignore the call of the office.

"*Uskalla*," as in "to dare" in English, points to a semantic field characterized by a certain leap of faith. One speaks in this register when what one is about to do flies in the face of common sense. Thus, in daring not to ignore the memo, Iiris gives up more than her labor. In daring not to ignore the memo, she not only departs from what is common to sense but also gives up her capacity to make sense.

But in Finnish, *uskalla*, more so than "to dare" in English, etymologically builds on the verb *uskoa*, to believe. It thus highlights the aspect of self-resignation and faith. According to Søren Kierkegaard, the act of not daring to dare is a moment in which one loses oneself. The hand of God takes over, as it were, as we resign ourselves—albeit with "fear and trembling"—to His will (Kierkegaard 2003).

Against what force does Iiris not dare transgress? To what divine authority does she offer the sacrifice of herself? What is it here that is absent and yet makes an effect?

This turn to divine authority, or authority beyond human reason, in thinking about Iiris here is not far-fetched. Iiris had a ledger in which she kept a detailed account of "who owed whom what," an account not intended for anyone other than herself (and me). Names of the worst offenders appeared so often in her accounts that I developed a familiarity with them. However, she never held these individuals responsible. They only appeared as figures in the litany of complaints Iiris levied against the office and never as actual foci of negotiation.

But every time I asked her why she expends herself against herself, she fell speechless. Why does she not use the ledger to demand a return for her gifts of labor? Why does she remain irritated?

A curious disconnect emerges between the ledger and the social field it promises to manage. Here, a form of relationality emerges in which the act of being in relation is illegible both to the giver and to the receiver of the gift of sacrificial labor. Iiris's ledger is neither a bill to be sent to the office nor a personal accounting of her own expenditure. Where the idea of a "balance" factors heavily in discourse surrounding stress (e.g., the risk of "depleting an energetic balance"), we see here that something beyond the logic of the balance moves Iiris. But what moves her? And why does she fall speechless?

The ledger maps out a social field and consigns within it what there *is* that circulates. But as we see with Iiris, there is a force irreducible to the ledger that moves her. Even though the ledger founds the possibility for negotiation, for a more equitable distribution of labor, and for Iiris to count herself out of any future favors the office may demand of its workers, it is silence and speechlessness that emerges. Through the space of silence opened in her attempt to communicate what authors her actions, something else altogether announces itself.

What is it that is counted toward the ledger and what remains unassimilated to its logic? There is a fundamental negativity within the concept of economy that moves exchange without making itself available to legibility. Moreover, this negativity becomes most evident at moments of economic transformation, when taken-for-granted imaginaries of exchange falls under conscious examination. It is to this transformation I turn to next.

## The New Economy

Where Iiris falls speechless, Finnish health experts speak. In 2006–2008 when I conducted ethnographic fieldwork for this book, Finnish health experts found particular interest in workers like Iiris who worked in excess and complained in private. With increasing complaints of stress, insomnia, and fatigue in the national work-life surveys the early 2000s, Finnish health experts set out to question what drives this unhappy excess.

Moreover, giving urgency to the complaints of stress was an increase in the ideation of suicide among the workforce. Together, these concerns mapped out a terrain state officials recognized as symptoms of occupational burnout (*työuupumus*), a chronic stress disorder that when taken to its extreme carried lethal consequences.[1] Research that showed affective symptoms of occupational burnout as being somewhat contagious added to the urgency of the issue (Korkeila et al. 2003). Given these concerns, Finnish health officials declared the stress disorder as a new hazard (Kalimo and Toppinen 1997; Lehto 2008).[2] In turn, naming occupational burnout as a new workplace hazard had the effect of directing national attention onto the challenges of the new economy (*uusi talous*) (Lehto and Sutela 1999; Rantanen 1999) and, more generally, to timely concerns of the here and now.

The new economy rose out of the worldwide economic crisis of the 1990s. With the fall of the USSR, Finland's then-largest trading partner, coinciding with a domestic banking crisis, Finland experienced the worst recession since World

War II. The crisis and the recession that followed put forth a discourse of national economic "survival" (Salovaara-Moring 2004) and legitimized preexisting perspectives that Nordic welfare ought to be recalibrated in ways that prioritize economic rationalism over the ideology of moral politics.

This pressure from within for the nation to transform itself was matched by pressure from without. The dissolution of the USSR hurt trade, but it also opened new opportunities, opportunities that put more pressure on an already strained nation. With the end of the Cold War, Finland released itself from the ignoble condition commonly known as Finlandization, a condition in which a more dominant nation-state (here, the USSR) exerts a deep influence over another nation's (here, Finland) foreign affairs and the media. As Moscow no longer had a say in its relationship with greater Europe, Finland could seek membership within the European Union (EU) on its own terms. This, however, meant that Finland had to fit the criteria set by the EU to meet its stipulations to qualify as a member nation-state. This meant a wide-scale restructuring.

By 1995, Finland was slated to become a member of the EU and, in 1999, the Economic and Monetary Union (EMU)—the only Nordic country to do so. Here, national economic administration became a number one priority. This transition meant sacrificing of long-standing ideals of reciprocity between the state, the nation, and capital (e.g., business) to realign Finland's economy, its politics, and its imaginaries of exchange to do so.

In the span of a decade, Finland emerged anew from the shadow of the USSR. However, while the euro took over from the Finnish markka in 2002, "being Euro" involved much more than flooding the Finnish banks with new currency. Where Finns held in their hands the tangible mark of a new economy and of a new identity in the greater European region, what counts as exchange, more specifically, what counts as fair exchange remained an open question. With the social contract shifting under the terms of the new economy, public opinion also shifted in terms of what responsibility citizens ought to have to the state and vice versa.

Moments interregnum not only interrupt business as usual, but they also carry within them a temporal element. Moments "inter" expose the absence of sense (i.e., what is sensible to do at any particular moment) before sense gains the contours of *what will be* and *what has come to pass*. In such moments when we strive to make sense of *what is*, the everyday emerges as anything *but* the everyday. In the loss of the self-evident and the given, the very basis for articulating what constitutes common sense melts into thin air.

Moments interregnum and what follows thus bring forth much thinking on the here and now. In reflecting on the social, political, and economic transformation that took place in the 1990s, Pauli Kettunen, a political scientist at the University of Helsinki, explains the speed at which the new economy unfolded in

Finland as stemming from the nation's long-standing peripheral position vis-à-vis Europe. For a nation that for some time in its history did not exist on the map of Europe (it was a grand duchy within the Russian Empire), officially becoming a member of the EU came with historic significance.

According to Kettunen, the economic recession could not have come at a worse time given the nation's aspirations to become a major player in the European region. Raising Europe as Finland's aspirational future, Finland placed itself in the past. Kettunen argues that the recession proved to the nation that the Finnish mechanism of welfare was "outdated" and that "'we' have to reject [it] . . . in order to meet the new challenges" (1998, 33). Thus, the move to adopt advanced capitalist ideals in Finland took place through the urgency of a nation that self-identified as an entity in the state of untimeliness. The new economy thus became part of Finland's national project to be timely.

This project for timeliness, however, required that the national workforce act in accordance with what matters and what counts in the here and now. It required that citizen workers give credence to a new sense of administrative order and to take it as the self-evident given of the everyday.

As Marxist scholar Kojin Karatani (2003) reminds us, the economy is more than infrastructure. It is not a mere mechanism. Quoting a passage from Karl Marx, Karatani undergirds this point: the economy "abound[s] in metaphysical subtleties and theological niceties" (5). The economy requires the public to give its "theological niceties" credibility. It is only through belief in what capital tells us as what counts—for example, what counts as exchange, what is to be counted, or who comes to count as a participant of exchange—that its objects gain value and exchange gains sense through "its" terms.

The regulative force of economy, its capacity to distribute, to balance, and to direct the ethics of exchange thus comes from how it relates the visible calculus of management with the "things" it purports to manage. The economy, thus, is an ontotheological vision that establishes what matters. *Mattering*, here, points to both an ontological condition as well as to the status of what counts. Each economic regime inaugurates what matter there *is* and how *it* is to circulate. Each economic regime demands that we sacrifice to its god, its "theological niceties."

Here, it is instructive to turn to Émile Durkheim. In focusing on the curious intersection between theology and economy, Durkheim argues that what a worshipper really sacrifices to the gods "are not the foods which he places upon the altars, nor the blood which he lets flow from his veins: *it is his thought*" (1995, 350, italics added). What makes economy possible, or put another way, what makes circulation possible, is not what is produced as sacrifices—for example, the foods, the blood, the valuable items slated for destruction. Here, both Durkheim and Karatani (via Marx) point to a less visible sacrifice necessary for the symbolic circulation of goods and currency to take hold. We must give credit, our thoughts, to the "metaphysical subtleties" that arise out of the praxis of economy that relates what there is to be managed with the instruments of management. It is here that our faith in what we ought to do (or dare to do) intersects the logic of the ledger.

Yet, without their followers, even gods die. And as old gods die, new gods emerge and with it, new imaginaries and duties of what matters, what counts, and what has credence. As what used to matter comes to matter less, we become captured by other matters. Mattering thus has a temporal element in which what matters has a finitude not visible in the moment in which it matters. But it is to this finitude, to what matters in the here and now, that we lose ourselves. And in being captured by the spirit of what matters today, we sacrifice the very enigma of what moves us. In being timely, we come to matter, to count, and to make sense in ways common to that moment, that time and space. In being timely, we become part of the circulation of time. We sacrifice that which is timeless.

It is those who fall speechless who teach us what those of us assimilated into timely being failed to see. What makes sense today may not make any sense tomorrow. Left out of the labor to make sense is a timeless negativity that resists finite pronouncements of a today and of a tomorrow. In fact, the labor to make sense today demands a distance from the here and now, an untimeliness. In an ironic twist, those who are timely are not those in sync with the present. Those who are timely are those capable of seeing the present from a distance, and from their untimeliness make out the contours of what makes sense as "today" (Erber 2013). Against those of us sacrificing our thoughts to the gods of today, those who fall speechless teach us what potential lies in making this very idea a sacrifice.

## Untimely Sacrifices

The new economy gave birth to a new type of worker—the "martyr worker" (*marttyyri työntekijä*). Arguably, workers who fit the category of the martyr worker may have existed before, but they came to figure more prominently in the popular media in the early 2000s.

Martyr workers pointed to workers like Iiris who fail to make their sacrifices count in ways other than in the extreme and sometimes terminal sense. Moreover, the coinage of the martyr worker circulates and gains currency in a nation alerted to the unhealthy and potentially lethal consequences of the new economy— occupational burnout.

Martyrdom pointed to a breakdown in sociality where communication came tinged with a certain hopelessness. One becomes a martyr, one gives the sacrifice of oneself, when one reaches the limits of communication.

Terry Eagleton, in making a clear distinction between those who commit suicide and those who commit to martyrdom, argues that unlike the suicide, the martyr does not wish death. Death comes not as the goal but as an inevitable consequence of a "cho[ice] to defend a principle to the death" (Eagleton 2018, 91). Building on this important distinction, however, here I explore what understanding of the martyr we could have should we replace Eagleton's word *choice* with *compulsion*.

Martyrdom thus counters the logic of the ledger which promises a certain balance, negotiation. Martyrdom results when the ledger gains no purchase. And yet, it is through coining as "martyrdom" that which the ledger fails to assimilate that the ledger gains its coherence.

Those who frustrate the logic of the ledger, however, figured heavily in the popular media in the mid-2000s. Often, the figure of the "martyr worker" appear in stories that showcase the Finnish workplace as having become "faster" and "harder," one in which workers who consider themselves to be "overly kind" (*liian kiltti*) fall sick (Sannemann 2006).

*Me Naiset*, a popular women's magazine, for instance, published an article titled "Kind or Just a Martyr" (*Kiltti Vai Ihan Vaan Marttyyri*; Myllyoja, 2012). In it, they turn to Anna-Liisa Valtavaara, a theologian who has published on the topic of kindness and sacrifice.

According to Valtavaara, those who are kind sacrifice themselves for the love of others. Those who are martyrs are so out of duty and thus demand to be recognized. Martyrs know they give more of themselves than others, claims Valtavaara, and when they fail to get what they believe as their due recognition, things turn ugly. "Tantrum and martyr-drama" (*kiukuttelua ja marttyyrikohtauksia*) follow, says Valtavaara, when martyrs do not receive the praise they expect.

Common to these stories is the issue of fair exchange. It is not the amount of work that is at issue. Rather, these stories—along with the official understanding of occupational burnout itself—highlight that spending one's energies without recompense, seeing others working harder than yourself—come with affective by-products not factored into the logic of the ledger.

Workplace precarity, workplace competitiveness, and unfair exchange of labor come with emotive and affective consequences. Juha Siltala, a historian of labor in Finland, argues that the increase in competitiveness between workers under the new economy has transformed the nature of workplace sociality.

In an article, Siltala (2004) analyzed the impact deregulating the labor market had on social interactions at work. Following the labor market from the 1970s onward, he argues that where aggression was once projected between worker groups and employer groups, the new economy brought tension between the workers themselves. This point not only resonates with Han's (2017) analysis I introduced earlier that aggression under advanced capitalism has turned violence inward but also undergirds how different economic regimes direct aggression in disparate ways.

The deregulation of the labor market has brought free market principles into areas previously protected from market forces. Where each sector provided similar compensation for workers doing similar work, new economic policies made compensation more competitive. With the aim to make what Siltala calls "lazy capital" more productive (2004, 46), not only was higher compensation given to more productive workers, but also huge cuts in personnel were made as a way to cut redundancies and to make businesses as a whole more competitive.

These moves, Siltala claims, have made workers watch other workers over their shoulders. Where workers once bonded together against administrators as paternal figures, today, Siltala argues, workers are locked into what he calls sibling rivalry (2004).

Discourses surrounding competitiveness go hand in hand with workplace efficiency and the speed of production. Moreover, businesses have found that efficiency, speed, and competitiveness come from happy workers, self-driven workers who love what they do, and are enthusiastic about their jobs. It is not enough that one merely does one's job. In the new economy, one must give it "everything": one must give it every bit of one's time. Businesses have found that happiness is the key to a workforce immune to stress, creativity, and speed. When we are happy, time flies. When we are happy, work is not work. When we are happy, we do not tire.

Yet, being happy requires both a psychological and physiological commitment. This commitment to the new economy has prompted a columnist from Finland's major newspaper, *Helsingin Sanomat*, to publish the following article.

In a poignant piece titled "Ants of Our Lord," Hannele Tarkke-Tierala (2004) writes, "The ideal worker is as happy and flexible as a rubber man—ready for change, ready to forget any dreams about early retirement, ready for lifelong learning. And above all, an employee should have a healthy lifestyle, allowing for a 100% commitment to the employer."

A "faster" world thus experientially goes hand in hand with a "harder" world—a world devoid of personal dreams—a world set for talking about stress. Hitting against a "harder" world, those who fail to sacrifice to this harder god shatter.

Besides martyr workers, occupational burnout gave rise to other avatars of untimeliness. In the clinic, it was the "conscientious worker" (*tunnollinen työntekijä*) that took center stage. Kirsi Ahola, one of Finland's leading experts on occupational burnout from the Finnish Institute of Occupational Health (FIOH), stated in an interview with YLE (the Finnish Broadcasting Company) that "conscientious people" are those "who have a tendency towards self-sacrifice and perfectionism" (YLE Uutiset 2004).

In the article, YLE remarked on the specific significance in Finland of the risks posed by conscientiousness as follows: "Alarm bells seldom ring when someone is overly conscientious, *especially in Finland* where diligence is regarded as a commendable characteristic among employees" (italics added).

YLE's report on occupational burnout is but one of many that appeared in the mid-2000s in which what motivates individuals to engage at work became a part of national debate. According to such reports, conscientiousness and diligence as "especially" Finnish problems chafe against current political and economic projects that attempt to redefine work as an activity liberated from such righteous convictions.

Historically, Nordic welfare traces its origins to Lutheran foundations in which work had theologico-ethical value (Nelson 2017; Trägårdh 1997). However, where work driven by a moral conscience once set a worker apart from his or her peers, work made profane under the logic of economic rationalism of the new economy sacralizes no one. Rather, self-expenditure in the workplace today makes sense as an expression of one's conscious calculus of what is in one's interest to do (career advancement, fiscal advantage, personal learning, etc.) and not, as Iiris puts it, as an act driven by what one "dares not" to do.

In such a context, occupational burnout epitomizes for the nation what ails the present. It is thus that occupational burnout becomes a part of the narrative of what makes the present distinct from the past. It is also through the understanding of occupational burnout as an emergent disorder that health experts reach out of the boundaries of "health" to speak to issues of the present in general.[3]

According to experts from FIOH, "Different models of burnout share the basic assumption that the discrepancy between the intentions of a motivated employee and the reality in unfavorable working conditions develops towards burnout via dysfunctional ways of coping. *Burnout can be conceptualized as a crisis in one's relationship to work*" (Ahola et al. 2006, 11; emphasis added).

It is a crisis, experts argue, that stems from "changes in worklife" (Rantanen 1999), changes one can overcome via adapting to the demands of the present. It is thus that "martyrdom" and "conscientiousness" stand out as dangerous excesses and as holdovers of an ideological past. In the tension that develops, stress mounts.

Burnout thus merges economic demands of timely exchange with the vital problem of timely self-management. In doing so, it sets in motion a narrative of the here and now as one beset by an untimeliness that is not only unproductive but also maladaptive. If economic policymakers presented the adoption of new economic ideals as a matter of national economic "survival" (Hietanen 1999), Finnish health experts in turn made literal this notion of survival. Those who cannot adapt suffer the potentially lethal consequences of expending one's energy in ways that fail to count in the present. It is a deficit, health experts argued, that not only deplete energetic resources but also our will, the fire, to go on. Depleted, we burn out.

The understanding of occupational burnout builds on a vital economy of human energy that must be managed. It is instructive here to unpack the very concept of economy.

Giorgio Agamben (2009, 8) reminds us that the concept of economy has a "theological genealogy" that can be traced back to its Greek roots as *oikonomia*. *Oikonomia* refers to the praxis of management and administration, and in early Christianity, it became the transcendent principle through which divine providence governed over humanity. Where modern economic thinking has erased the aspect of the divine, economy still operates under "its" ethics, "its" management, and "its" administrative purpose to which we must sacrifice. Although God no longer names the core of what drives how and why we labor, economy continues to revolve around what Agamben calls the "theological device" that gives sense to what we dare or dare not do.

Included in this theology of economy is a temporal element. Economy is, moreover, a praxis that makes visible social exchange as unfolding within set time and place. What is fair and what is to be expected as exchange only gain articulation against the ethics, technology, and an ontology of what there is to be managed as they emerge within different administrative-cum-economic regimes. Activities thus gain sense via the telos of the economy. Economy is that which gives sense to how we spend and how we save our energy. It is, moreover, when one economic regime ends and a new one takes over that we become disenchanted from the economic-cum-administrative imperatives of the past. It is also at this moment when new gods take over that that which obstructs the inauguration of new forces gets marked for rehabilitation or domestication.

Being timely demands certain sacrifices. It demands that we give our time and energy in a manner in line with what makes sense given the needs of the economy. It points to a specific way in which the economy recalibrates what sacrifice there is to make. Going against this flow of time becomes a waste of energy—energy, an economic thinker would say, that could be used more productively.

Fatigue, more recently stress, has become part of this shifting landscape highlighted for treatment. For example, occupational burnout is not a primary diagnosis in Finland. It is, however, identified as an antecedent condition to many of the ailments that affect work such as cardiovascular diseases, suicide, and addictive behaviors. It is thus a dis-ease that challenges productivity, one that must be kept in check through the observance of everyday habits (e.g., sleeping well, eating well, exercising well, etc.). It is a disorder that turns our attention toward not only health but also toward life choices, lifestyles, and to oneself as an ever-perfectible entity.

Fatigue, stress, and unhappiness become effects of poor choice. One exists as if on a spreadsheet open to self-management.

In Finland, self-management took specific form as "maintenance of work ability" (MWA). In fact, the Finnish government redefined the main goal of occupational health services as the promotion of MWA (Peltomäki and Husman 2002). According to Peltomäki and Husman, "the workforce needs maintenance and promotion of work ability to manage high demands of today's working life" (263). And for Finland, shouldering one of Europe's oldest workforce, and with many workers slated to retire in the next decade, the maintenance of a worker's ability to work—that is, the worker's labor power—posed a major challenge to Finnish policymakers (Hätinen 2008).

MWA, together with another neologism of the 1990s—workplace well-being (työhyvinvointi)—became key concepts through which experts could streamline personal ambitions, career goals, and desires together with physical and nutritional needs for a healthier workforce that would not buckle under the pressure of the new economy.

It is under such context that burnout, a disorder with no official disease category, came to the fore of public health discussions in Finland. In the World Health Organization's International Statistical Classification of Diseases and Related Health Problems (ICD-10), a classification system on which Finnish medical and social insurance nosology is based, burnout is listed as a factor that influences health. Burnout in Finland also mirrors this focus on maintenance, optimization, and promotion of workplace well-being.

Despite its use in everyday conversations and even within the space of the rehabilitation center, the Finnish idiom that closely resembles the English for "burnout" rarely appears in official texts. In the place of the Finnish idiom *palaa loppuun* (to burn to the end), the official term *työuupumus* (literally, "work exhaustion") makes no reference to finitude or to an "end" (*loppuun*). Experts also specified as the official English translation of *työuupumus* as "*occupational burnout*," not merely "burnout."

In the field, however, my repeated usage of the term *työuupumus* in my everyday conversations with experts at the rehabilitation centers elicited laughter. "No one uses that term!" Satu, a physical therapist at one of the centers told me. "It is used in official documents, but when we are just talking like this, we say 'burn to the bottom' [*pohjanpalanut*] or 'burning to the end' [*loppuunpalaminen*]. Sometimes it makes more sense to just use the English 'burnout,' but we rarely use the term *työuupumus* in day-to-day conversations! It's just the official term."

I mentioned this incident to Jari Hakanen, a leading researcher of burnout at FIOH, when I interviewed him. He explained to me that the term *loppuunpalaminen* used to be the common term for burnout. But this was in the 1980s, a decade before the official translation of the ICD-10 into Finnish in 1996 and also before the disorder became a matter of national concern. He told me that his colleagues had written about burnout before the 1990s (Valtiovaara 1987) but that the disorder gained the current level of national attention only after his institute published a report in 1997 stating that over half the Finnish workforce suffered from some symptoms of the disorder. It was in this publication that experts used the term *työuupumus*, and it was since then that it replaced the more colorful idiom of "burning to the end" as the official term.

According to Jari, the conflict over how to translate "burnout" into Finnish caused a stir among public health experts, even to the point of it being presented to Finnish language experts at the Finnish Academy. Opponents of the use of Finnish idioms similar to that of the English "burnout" finally won this contest by arguing that the idioms—"burning to the end," "burning to the bottom," and "burning out"—all had negative connotations of death and terminality not conducive to the public health goals of promoting work maintenance and self-management. Instead, the term *työuupumus* focuses on "work" (*työ*) and "exhaustion" (*uupumus*), both conditions amenable to techniques of rehabilitation and the chance to work on oneself. Where fatigue can be worked on, nothing can be done with an individual who has reached the "end."

In dealing with burnout, the Finnish Insurance Institution (KELA), the public agency responsible for providing social security programs, plays a key role. Their program for occupational burnout is premised on "self-awareness" (*tietoisuus*) as the basis for rehabilitative success.

"Self-awareness," as KELA sees it, translates into the reclamation of timely belonging via an awareness of self-limits. These limits specifically refer to social limits—the amount of time one can spend on friends and family, as well as time spent on doing favors for colleagues at work; professional limits, limits of one's capacity to do a particular task; and finally, physical limits, the limits one may have to working late, to lifting heavy machinery, to doing too many tasks at one time. Self-awareness was also meant to push individuals to become more attuned to the limits of the workplace. Given the limits of the workplace, individuals were to reconsider giving the gift of sacrificial labor. Rehabilitative experts, for example, might have told Iiris that had she more self-awareness, she would not have given herself so repetitively. According to their logic, she would not have become so "irritated" had she been more aware of the limits of her colleagues.

This push for self-awareness, as I understand it from the interviews I held with health officials, was also a push for an internal balance—a way to keep an eye on the level of their "energetic depletion" (Ahola 2007; Shirom 2003). Via transforming worker citizens into accountants of their own vital energy as set against an ever-dwindling resource, rehabilitation proceeds by pitting the logic of the ledger against the supposed ideological excesses of the past.

Contra the welfare ideals of the past where work tested one's moral standing by one's willingness to contribute to the common pool, the workplace today demanded a different sort of sacrifice. No longer did proving one's moral worth amount to accolades in the workplace. The workplace today required that one proves one's economic worth via the use of the ledger. It is here at this disjuncture that the martyr worker comes to figure prominently in the media.

But what units of care, moral politics, and ethics of labor does this figure of the martyr worker mobilize? How does the shift in public health from its traditional attention to conditions of dis-ease, to its current concerns over the maximization of wellness affect the understanding of sickness? Wherein lies the responsibility and the need to change? These are but a few of the questions I explore in this book.

This book, moreover, attends to occupational burnout as a *disorder that orders the present* in contradistinction to health experts who present the stress disorder as an effect of the new economy. Through making visible the here and now as a particular moment with "its" challenges, with "its" threats, and so forth (yet a moment that is inevitable and normalized), occupational burnout enables policymakers, economists, and health experts to mobilize an administrative force based on this timely vision of what matters, what counts. Rather than an effect of the present, occupational burnout is part of the new economy; it inaugurates the present.

It is through naming something new, a "new hazard," for instance, that we distinguish between *this* time from *that* time. It is through separating time into different moments, or as Jean-Luc Nancy puts it, through spatializing time into distinct "suspensions" (1993, 150) that we step into the present as timely beings.

According to Nancy, it is only through *giving space to time* that we can conceptualize how events *take place in time*. It is through giving space to time that we make sense of how things take place. In this labor to suspend time within finite spatial units, naming occupational burnout as an emergent disorder does much to make visible the schism necessary to space time, space necessary to make sense of time and existence now as one with "its" own sense of order.

Those who go against the common sense of being in the here and now fall untimely, some fall speechless. This negativity of the speechless is one advanced capitalism attempts to rehabilitate and make productive via its containment within the medical register. Negativity defanged as an illness falls short of opening a space for critique.

Diagnostic categories have a way of domesticating the enigmatic force that dares us to act. Such a domestication sheds light on the abyss at the core of why we do what we do and brings forth an illness. The formulation of occupational burnout disavows the horror of the social by foreclosing the very possibility that some other force moves us to give the gift of labor. Where Iiris falls speechless, the diagnosis speaks for her and offers rehabilitative promise and safe passage to a timely state of being. The diagnosis makes safe the negativity of speechlessness and transforms this radical void where no explanation takes place into the very space of intervention.

Moreover, occupational burnout as a marker of untimeliness articulates not only what it takes to belong to the here and now but also what counts today as an exchange that matters. The technomedical intervention, then, shifts the enigma of what moves us to a technical register and through it, promises to render the social field open to administrative control.

However, as Marcel Mauss reminds us, the notion that we sacrifice voluntarily is but "a polite fiction, formalism, and social deceit" (1990, 3). As he puts it, there is a "force" that resides in the gift that compels the recipient for its return. Naming the thing that is reciprocated as "gift" allows for exchange that is only voluntary "in theory" (3) to take place *as if* it were otherwise in practice. How might we see occupational burnout anthropologically through the logic of sacrifice? How might we rethink stress disorders that arise from self-expenditure by opening it up to ideas beyond its traditional field in the health sciences?

James Siegel (2006) sees naming as an act intent on mastery that nonetheless falls short. For instance, naming as "gift" the force of the thing that moves us to reciprocate enables the semblance of its domestication. However, he shows through his account of witchcraft accusation in Java that this act of naming produces not stability but anxiety.

The "polite fiction" in this case is nothing but polite. In his observation, naming the witch does not bring an end to witchcraft accusations. Naming one witch brought forth yet another and another. No mastery emerges over the witch as such. The category of the witch, he argues, comes to mark the space of tension between what we could bring into social understanding and what remains out of such formulations. No social structure, no certainty emerges from this socially determined understanding of "witch." Naming the witch, he tells us, ironically feeds into the very menace the act of naming attempts to domesticate.

Naming, thus, is an act productive in its nonproductivity. Naming is an act that touches on the limits of what we can grasp and incorporate into our "polite fictions." In touching this limit, however, what we attempt to domesticate through the name is always already contaminated with the negativity of that which resists the name. Giving something a social origin via the conferral of a name does not allow us to manage its power.

Iiris, for example, complained that her coworkers called her a martyr worker. Being named a martyr, however, she still dared not to ignore calls for help from the office. What moves her bears no identifiable name. It fascinates.

What fascinates gathers many names. For instance, the bear has many names owing to Finland's long tradition of bear worship. So, too, with modern figures of wonder.[4] But in relegating those who make us question "why we do what we do" into the category of the mentally ill, the sacrificial martyr, or the conscientious worker, all untimely in their particular ways, we close the necessary space through which sense gains contour as *sense*. Here, I opt to keep this space open, if only to keep the spirit of the gift—the spirit that moves us, lights our inner fire to give—alive.

# Rehabilitation

In the spring of 2007 and 2008, I followed patients, or clients, as they were called, as they attended in-patient rehabilitative programs for occupational burnout. Funded and developed by KELA, such programs for burnout reflected the multifaceted nature of the disorder by bringing together a motley crew of experts.

Each program came with an attendant psychologist, general physician, nurse, nutritionist, social worker, physical therapist, and an activity expert responsible for organizing recreational activities for clients during their time off from the daily schedule at the center.

Such programs came with a cap of ten or twelve clients each and had a full schedule from eight o'clock in the morning until the late afternoon. Although I was barred from attending the private sessions clients had with the psychologist, I was allowed to join in the recreational activities as well as the physical therapy sessions and the creative cognitive behavioral sessions.

To gain a sense of how clients cope with life after the initial program, KELA provided a follow-up session that invited clients back to the respective centers where they had begun their care work to spend another week with the experts. There, reunited with their cohorts and with the center staff, clients were to reflect on the year that they had spent at home since their first admission to the program. Uniting the two stages of the rehabilitative program was what KELA called their empowerment paradigm.

The rehabilitative concept of empowerment had a lot to do with keeping individuals in control over the mechanism of labor. The term *client* also reflected this strategy. As clients, individuals were active consumers of health services; they were not passive recipients, patients worked on by the rehabilitation experts.

Clients work on themselves through the use of techniques offered by the state and, thus empowered, gain the capacity to return to the workforce.

I see spaces of rehabilitation functioning as "zones of pure logistics" (Bratton 2006, 19). They are sites that regulate the rehabitation of individuals as productive citizens, and as such, they become necessary nodes within the virtuous economy. Rehabilitation programs ensure that clients get their full wages as well as free room and board during the length of their stay; they also assure the public the value of their tax expenditure by promising the return of productive individuals whose stress symptoms would less likely progress into more serious diseases that would require further public expenditure. The welfare state thus legitimizes public expenditure by the reproduction of a well-adjusted citizen worker.

Methodologically, KELA's techniques of empowerment came from getting clients to be "aware" of themselves and specifically as being out of joint with what constitutes productive citizenship under the present context. Through meditation, mindfulness, and stretch exercise sessions, experts made explicit the importance of getting to know one's body and its limits. "Listen to your body" was a common motto at such sessions, and it was often transposed onto situations beyond the center.

"Honesty is one thing we value in Finland," said Satu, a physical therapist who was part of the team at one rehabilitation center. "And my clients are people who feel tremendous guilt when they can do something to help others and they do not offer it. Here, I am telling them not to listen to that voice that tells them they are bad, dishonest people and to listen to their bodies instead."

Physical therapists, like Satu, took special notice of clients with pain in the neck, the shoulders, and in the back. The accumulation of pain in such places of the body, according to therapists, revealed the imprint of pressure workers placed on themselves. Therapy aimed at the body was thus conducted with an eye toward changing individual attitudes to work.

"When the body screams in pain," said Satu, "it is best that we listen. We must not override our bodies. It just makes more sense." Moral ideals such as "honesty," "conscientiousness," and "loyalty" no longer mutually obligate employers to respond in kind. I followed therapists like Satu who argued that workers needed to work in ways that took heed of such changes.

Daily schedules at rehabilitation centers stitched together sessions with physical therapists with group counseling sessions into a seamless continuum rendering multiple spheres of life accessible to technomedical intervention. Moreover, an intervention based on the paradigm of empowerment focused on getting clients to rehabit the position of subjects capable of making sense in the present. Power, here, came from making sense and from the capacity to negotiate one's position via the use of reason in line with the limits and rewards of the present. One empowers oneself via developing the capacity to participate in the flow of ideas and reason as they circulate within time and space. Empowerment in this paradigm comes from regaining the capacity to speak and to be a part of the fabric of "today."

Together with KELA's focus on self-awareness, rehabilitative experts took the notion of empowerment to help rehabilitees overcome their speechlessness, their inability to negotiate, and their sense of hopeless despair by making sense of why and how they got to where they are. This meant that individuals must not only rethink why he or she may not "dare" to say no to certain demands to work but also reimagine "today" as grounded on a different notion of what is given as the self-evident. Rehabilitation thus tinkers with the sense of exchange as it shifts together with the mode of exchange.

The rehabilitation center, this zone of pure logistics, then, stages the changing interest of capital and works together with state and national concerns of survival to reshape the topography of what moves individuals to do what they do.[5] In this national project, the language of the here and now works as a catalyst to create urgency in its logics to produce the citizens of today.[6]

Examining how medical institutions become a part of political and economic projects to shape the fabric of time would appear to extend Michel Foucault's (1972, 2014) analyses that what it means "to be a living being" increasingly falls under the mechanics of power. Such mechanics, or apparatuses (*dispositifs*), as Gilles Deleuze reminds us, are "machines of visibility" (1992, 160) that lights the world and makes us see in specific ways. Rehabilitation centers become part of the machine that renders oneself in the here and now visible. However, I argue here that shedding light on oneself as a certain product of history illuminates and also blinds.

Joining clients in their physical therapy routines, meals, and off-times at the rehabilitation centers, a process of gaining tighter control over oneself is not what I saw. Individuals told to liberate themselves from the morals of a past economy did not find new points of reference from which to reproduce a sense of themselves. Articulating the terms under which sense makes sense as *sense* does not empower or enable individuals to gain ownership over the cause of their self-expenditure. Rather than find the capacity to make sense of their excesses, clients questioned the basis on which we produce sense. Moreover, in having lost a sense of themselves, they spoke to me of being exhausted from this very labor to make sense.

This book attends to spaces of silence that open against a demand to make sense. Speechlessness as I witnessed, however, is not mere refusal to speak. The resistance to speech as I approach it here is one that ruptures the coherence of common sense and timely formulations about existence. It is one that makes evident the senselessness of a senseless support of sense.[7] Those who fall silent show us this senselessness when we no longer can. Those who fall speechless teach us how to radically break out of the here and now and to engage with what is timeless.

In speaking of senselessness here in no way references the works of rehabilitative experts, however. The chance to work on oneself and to gain some respite from a stressful workplace is an opportunity one would be hard set to argue against. However, when we treat happiness, well-being, and creativity as conditions that can be "produced" via the right lifestyle, proper career choice, and workplace environment, what notion of the human do we put forward? When we reduce human experiences to manageable techniques and workplace profiles, what do we leave out of this formulation? How can classic anthropological scholarship on sacrifice and the gift help us rethink the potential of negativity in the face of positive psychology and its telos of a capitalist subject intent on saving and conserving energy?

These questions are not meant to discredit the efforts of rehabilitative experts in the least. In fact, many of the clients with whom I interacted at these rehabilitation centers expressed how much they owed the experts for giving them an official category and space through which to work out what ails them. What I wish to call attention to here, however, is the dangers posed by the promise that we could tinker with our minds and feelings for the sake of productive expenditure.

## Technologizing Happiness

Every industrial age comes with its own afflictions. The introduction of the railroad in Victorian England rattled sensitive nerves. Newspapers at the time reported some travelers lost their minds (Milne-Smith 2016). As cases of individuals losing their composure on the train only to regain it once off the train became a figure in popular imaginary, Victorian medical professionals named the mania incited by the power of the steam engine "railroad madness." The railroad, one of the most significant developments of the nineteenth century allowed travelers and commodities to move from one point to another at unprecedented speed but at the cost of "nerves." Where technological advancement enabled ever faster circuits of exchange, the human nervous system emerged as a limiting factor.

This issue of nerves also had a central role in the United States, where the fledgling use of steam to power industry radically transformed the speed of production and the rhythm of life. In the United States, the imagery of nerves and its electric transmission of mania went hand in hand with Thomas Edison's invention of the electric light bulb and the popularization of the use of the telephone. The widening importance of electricity to drive communication and the ease at which the electrical circuit closed vast distances, however, made some Victorians "faint" and even "hopeless" in the face of new demands placed on us by technology (Beard, cited in Abbey and Garfinkel 1991, 1640). Against the promise of new inventions, humanity balks at its own creations.

World War I and its horrors further cemented the link between energetic expenditure and fatigue to the development of a psychophysiological response (Abbey and Garfinkel 1991, 56). By World War II as a remedy for the psychological and emotional impacts of war, the military-industrial complex developed hormonal treatments to boost the adrenal mechanisms of the fighting force. Against fear and fatigue, endocrinologists found that in moments of danger, adrenal glands released stress hormones that allow individuals to accomplish superhuman feats of endurance, strength, and speed. The invention of hormonal treatments rendered visible human courage as steroidal compounds available for manufacture in the lab (Jackson 2013).

Shift in attention from the nervous system to the endocrine system thus lay the foundation for the possibility for self-management on a general scale. Stress management demanded that workers push themselves but not to the point where they offset the homeostatic balance.

The management of stress encompassed everything from eating well, resting well, exercising well, as well as dreaming well. One's dreams and aspirations had to be just right; one ought to not overstep the boundaries of one's capacities nor aspire below what one is capable. Boredom came with its own stress.

If neurasthenia provided workers with an image of energetic expenditure through the idiom of "nerves" and worn-out electric circuits, stress and the turn to the endocrinal system mobilized another imaginary of energetic expenditure. It, moreover, came with its own techniques of management.

Hans Selye, one of the chief endocrinologists responsible for popularizing the concept of stress, found that long exposure to situations that cause emotions such as fear, anxiety, and uncertainty led to high levels of the stress hormone, cortisol. Where cortisol plays a key role in the body's "fight or flight" response to danger, Selye discovered that cortisol also repressed functions in the body nonessential to this response. Cortisol curbs immune responses and suppresses the digestive system, and together with regions in the brain that controls mood, it signals to the body that it is in danger. Where previous examinations of the fatigued body focused on specific syndromes and/or disorders, Selye's genius resided in turning our attention to health as existing along an ever-perfectible continuum.[8]

The concept of stress, thus, lends itself to the micromanagement of the self as individuals can always be happier, healthier, and/or more productive should they exercise more, eat more nutritious foods, sleep better, develop better stress-coping strategies, and/or challenge themselves more. With stress, it is not the prevention of disease that matter but the promotion of more health. Under advanced capitalism, this promotion of more health took specific form as the promotion of happiness.

Yet, as William Davies (2015) claims, the attempt to instrumentalize feelings, lifestyles, and tastes can be traced back to the Enlightenment. Notable figures from Gustav Fechner, Sigmund Freud, to Jeremy Bentham have all left their mark on the techniques and methods we use to measure and to profile the human psyche. Yet, our current obsession with happiness points to a new horizon of such efforts. Indeed, Davies argues that our recent focus on the economic advantages on having not just healthy workers, but also happy workers has brought economic policymakers and mental health experts together in new ways.

How one feels about work has become vital to an economy increasingly dependent on technological innovation, creativity, and affective service. With such "immaterial" and "cognitive" aspects of labor at the forefront of production (Hardt and Negri 2004; Lazzarato 1996), the benefits of having a positive, enthusiastic, and stress-free workforce have not been lost to capitalists. According to Maurizio Lazzarato, "What modern management techniques are looking for is for 'the worker's soul to become part of the factory.' The worker's personality and subjectivity have to be made susceptible to organization and command" (1996, 133). Thus, the labor power in question here no longer only concerns the power of the worker to reproduce the means to satisfy his or her material means of subsistence as argued by Marx. The immaterial nature of labor calls into question what the worker needs to sustain a positive outlook on life—an outlook conducive to creativity and the "can do" attitude this economy needs.

This upsurge in the interest in the relationship between one's emotions and productivity can be seen in recent corporate interests in holding yoga and meditation retreats as well as in the introduction of concepts such as mindfulness into their executive training modules (Cederström and Spicer 2015). Since 2007, Google, for example, has offered a course called "Search inside Yourself" that teaches its employees how to be more mindful (Baer 2014). Chade-Meng Tan, the developer of the course, has established himself as the resident "Jolly Good Fellow" in chief and has described the objectives of the course as getting people to better relate to themselves through a combination of methods that brings mindfulness together with emotional intelligence. Corporations are not alone in the attempts to optimize their workers' feelings. Carl Cederström and André Spicer (2015) note how the sale of a lifestyle that gets workers feeling better, eating well, and exercising more are common features of organizations from Danish municipal workplaces to Swedish truck manufacturing companies.

There now exists a global market for the sale of personalized fitness and mood-assessing gadgets. Where Apple dominates the market, this growing market is not lost to Nokia, Finland's information technology giant; it has its own digital personal fitness gadgets. The commodification of health and feelings finds fertile ground in Finland as well.

Yet, in the shadows of a booming "happiness industry," scholars are talking. Sara Ahmed, for example, demands that we take a minute to ask what the discussions on happiness bring into focus and what they occlude. In her book aptly titled *The Promise of Happiness* (2010), she pushes us to examine what politics the "consensus to use the word happiness to describe something" mobilizes (4). Happiness is "promised" rather than given. A promise is but a promise. The happiness industry develops around this very uncertainty to sell its various techniques and technologies. More ominously, as William Davies (2015) reminds us, when the influential and the prosperous of the world are seduced by the technologies that promote happiness, we need to be aware that their primary concern does not revolve around the well-being of others.

Besides creativity and innovation, a happy worker is a tireless worker, a worker capable of answering to capital's ever-increasing demand for speed. Where time cannot be slowed to suit the needs of production, human labor in contrast point to a plasticity ever pliable to the demands of speed. Timeliness is also a matter of speed—more specifically, of the speed necessary for production within set time and space. Economic rationalism under advanced capitalism dictates that efficiency lies not in employing more hands but in digitization or making existing hands work faster to meet demand.

Capital has a way of accelerating human time by hitching it onto mechanized time. In the digital age, we can lose and make millions in a blink of an eye. Paul Virilio (2006), for instance, rewrites the history of industrialization as the history of speed. Dromology, as he calls it, sees human labor as the limit to unlimited speed achievable by technological advancement. It is a limit, as he shows, that demands careful regulation.

Analyses of this nexus between the human, the machine, and the demands of capital often turn to the disciplinary logics and strategies taken to optimize the relationship between entities to make for a smooth productive surface. In his seminal essay titled "Time, Work Discipline, and Industrial Capitalism," E. P. Thompson (1967) shows how the question of how best to harness human energy, a concern he says that goes back to the medieval era, manifests as time discipline that shifts through time.

Where time discipline alone fails to meet the requirements of the speed of capital, medicotechnical experts have infused the workforce with chemicals, most notably caffeine, methamphetamines, alcohol, and opiates as ways to augment human capacities for speed or to numb the pressure speed places on human bodies (Pine 2007). As Marx famously puts it, under industrial projects to improve operational efficiency, the human becomes a mere cog in the circuit of production. In this scenario, the medical register joins the technical and the machinic to make visible human limits as something that could be worked on and managed for the sake of speedy production—a self-evident good in the competition to save time and to save money.

"Time saved in the most absolute sense of the word" amounts to speed, says Virilio (2006, 46). Where time is money and money is time, saving time or shrinking the span of a moment it takes to conduct business becomes of utmost importance. Efficiency and a positive self-driven workforce become essential to this economic and political project for the production of speed. Under such circumstances, timely being becomes synonymous with going with the flow of time—the accelerational promise of speed on which capital banks its potential for growth. Anything that obstructs the optimization of speed becomes untimely. Anything that stymies acceleration becomes part of the challenge of the here and now.

In an era devoid of the right to universal employment, workers who fail to keep up with technological advancements suddenly lose their place in the workforce. Finland, for the first time since the end of World War II, began to see inherited forms of unemployment (Uusitalo 1996). The social security net long in the making starts to unravel, and those who fall, fall at great velocity.

Stress then emerges between the tension between economic visions of expansion and human limits to keep up with such technical thinking. Human limits to both industrial speed of production as well as to the expansionist ideals of capital become part of the disorder and malaise open to medical-psychological intervention.

Yet, it appears that this promise of happiness can be fatiguing itself. As Iiris shows us, there is indeed life beyond the logic of the ledger, and we ought to be skeptical about the technological thinking. Happiness is not something that emerges out of strategic calculation. Comfort, maybe, but happiness, exuberant happiness, comes from somewhere else.

Continental philosophy has much to offer us in terms of such skepticism toward technological thinking. Martin Heidegger poses the danger of technology as our potential enslavement to its "framework." In his piece, *The Question concerning Technology* (1977), he presents technology as something more than "a means to an end" and claims that its essence lies in its capacity to "reveal" the world to us in specific ways. Technology thus refers not to specific tools and structures of utility but to the manner in which it reveals rivers, forests, and even humans to us as particular objects. It places individuals within a technological framework, a relation, with other objects, through which it produces a sense of existence—reality. This reality, however, has nothing to do with reality "in itself." The reality in which humans and forests exist as "standing reserve" for economic activity is real only insofar as we are captured (*Gestell*) by the technology of capital.[9]

According to Heidegger, we do not control the conditions under which we contemplate existence and its realities. We are always already oriented to the world around us by specific technological frameworks into which we are born. Thus, we are deluded in thinking that *we* have technology. It is technology that has us. We do not act on the world per se: technological thinking operates us.

Heidegger points to the power plant on the Rhine as an example. Where does the decision to build the plant originate? For Heidegger, we can build the plant only because technology reveals the Rhine as raw material. We do not see the Rhine as it *is*; rather, we see it as it is revealed to us through technology. Thus, the plant is a product of a technological thinking already in place.

Technology "orders" (Heidegger 1977, 33) the world by bringing forth "something concealed" into "unconcealment" (11). The Rhine is unconcealed in its productive potential by this very process. Yet, he notes, unconcealment, or revealing, is in itself a form of concealment. In making us see, technology also paradoxically makes us blind. By unconcealing the Rhine as standing reserve, we can only see a technologized river. We forget the river as something other than a resource. Seeing through the eyes of technology becomes increasingly hard for individuals to see the world from "outside" its framework.

Moreover, Heidegger argues that every attempt to turn away from one form of technological thinking brings forth another. Although this is horrible in itself, he paints an even more disquieting condition. Installed as we are in the technological framework, we can never quite tell if we are seeing the world with our "own" eyes. The "will" to see differently, according to Heidegger, is disconnected with the essence of freedom. Freedom, for Heidegger, comes from relinquishing "the will to master" technology and from recognizing the dangers of finding comfort in seeing oneself as a master of our own optics.

What we learn from this seminal piece is that the notion that we could optimize well-being reveals our capture within the technological framework of the present—one that orients us to ourselves as raw materials of a particular kind. However, lacking ethnographic insight, philosophy falls short of elucidating exactly *how* the dissolution of a world we take to be self-evident and given carries the potential for radical change. It is a shortcoming anthropology is uniquely suited to address. The larger conceit of this book thus consists in the examination of how anthropology might challenge philosophy's dominion over thought.

What I believe those who fall silent teach us is not a truth beyond what technology allows us to obtain. What they teach us is the unreason of reason that tells us how we are to find happiness in an undoubtedly unreasonable world.

Back to Iiris.

## Speechlessness

That particular night, Iiris broke the silence first, when usually that task fell to me. "I have a friend who's worse than I am," she said.

"Worse?" I asked.

"Worse. She makes less sense than I do," she explained and added, "She worked like *mad* [*hullu*]." Iiris, here, referred to her friend, Saija, who had been recently diagnosed with occupational burnout. According to Iiris, Saija sought professional help after she started to suffer from depression, severe insomnia, and a kind of fatigue that no amount of bedrest could take away. For Iiris, who had been Saija's confidante and had long worried about her friend's increasing social isolation, alcohol intake, reckless behavior, and emotional imbalance, Saija's diagnosis came as a relief.

Something was indeed wrong with Saija. The conferral of her friend's medical diagnosis provided a point of identification, a handle on how to intervene on Saija's various excesses. Giving Saija's distress a name, however, did more than merely open Saija up to technomedical intervention. Where Iiris remains silent about her own "madness," when positioned against Saija, she regains her capacity to speak. Iiris can temporarily disavow her own lack of sense by positioning herself against Saija, someone whom Iiris says is "worse" than her, someone with a diagnosis.

The topic of Saija made Iiris talkative. Iiris joked that Saija was the "office garbage bin." "If there is something that needs doing at the office, it will just end up on Saija's desk," she said. It is here that Iiris turns to the figure of the martyr worker. Iiris described Saija as not only a garbage bin but also as a martyr worker, a kind of worker, she said, that was "common in Finland today."

However, although Iiris draws a clear distinction between Saija and herself, it appears that the excess of martyrdom (or madness, as Iiris puts it) also claims Iiris. Unable to explain herself and yet unable to renounce the memo's demand to give herself, Iiris shows that she, too, is under the spell of an injunction beyond her comprehension.

Falling speechless, however, does not necessarily mean the lack of a desire to speak (Siegel 2006). Every time Iiris fell silent, she gave every sign of someone wanting to speak. She gesticulated wildly with her hands, and although she never produced words, she mouthed contours of words. At such moments, she would sigh and shake her head. That evening was no different.

As she fell silent, we sat mute, looking at each other from across the table, each reaching for the distant shores of comprehension and not quite understanding that we had already reached a destination. In my eagerness to understand what moved Iiris, I mistook this moment of silence as a void to be filled, an empty wasteland to be traversed until she spoke again. It is in going back to this moment via writing this book that I now understand it as not an absence as I had once believed. Speechlessness is no *no*-thing but an experience of negativity ordinarily covered over by speech.

Speechlessness despite the desire to speak marks a limit of speech to formulate. Speechlessness is not a mere inability to speak; it is not a condition we can produce at will. Rather, it is an instance of negativity that makes itself felt when we come in contact with that which resists being put into words. Speechlessness thus marks the place where something, the self, what moves us, the event, and so forth, remains beyond one's grasp.

Silence, according to Max Picard, is not the mere suspension of language; it is an "autonomous phenomenon" (2002, 17). Silence has an independent existence that allows it to intervene on language. Silence ruptures the smooth surface of a world wrapped in the "polite fictions" and formulations we make of it. It is through the spaces opened by silence that we come to question what sense we make of time and being. It is moreover through falling speechless that what could be said can be questioned, can be theorized. Here, this problem of speech revolves around naming the origins of what moves us.

In reflecting on the works of Mauss and others on sacrifice, George Bataille argues that although French sociologists accounted for "the effects of sacrifice," they fell short of explaining the enigma of what moves men to give and to give in excess (1985, 62). Bataille posited this question as the "ultimate question" and as one that holds the secret to why individuals expend themselves against their best interest.

This question of what moves us is one echoed by scholars of burnout. Although they see wasteful energetic expenditure through the lens of a stress disorder, they nonetheless take up the problematics of human excess and the conundrums that then follow. In the remaining pages of this introductory chapter, I thus wish to trace the history of burnout and some key thinkers on the subject.

According to Ayala Pines (1993), to burn out, one must first be "on fire." Despair and exhaustion characteristic of burnout, for Pines, emerge as a consequence of unrequited passions. Burnout results as a consequence of having one's very desire to realize one's ideals snuffed out and nothing remaining to spark an interest in life. Burnout is thus distinct from other stress disorders like work stress. Where work stress highlights the exhaustion of those who have worked too much, burnout stems from a toxic concoction of hopelessness, cynicism, and exhaustion that at times leads some to suicide.

For individuals "on fire," the moment of having done enough appears to constantly vanish into the distance. Where working toward an ideal might keep the fire alive, having to rethink the very ideals for which they are on fire—for instance, the death of a charismatic leader (Freudenberger 1974)—threatens the very source of energy that keeps such individuals going. What burns out, then, cannot be reduced to the physicality of stress science nor to an idea. What burns out is the relation or bond between the individual and a certain orientation to the world that leaves him or her empty. Social, political, and economic transformations thus can burn away at such a bond making untimely individuals particularly vulnerable.

Herbert Freudenberger documented the first profile of those most likely to burn out in his seminal paper titled "Staff Burn-out" (1974). In it, he wrote about his own experiences with burnout while a volunteer psychiatrist at Saint Mark's Free Clinic in New York City. The Free Clinic catered to patients who fell out of the mainstream health system, and many experts who worked at the clinic, like Freudenberger himself, were individuals who cared strongly about the provision of health care as an issue of social justice. These experts offered their time on a voluntary basis to care for individuals who would otherwise not be receiving any treatment. Although the Free Clinic sustained itself by the collective energy of the volunteers, Freudenberger, however, noticed that the most "dedicated and the committed" among them "walk into a burn-out trap" (161).

Burnout, according to Freudenberger, has a tripartite character. It not only affects the individual physically and emotionally but also behaviorally. He kept a journal of his own struggle with emotional exhaustion and also made observations of other volunteers. Based on his notes, he saw a pattern emerge. The "burn-out candidate," as he called them, were individuals who put in long hours and took personal interest in their patients. But because of their sense of dedication, these were individuals who failed to be satisfied with what care they could give. Freudenberger observed how under intense pressure "from within and from without" to "give" themselves, seeing any bit of their efforts overturned by the very institution for which one works, or worse, the very individuals under their care, very quickly turn colleagues into "house cynics" (161).

Guilt plays a central part in the making of burnout as a pathogenic condition. As Freudenberger puts it, a burnout candidate is someone driven by "a need to give" and is never sated with what they can give (162). For such an individual, guilt at not being able to give enough promotes "even further 'giving' and ultimate exhaustion" (162). This toxic combination of guilt, cynicism, and exhaustion turns feelings of aggression onto the self.

Freudenberger observed how colleagues who were once driven and dedicated not only self-medicated themselves in the form of heavy drinking, smoking, and use of tranquilizers but also took risks with their patients. He describes the "burnout candidate" in the following passage:

> He cries too easily, the slightest pressure makes him feel overburdened and he yells and screams. With the ease of anger may come a suspicious attitude a kind of suspicion and paranoia. . . . The paranoid state may

also lead to a feeling of omnipotence. The burning out person may now believe that since he has been through it all, in the clinic, he can take chances that others can't. He becomes overconfident and in the process may look foolish to all. (162)

Emotionally exhausted and racked with guilt, the burnout candidate breaks easily should any new pressure be placed on him or her. And with the halo carried by one who believes he or she has sacrificed everything, such an individual becomes impossible to discipline, should his or her risk-taking behavior negatively affect the patients.

Where Freudenberger's influential paper provides the first profile of the burnout candidate, it came down to Christine Maslach, a social psychologist from the University of California, Berkeley, to develop the diagnostic index that would be used around the world today. By standardizing the components of the disorder as cynicism, decreased professional efficacy, and exhaustion (Maslach 2001), Maslach allowed experts to distinguish between "normal" levels of emotional stress from its pathogenic forms.

Moreover, this index also allowed experts to "discover" burnout in workplaces across occupational groups. Contrary to initial assumptions that only certain professions with high demands for emotional labor—for example, health care, teaching, and police work—experts found that no group was safe from burnout as long as there was a potential for conflict between the realities of the workplace and personal ideals of work.

Although studies on burnout focus on what sparks the flames of the disorder, they nonetheless fall short of providing a theory of relationality based on loss. Rehabilitation programs and therapy provided for occupational burnout focus on the resurrection of individuals as authors of exchange. The "cure," as it were, resides in disenchanting the individual from what "dares" one to work, from work ethics of the past, and from other ideological forces that impede with the capacity of the individual to balance his or her energetic discharge.

However, in treating burnout as a disorder of martyrs, the untimely, and the workaholic (Salmela-Aro and Nurmi 2004), for example, we overlook the power of what burns, what sets us on fire, and how this force inheres in the very instance of social engagement. Where those with ideals that go against the times may experience the friction and stress that may slowly wear them out, there are those "on fire," as Pines puts it, who are favored by the times and have the resources necessary for them to keep going. In either case, it is through believing in something, in someone, in an ideal, in a future, that propels us. The force that makes us dare to expend ourselves comes from outside ourselves. It is not that we are "on fire," as Pines puts it, but rather that we *catch on fire*.

Burnout shows us that relationality depends on this capture, this contagion of fires to spread. It is a fire to which we sacrifice the balance sheet and the ledger. It is a fire to which we give our time without calculation. Without it, we would be subordinated to a utilitarian existence, an existence of a tool.

There is thus something sacred to this burn that resists being smothered by the profanation of ledgers and the balance sheet. Those with burnout highlight for the rest this tension between the enigma of what moves us and an economic project bent on the preservation of one's energies. Turning again to those with burnout as teachers, it is they who teach us how to think the human implications of an economy bent on preservation as opposed to one driven by loss. Finally, it is those with burnout who reveal to us the indeterminacy of what moves us, that we do not author our own actions, and of the horror of this condition on realization.

## Thesis on Negativity

In witnessing Iiris repeat the cycle of giving her time and energy only to complain about this gift of herself, I was seized by vertigo. It made no sense. Iiris's repeated sacrifices not only made her speechless but also had the contagious effect of making me, the witness, silent as well. The impulse to write comes from being drawn to this void, an existence without sense.

The void captivates and possesses. What is ethnographic writing that begins at this space of nonsense in which I author and yet I am compelled to write. What does writing from this place of displaced authority entail? How might we challenge ethnographic writing as a disciplined technique of seeing should we reframe communicative contact as horrific contagion?

Didier Fassin points to the authority of ethnographic writing as capable of putting the world into place like a "jigsaw puzzle" (2014, 43). He thus affirms the function of the anthropologist as the one capable of "speaking for" those suppressed of speech by connecting singular and individual experiences of dispossession with broader political and economic events of historical significance. For Fassin, ethnographic writing "captures life" (41). The anthropologist occupies a place of authority weaving together elements into a narrative whole. What I mean by the ethnography of the negative in contrast refers to instances in which no such position can be held.

Ethnographic writing here takes place through an inability to ignore that which continues to haunt. These ideas on writing stem from my witnessing individuals like Iiris fall silent and becoming myself affected by this limit of language. Maurice Blanchot describes the literary experience as a certain "sickness" (1982, 25). Mastery over writing exists not in the hand that holds the pencil. The hand that holds the pencil "cannot let go" (25), seized as it is by the compulsion to write. Mastery exists in the other hand, the one capable of intervention, of laying down the pencil, and thereby restoring to the writer as sense of him- or herself.

The ethnography of the negative attends to moments in which communication yields no access to oneself or to the other but nonetheless leaves an effect. Iiris offers herself to the office repeatedly, yet she gains no power to impose her will on the memo—she dares not ignore it and knows not why. It is in this moment of self-erasure when her own actions do not make sense to herself that we can finally question sense from "outside" sense.

But what does writing from this place of self-loss entail? What is data? Who writes? What place can we give to ethnography moments that give sense its necessary contours but lacks sense in itself?

Iiris's speechlessness infects every aspect of this book. Those who appear in this book do so as agent provocateurs who pose a threat to our boundedness as subjects with a place from which to name our experiences as our own.

As provocateurs, they set off a chain reaction in which the supposed "scene" out there is anything but external to the observer. They secrete anxiety into the very mechanisms of our anthropological distance. What is silenced is not Iiris herself but ordinary speech and the discursive techniques aimed at making sense. Provocations lacerate, they "wound" (Bataille 1988). They open us up to the outside to allow our fears, anxieties, and laughter to mingle in communion with others.

Here, I follow agent provocateurs I encountered during my fieldwork to explore how moments of speechlessness, silence, and the retreat of common sense free us from seeing relationality from the telos of the already self-evident. I aim to keep the wound from closing.

Ethnographic writing in this sense is one haunted by that which resists comprehension. It is thus a genre of writing driven not by a desire to reduce negativity back into the positivity of comprehension but one captured by that which fascinates. Fascinated, it can but speak in the spirit of that which appears at the edges of everyday language. Ethnography, then, is an endeavor that takes as its primary task the interruption of attempts that aim at determining what "passes in between entities" (Ffrench 2007) as part of conquered territory that gives closure to the uncertainty of being. The ethnography of the negative—here, speechlessness, stress, retreat—seeks not to historicize the context in which it appears, nor is it concerned with how individuals make sense of their condition. It concerns what agent provocateurs unleash, what they inspire, and what analyses can then follow. They wound in ways that take control of the direction of this book, but they remain as points of provocation, not entities opened to investigation. They retain their mysteries to themselves.

Seeing ethnographic writing as work provoked and work that provokes then provides an alternative framework. The image of the anthropologist as an authority that threatens to place individuals under examination, bolstered as it were by the academy, ought to be replaced by one in which the anthropologist places anthropology under examination through the encounter. Anthropology here does not remain out of the picture. It and the philosophies and methods that contribute to it are what become the object of study through the interactions begotten through fieldwork.

Moreover, ethnographic writing picks up what is exposed to analysis. It thus deals not with the "they" out there but the ethnographer who has been provoked into writing by her very exposure to the tensions and anxieties born in her very presence. It thus deals not in the description of what happened or how "they really" are; rather, it is concerned at its core with what provocations in the field can contribute to theoretical thinking. Theory lacks force without a basis in human relationality.

Meeting Iiris provoked certain anxieties. Being present, sitting with her, and seeing her silent struggles exposed me as well to the limits of what we can know as an experience. Facing such a struggle, I was also caught up in the enigma of why she could not make sense of her actions herself. Fascinated, I fell silent myself. This book attempts to rethink what spills out of such moments of negativity as fundamental to understanding how a politics and an ethics of self-recognition and self-affirmation are even possible.

# EMERGENCE

*Finland, especially Päijät-Häme, are [sic] now officially poor. The rest of Europe is sending wheat, milk powder, butter, and meat as food-help to Finland. . . . Finland was the only one of the new member countries that applied for food-help from the Union's charity funds. On the basis of the unemployment rate and gross national product, Päijät-Häme is among the poorest [regions] in the EU. Food-help was felt as degrading. The wealthy North is receiving grain from Europe to face their hunger! It feels like after the war, when care packages containing marbles were sent from America.*

—"Food-Help to Päijät-Häme," *Etelä-Suomen Sanomat*, cited in Inka Salovaara-Moring (2004)

The food aid that *Etelä-Suomen Sanomat* describes here came following the collapse of the Finnish economy following the end of its chief trading partner, the Soviet Union. The subsequent recession of the 1990s did more than challenge the viability of Finland's welfare model. As the *Etelä-Suomen Sanomat* article and many others like it indicate, the arrival of food aid from the charity banks of the European Union (EU) sank the country into a moment of national self-reflection. With confidence in the state at an all-time low since the end of World War II, the state of "we, now" gained center stage in national debates.

Social scientists writing on this period of economic and existential crisis argue that the transfer of power from state-bound politics of the welfare state to economically driven forms of governance occurred through a sense of "powerlessness" against global market pressure (Aslama et al. 2001, 167). Interviewing politicians and policymakers during the late 1990s, Minna Aslama et al. (2001) remarked how political elites often underscored the inevitability of making radical changes to the mode of exchange between state and citizen developed through the ideals of Nordic welfare. Political elites, according to these researchers, saw the recession as evidencing the inefficiencies of nation's economic-political model and that the country "had to" follow "the world outside," which, as one policymaker put it, was "many times . . . ahead of us" (171).

Moreover, the media representation of the economic crisis of the 1990s as a moment of "collective shame" (Salovaara-Moring 2004, 143) accelerated the palatability of making the economic competitiveness of the country a primary concern and also legitimated the sentiment among policymakers that the Finnish mechanism of welfare was "outdated" and something that "'we' have to reject . . . in order to meet the new challenges" (Kettunen 1998, 33).

With this in mind, Finnish leaders, formerly on the geographic and ideological borders between Western Europe and the communist world, courted membership in the EU. With the collapse of the Soviet Union, Finland could finally free itself of the ignominy of an eponymous condition—"Finlandization"—and make its own foreign policy decisions without fear of rattling Moscow. However, the economic crisis exacerbated a long-standing sense of "inferiority" vis-à-vis the rest of Europe (Kemiläinen 1998; Raunio and Tiilikainen 2003, 120; Tervo 2002).

Here, I do not seek to recapitulate the story of the EU's mid-1990s expansion or the collapse of communist regimes in Europe from the perspective of geopolitics. This ground has been well tread. Instead, I am interested in the everyday aspects of such a shift. As the Finnish government sought to recalibrate its own status within Western Europe, as I show here, individuals likewise began to rethink what it meant to be a member of the nation at the present moment.

I argue that the idea of a "we, now" has a directional element. In inscribing the "now" as a moment of difference, such a temporalization gives purchase to the notion of a novel way of being in common. Here, I attend to how marking time thus provokes articulations of "who we are" and mobilizes a particular idea of a "we." Moreover, I ask, what escapes such formulations of time as the present and of a "we" that supposedly dwell within it? What remains as the given and the self-evident when the present presents itself as an idea? What escapes?

According to Maurice Blanchot, we are "engulfed within and deprived of the everyday" (1993, 239). The moment we analyze what is given, it ceases to exist as a "current of life" (239). The everyday is what is given and what we fail to give ourselves; for in giving it to ourselves as an idea, a category, or a moment in history, we sacrifice the very thing we attempt to give. This current of life, then, is that which, as Blanchot tells us, has this fundamental character: "it allows no hold. It escapes" (239).

This, however, does not mean that no relation between the current and the idea of the present can be made. Blanchot calls the passage between the vibrant and spontaneous current of life and the controlled flow of history as "the very movement of society" (1993, 239). How do we relate to such a movement? In this double bind of stasis (e.g., the everyday as the space where nothing happens) and movement (e.g., the everyday as the current of life), how do subjects find their footing?

Here, following Blanchot, I turn to the everyday as the sphere charged by a given idea of the present but one that nonetheless provides no solid ground. Through a series of instances in which I witnessed individuals take issue with the very constitution of the present, I explore what such an awareness of the everyday as the everyday renders visible but also obfuscate. I do so by tracing thought provoked by encounters with individuals, each of whom came to question their very place within the here and now when the everyday appeared anything but the everyday.

# Viivi

Viivi lived on credit. Sometimes she borrowed money from her brother to pay her rent, but she still went to her office every day. As a master's student with no source of income, she worked at a government-subsidized student job during the day but with no hopes of getting paid. She had signed onto this job after losing her temporary work contract at her old workplace, but due to an error, this job became an unpaid position.

What had happened was this: the Employment Office of Helsinki told Viivi that her new employer did not have an employment office code that would allow the Employment Office to pay her. Even worse for Viivi, her new employer gave her this position as an office receptionist on the condition that the government subsidize her paycheck and thus, when the Employment Office disqualified her for wages, her workplace refused to pay her *or* let her renegotiate a contract that she had already signed.

She noted the irony of her situation. She needed work to pay her rent; she succeeded in getting a job but one that could not pay her wages. As Viivi said, "I am proof that we now have big holes in this security net of ours."

It was election season then in 2007, and she offered to walk with me through the city squares of Helsinki where different political parties amassed to hand out pamphlets, coffee, as well as other knickknacks in order to win voters for the upcoming election. After a morning of stopping by to listen to several groups, we sat down at our usual café on Mannerheimintie.

When I asked her what she thought of the election that year, she pulled out from her bag a political cartoon. The cartoon had eleven frames, and in one, a caricature of Jyrki Katainen, the head of the conservative National Coalition Party (Kansallinen Kokoomus [NCP]), stood pointing to a soccer field where two teams jostled to kick the ball into the same goal. Referring to the increasing power of the NCP and the Center Party (formerly the Agrarian Party), Katainen explains, "Finland has two teams, but as they both play into the same goal, we are all winners!" (*Joukkueita on kaksi, mutta kumpikin pelaa samaan maaliin. Kaikki ovat voittajia!*) (Kuukausiliitte 2007, 103). In another frame, Finnish lyrics to the anthem to the Soviet Union pours out of a gray compound obviously meant to represent the headquarters of the Central Organization of Finnish Trade Unions (SAK). However, instead of the official title of the building, it carries a more ominous title, "Armaqedontec OY" (Armageddon Incorporated).

Following these sequences of frames, a caricature of Oiva Lohtander, the actor made infamous for his role as the "greedy" capitalist in an advertisement made by SAK, a political group with strong connections with the Social Democratic Party (Suomen Sosialidemokraattinen Puolue [SDP]), is shown hauled away by two policemen.[1] Katainen's head complains to the reporter of left-wing propaganda in the next frame.

Where Viivi sees her condition as "proof" that holes exist in the security net, she pointed to the cartoon and to the statistics that give grounds to it as articulating politically why such holes now exist. Pointing at the cartoon, she claimed, "It wasn't like this during my mother's time." Something fundamental has changed, a change reflected in the spirit of the political left.

Specifically, she interpreted the satire as underscoring how unpopular the left—especially the SDP—one of the strongest parties in Finland's history, has become in recent years. According to David Arter (2006, 73), the SDP in Finland has been the largest party in parliament since World War II, and only in 1962, 1991, and 2003 has it lost this status. But in the election season of 2007, the SDP seemed to be in trouble yet again. The economic and political compromises it made to make the national economy more globally competitive had the consequence of turning its constituents against itself. This shifting economic and political position of the SDP was significant enough that the bourgeois parties (*porvarihallitus*) used the phrase "No Opposition Anymore" as their slogan.

I questioned Viivi on her own perception of the decline in support for the SDP, a party I knew Viivi spoke of approvingly on occasion. "Well," she said without looking up at me, "even when we had a center-left government, the SDP did nothing to stop the trend toward—I'm sorry—'American-style' politics. Workers have actually lost faith in the SDP and this is what remains." She went on to explain what she meant by "American-style" politics: a system of governance in which only those with money can obtain what in Finland is considered a basic human right. As an example, she told me of the hardships she encountered when, as an exchange student in high school, lived in a small town in Connecticut and, without a car or a driver's license, found herself stuck in the residence of her host family with no means to go anywhere.

"I had no way of getting around unless I asked my host family for a ride. It was embarrassing! In Finland, we have a basic right to the independence of travel no matter how young or poor you are. We love our public system, and our transportation system can get anyone anywhere. In *our system*, you don't need to buy a car to have the freedom of travel. In Finland, individual independence is maintained through the public."

Against changing political allegiances, the welfarist past emerges more coherent than ever. Moreover, Viivi follows a trend in the media to name this past "Finnish" as against the present that has taken on a distinctly "American" vibe. The past is one in which a moral politics sustained a collective system that allowed members of the national community access to transportation, dignity, and freedom. Viivi presents a conflict between a previous time, when "we" Finns had a moral obligation to contribute to the common for the good of the collective. It is a "we" based on trust that none should freeload on the sacrifices of others. This "we" she refers to is the collective of Nordic welfare, a secularized avatar of state Lutheranism, a collective dependent on this moral politics of honesty, trust, and self-sacrifice for the sake of all.

But the political tension that Viivi points to shows how this sense of trust in the other is being challenged. It is a tension that she also points to as giving sense to her everyday financial hardships and her constant struggle with the Employment Office that refuses to (or fails to) fix her paperwork so that she could be paid for her labor. Where annoyances of the everyday fall short of a name, a point of origin, or cause, shifts in the makeup of traditionally strong political parties (e.g., SDP) provide coherence as to why things fall apart.

But what is it that Viivi means when she refers to "our system"? To contextualize this notion of trust and honesty and how it works within the particular mode of exchange between state and citizenship, I now turn to examine the specific edicts of Nordic welfare.

## Welfare (*Hyvinvointi*)

Sociologist Erik Allardt reminds us "the word 'welfare' (in Swedish *välfärd*, in Danish *velfaerd*, in Norwegian *velferd*, and in Finnish *hyvinvointi*) also stands for well-being, and that it relates to both level of living and quality of life" (1993, 88). Moreover, according to Allardt, the ideals of Nordic welfare make explicit well-being as the satisfaction of universal basic needs: the satisfaction of which he argues is maintained by state intervention and a moral-communitarian-politics that demands that individual excess be sacrificed for the benefit of all. The role of the welfare state in redistributing wealth, then, cannot operate without the accompanying moral sentiment of mutual sacrifice that makes up the community.

Gøsta Esping-Andersen (1990) underscores this special relationship Nordic welfare states have vis-à-vis the market and the national community. According to Esping-Andersen, what characterizes social democracy or state capitalism in Norden (a term some scholars use to refer to states such as Norway, Sweden, Finland, etc.) is the role of the state in diminishing market power over labor. He argues that the power of the state to "de-commodify labor" also authorizes the moral-communitarian-politics of state welfare that prioritizes the well-being of the national community over that of the economic success of set individuals. Where the welfare state keeps individual economic liberties in check, the mutuality of sacrifice keeps the national community together under the state.

Such a relationship between the state-nation-capital triad stands in stark contrast to the "Anglo-Saxon-style" or "liberal" regime of welfare.[2] In the liberal regime of welfare, social reform is "circumscribed by traditional, liberal work-ethic norms . . . [and] the state encourages the market, either passively—by guaranteeing only a minimum—or actively—by subsidizing private welfare schemes" (Esping-Andersen 1990, 27). Esping-Andersen argues that such a regime model minimally decommodifies labor and creates a market-dependent provision of social rights and social security.[3]

The differences between the liberal strategy and the strongly welfarist one of social democratic regimes are exemplified in Juha Häyhä's (1993) comparison of contract law between the two. Häyhä argues that the biggest difference lies in the role of the state in protecting either negative or positive rights. Häyhä describes how the idea of negative rights, most closely associated with liberal ideology, enforces a legal framework necessary to put in place the moral imperative for others to refrain from impinging on other's rights. This protects individuals from the will of others and from the illusion of freedom as choosing one's own strategies in life. The role of the state in this case is to "guarantee that private contracts [a]re respected" (Häyhä 1993, 28). This ideal role of the state per liberal ideology builds on and promotes the premise that a citizen acts on his own self-interests and that the state must provide protection to its citizens from "others' and [from] the state's interventions" (28).

The welfare state, in contrast, has "the positive task of ensuring the material preconditions of the social and cultural autonomy of the members of the society" (Häyhä 1993, 26). And thus, unlike the liberal theory of society prevalent in the "Anglo-Saxon states" where "positive" tasks given to the state are seen as meddlesome and antagonistic to individual autonomy, citizens of Nordic welfare systems see state interventions not as "interference" but as the state fulfilling its role as the mediator between nation and capital—recall Viivi's indignation that the United States did not ensure that all citizens had access to reliable public transportation.

This is because the welfarist model of the state operates on the assumption that the state must provide positive rights for its most disenfranchised citizens, thereby taking up an interventionist role. Here, the assumption is that the "open" or "free" market is never a level playing field and that contract law must "limit the scope of freedom of contract in favor of the weaker party" (Häyhä 1993, 37). According to Häyhä, the duty of the welfare state is to "cure the problems caused by the open market," while keeping "the basic structure of the open market mainly . . . untouched" (34).

This difference in the fundaments of what constitutes the responsibility of the state (either to act as the protector of positive or negative rights) stems from how the need of the addressee within the national community is imagined. It further reflects the difference in the nature of social antagonisms germane to the particular political structure of both liberalist and welfarist societies.

According to Häyhä, the vision of law developed by liberalist states stems from a history of the oppression of general society under the perceived despotism of absolute monarchs. He argues that it is from such a perception of tyranny and the "unpredictability" as resulting from living under an all-powerful monarch that law developed as a measure to provide predictability and protection from not only powerful others but also from "others" in general (1993, 34). Or, to rephrase his formulation, the idea of the subject as desiring liberty from the imposition of others developed as a complement to and only because of the perception of the big Other (the state, society, etc.) as enjoying this freedom in our stead. Law, then, in this case, constructs subjects as already interested parties, free to enter into contract with others but owing nothing beyond what is deliberated by law.

In contrast, in Norden, especially in the case of Finland, Pauli Kettunen (1998) argues that a history of a free peasant society without a monarchy and without religious conflicts with the state placed the initial need for law on a different trajectory. The law is not put in place to protect individuals from a tyrant or the collective in the Nordic welfarist system, as the law is made commensurate with collective interests. Unlike the push for liberation from an intervening state, welfare law presumes that without the state, the logic of the market will take advantage of the weaker, less informed party of a contract. Häyhä summarizes these differences by two slogans: "Legitimate expectations based on contract" for liberalist contract law and "Contracts based on legitimate expectations" for the welfarist model (1993, 43).

However, despite the weakly liberalist vision of social democratic welfare states, Häyhä and Esping-Andersen both reveal that an interventionist state still keeps the market intact. Although the highly universalistic provision of social services "constructs an essentially universal solidarity in favor of the welfare state" (Esping-Andersen 1990, 28), this is not set up in opposition to the basic liberal principle of market success. Esping-Andersen (1990) claims that the most "salient characteristic of the social democratic regime is its fusion of welfare and work" (28). The universalistic and decommodifying principles of Nordic welfare require full employment and the minimization of people living off of the system: this way, "all benefit; all are dependent; and all will presumably feel obliged to pay" (28).

What lubricates the redistributive mechanism of the welfare state, then, is the affective and communal bond individual members imagine they owe to the national collective. Kojin Karatani (2005) argues that moves to counteract the commodifying power of capital by the state always mobilize an affective response at the level of the nation. Finding the hyphenated relationship of the nation-state lacking, he contends that should we attend to what he calls the "trinity of capital, nation, and state," we would better understand how capitalist commodity exchange operates within the imaginary of a community held together by an authoritative referee (17). Capital nation-state is an interrelated system in which each exists to limit the excesses of the other. Like a Borromean knot, it can only be complete in its relation to each other. This system works full force under the Nordic welfare regime, where the state implements laws of redistribution against the exploitative reach of global capital and finds justification by an appeal to national moral sentiment.[4]

Exchange thus occurs within the moral bedrock of a national communal obligation to sacrifice one's interests. Pekka Kuusi, one of the architects of Finland's model of welfare, advances the notion that the attempts to regulate the inevitable inequality that results from capital at the state level can only find legitimacy in a national community that values "mutual solidarity among men" (1964, 31). It is a solidarity maintained not via the force of state law but by the communal power to shun, shame, and to reward. It is the rule of the community that communicates what constitutes legitimate need, and it is again the community that identifies freeloaders who can be punished. The welfarist model of "contracts based on legitimate expectations," then, builds on a sense of exchange stemming from the political, economic, and social sentiments of the time (Häyhä 1993, 43).

In light of the significance of affective experiences that play a crucial role in the moral politics of the welfare state per these Nordic scholars, it behooves us to rethink Mary Douglas's (1990) critique of Marcel Mauss's take on social democracy in her introduction to his essay on *The Gift*. There, Douglas argues that Mauss's use of the logic of the gift to examine the mechanisms of redistribution in social democratic states as "really jumping the gun" (xv). According to Douglas, the elected bodies of the modern welfare state that redistributes wealth collected via taxation "utterly lack any power mutually to obligate persons in a contest of honor" (xv).

However, should we take Karatani's approach to expanding the nation-state to his triptych, capital-nation-state, we see that while the state lacks such a power, the moral code of the national community could be incited to induce feelings of obligation, shame, and indebtedness among its members. For instance, in his oeuvre, *Plan for Finland*, Pekka Kuusi (1964) emphasizes the affective role "envy" plays in pushing public policy forward.

Drawing on Eino Kaila's (1934) work on the affective dynamics of social equalization, Kuusi argues that the redistributive mechanisms of welfare ride on not the "lofty ideals" of universalism and the rights of man but "psychic forces of egoism and envy" (1964, 32). Kuusi cites Kaila, who states,

> It is peculiar how there is less social rancor and envy, less psychic dynamite of resentment, in a caste society than in a democratic society. For man only envies his peers; the slave does not envy his lord, with whom he does not compare himself. But as civilization reaches the lower social strata as a result of *social capillarity*, this kind of comparison is rendered possible. (33; italics added)

Capillary movement moves liquids up a tube. In "social capillarity," redistributive mechanisms level the surface tension of society by bringing every one of its members up the social hierarchy. Giving power to the equalizing policies of the state, according to Kuusi, gives rise to higher levels of aspiration and resentment that spares no one—not even "lords" who until then remained above the fray. Where the state lacks the power to enforce shame on those who take advantage of the system, these psychic forces of the community will. Psychic forces of envy, resentment, and equality bind individuals together if not for the mutual contest for the greater good but to ensure that none benefit at the cost of the other.

Citizenship in a social democratic welfare state therefore gains experiential sense through communal moral codes rather than of the polis. In contradistinction to citizens of liberal states where the state already represents a tyrannical and interfering "center," the Nordic state plays the significant role as referee that maintains a balance "between me and you, between egoistic and altruistic aspirations" (Kuusi 1964, 31).

Moving away from the notion of social struggle per Kuusi, Henrik Stenius (1997) argues that the redistributive mechanism of the state is upheld through the North's religious history. According to Stenius, in Nordic states, both the Lutheran tradition of equating self-sacrifice and humility with the path to salvation and the agrarian spirit of communal hard work strengthened the social fantasy of individual responsibility toward receiving welfare benefits. The social democratic society represented by the redistributive state is not tyrannical. Like Esping-Andersen (1990), Stenius sees work as "the main principle of Nordic societal organization and the force that holds the association together" (1997, 164). Citizens enjoy universal education, health care, sickness, and unemployment insurance only based on the faith that everyone works, is "honest," and will burden the community with only the most "basic needs."

The success of and the legitimacy of redistribution of wealth, universal coverage of social services, and benefits rest on the presumption of a citizenship well attuned to the religious principles of self-sacrifice, "humility," and "honesty" that merged with secular virtues of state welfare. Supplementing the authoritative power of the welfare state to intervene on the side of the nation against capital, then, is faith that all suffers but all benefits. Doubt, however, is never far behind faith. Stenius critiques welfarist communities as grounded on "intolerance" for letting others be. According to Stenius,

> What abounds . . . is common sense itself, a straightforward modern sense that feels competent to decide what is natural and normal. "Society," that which is shared, the *Gemeinschaft* that never completely vanished, knows no bounds. All the doors are open—to the living room, the kitchen, the larder, the nursery, not to mention the bedroom—and they are not just open: society marches in and intervenes, sometimes brusquely. (1997, 171)

The national community (*Gemeinschaft*) reproduces itself through the tacit rules of honesty, hard work, and self-sacrifice, and it imposes itself on individuals in ways more intimate than any law of the state. Where the laws of civil society (*Gesellschaft*) mediate between oneself and one's neighbors and thus exist as an external force against which one could take a position, the rules of the community in contrast remain opaque and barely visible in its very pervasiveness. It is this all-encompassing rule of the community that grounds the self-evidence of common sense and gives force to what one dares not transgress. It is here significant to note that the term *kansakunta*, the term for "nation" in Finnish, is made up of the word *people* (*kansa*).

Whereas Viivi points toward the explicitly articulated shifts between labor and state, in the examples that follow, I draw on moments when my interlocutors addressed the ways that changes in nationally imagined tacit rules had an impact on everyday ways of being.

## Kirsti

The spring of 2007 was not just a time of elections. It was also a season of scarves. In the fashionable districts of Helsinki, a certain segment of the nation's women sported Burberry's camel brown tartan check luxury scarf from England. Having witnessed four such women pass me on the streets on my way to an appointment with Kirsti, a freelance journalist, I started the conversation by asking her what she knew of this fashion. Incidentally, her work focused on investigating Finland's growing income gap, a topic coincidentally appropriate for the discussion on scarves.

Instead of addressing the scarf phenomenon head-on, she shared with me how she had been noticing a marked difference in how people enjoyed wealth. It was a difference she said that provoked "resentment." In the past, according to Kirsti,

> if you made a lot of money, you didn't want to show it because you would feel like *something awful would happen*. In eastern Finland, people are shyer about showing happiness than in western Finland. And people are more willing to show wealth in the south where there is a bigger Swedish impact. People just don't want to tell anybody if things are going too well, because, well, I think they fear *envy*. And this kind of dynamic goes way back. For instance, my parents live in between Kuopio and Mikkeli [towns in eastern Finland]. When they bought new furniture, they put a carpet on the window so that people couldn't see. . . . In Finland, you have to *deserve* everything—for example, even a glass of wine. That only comes on Sunday!

Her response to my casual observation about a scarf by a luxury brand triggers a memory that renders visible the present as a space of experiential difference. Kirsti's message to me was clear: the denizens of today enjoy themselves in quite different ways.

Transformations in Finnish welfare since the economic recession carry ripples beyond immediate shifts in policies to affect more intimate forms of relationality that contextualize how individuals experience the less articulable aspects of life such as fear, dread, and enjoyment. Enjoying one's wealth no longer needed to take place behind a "carpet" safeguarded from the prying eyes of one's neighbors. Wealth, under the new economy, no longer had to be morally justified or "deserved." Moreover, in a time and space in which having wealth has become dissociated from the notion that "something *awful* would happen," nothing barred the way to displaying it for all to see.

Enjoyment, according to Jacques Lacan (1986), contrasts with pleasure (*plaisir*) in that enjoyment, or jouissance, has nothing to do with the comforts of pleasure and everything to do with psychic tension. Jouissance is a condition that resists the labor of sense making. It springs from the register of the negative in which horror as well as the ecstatic finds its home. It is a self-destructive and compulsive form of pleasure that comes at the risk of unraveling one's sense of reason. Lacan provides the example in seminar VII of jouissance as the transgressive thrill of going out with a forbidden woman knowing full well the social and/or moral consequences that will result. The thrill is compulsive, and it is here the difference between pleasure and enjoyment lies.

Buying new furniture at pain of negative social judgment has elements of the destructive force of jouissance. Kirsti's parents do not simply get pleasure out of their new furniture; rather, their new acquisition has an added value, a psychic thrill of a taboo object, an object one ought not to have purchased and yet one feels compelled to have despite the risks of retribution. The space of enjoyment created behind the carpet on the window has the perverse intensity that comes of the knowledge that one might suffer for it. It is the coveted pleasure of those who dare break a communal rule. The wearing of the Burberry scarf in public with no attendant shame or attempt to conceal, then, not only makes such a dare irrelevant but also untimely. As Manuel Castells and Pekka Himanen put it, visible in the landscape of today is "the culture of the new technology option millionaires who enjoy their work and show off their wealth by driving Lamborghinis" (2002, 160). Public display has come to take the place of intimacy to become part of the fabric of the everyday; the new economy has shifted the relation not only between people but also what passes between people and things.

However, inequality, though much restricted during the golden age of welfare, is not something that emerged with the new economy. As we see from Kirsti, differential purchasing power existed "before," but only "now" do people feel free to show it. Each instance of exhibition (e.g., the luxury scarf and/or the Lamborghini) reveals the secret behind the carpet that Finland has always had internal differences. Moreover, each of these instances reveals a weakening of the social institutions that had impressed themselves on the individual that they need to cover up their items of luxury. What Kirsti calls the "fear of envy" has shifted into a demand to exhibit. The "polite fiction" has shifted from "we are all equally limited" to one of "we are all consumers of European luxury." Where luxury had to be covered over at one point with a carpet to be a member of the virtuous circle, the dictates of today demands that one must show one's purchasing power.

Yet, rather than finding pleasure in the freedom to display one's wealth, Kirsti speaks of "resentment" of her own. "How people flaunt themselves today just goes against everything that feels *right* to me," she said. What is "right" (or "wrong" for that matter) as it concerns enjoyment? And how does such a sense of what is right coalesce?

It is instructive here to return to Mauss. According to Mauss, what mediates the gap between gift exchange as it unfolds in practice as opposed to how it is conceptualized in theory is the "polite fiction, formalism, and social deceit" that provide the coordinates to how one ought to feel regardless of how it "really" is (1990, 3). Should we see "resentment" against those who flaunt their wealth as resentment against shifting social deceits necessary for the present to develop its own "polite fictions," we might understand how a shift in the narrative of what feels right and wrong may be cause for disquiet. The impact of the Maussian total social fact becomes an anxious point of self-analysis especially at moments of transformation when the fictions and social deceits that make up the fabric of the everyday fray at the edges and the threads start to unravel. It is at such moments that we cling to a coherent image of who we are—a chronotope with a set spatial temporal dimension that provides us with a sense of why we do what we do.

For instance, Kirsti makes it a point to identify her parents as both natives of the southeast, or Etelä-Savo region, a region, she says, less influenced by neighboring Sweden to the west. In the east, she says, people are "shyer" about "showing happiness." Against the west and Helsinki, the cosmopolitan capital to the south, the east retains something of an older, more "Finnish" character.

This idea of the eastern regions of Finland as being "particularly" Finnish can be traced back to the nineteenth century, an era of national awakening in which eastern Finland, especially Russian Karelia, became the inspiration for "Finnishness." This eastern and contested corner of the country provided not only the runes that became the basis of the national epic, the *Kalevala* (1835), but also the romantic point of origin for all things Finnish.[5] In thus constructing Karelia as the untouched baseline for national culture, cosmopolites of the late nineteenth and early twentieth century traveled from Helsinki to make pilgrimages to Karelia in search of their roots (Anttonen 2005; Sihvo 1989; Wilson 1976).

This fetishization of the east as the seat of "primordial Finland" makes possible a chronotope in which the east holds in place an originary way of being against which the nation can communicate what it is to itself. What "feels right" for Kirsti stems not only from her upbringing in the east but also what the east represents as a genre of thought. Referring to her parents' "eastern-ness" already contextualizes a set moral tradition identified as "Finnish." Against this, Kirsti sees new forms of enjoyment of which she has yet to be a participant as somewhat suspect.

Under advanced liberalism and its triumphal call for transparency, the transgressive pleasure of enjoying something behind a screen becomes obsolete. Transparency no longer demands such discipline over oneself as it peels away the moral fabric that covers over one's acquisitions as something one must "deserve." Instead of asking whether one "deserves" the envy of one's neighbor or not, transparency demands that one exhibit one's purchases. It is a point increasingly felt by the highly digitized methods via which we are tracked as consumers. Individual purchases fall under the mechanistic purview of consumptive data. In such an era in which no prohibition stands in the way of enjoying what one has, there is no jouissance in consumption as such. The perverse element of jouissance comes from the need to hide this fact. But this question of what gives pleasure only becomes a problem when faced with an everyday in which we suspect something most intimate to oneself has been lost.

## Jyrki

What is the sense of the everyday? Or does it only become a question when this very indivisible experience becomes just that, a question?

I turn now to Jyrki, a friend with whom I had no agenda, no question, and no motive for engagement. Without my usual list of questions or my notebook, I joined him and his partner for everyday niceties such as walks along the beach, shopping for a used stroller at the flea market—events that are not events and thus often forgotten as part of the everyday. However, by being a part of such nonhappenings, I also latched on to the social fabric of a small group of people, albeit on the very fringes. Through them, my social circle grew, as well as opportunities for further exposure.

"Hanging out" was never neutral, even with the closest of friends. The fact that I brought my "ethnographic research" to Finland to examine "Finns" and "stress" were notions that never strayed far from our relationship. Although such a framework horribly reduced the aim of my project, it was the way people read me. This tension was most evident in the reactions of people who did not care to know me but cared enough to be curious about my business in Helsinki. At parties, at coffee shops, at bus stops, at any public space where the presence of an unfamiliar Asian face sparks conversation, people never failed to ask me "What are you doing here?"

Although my fieldwork in Helsinki went without much comment, people were fascinated that I should want to conduct part of my project in the easternmost region of Karelia in Ilomantsi. Indeed, the mention of Ilomantsi, a region known for its beautiful rune songs and musicians skilled at playing the kantele, elicited comments from even those who cared little for my project.[6] Even though the rich traditions and the wonderful hiking to be had there were obvious comments to be made, many also noted how appropriate it was that I should go east to seek traces of mental illness.

"That is a place fit for mental illness," said Lena, a woman I was introduced to through Viivi. It was the first time she revealed to me that she was a native of Ilomantsi. Lena described Ilomantsi as a lonely place, where farmers lived there in isolated farmsteads with only their sheep and alcohol to keep them company. She told me of a time when she went to visit some relatives of hers and how she had a hard time finding a studio where she could keep up with her daily yoga regimen. As we sat sipping our cups of espresso at a bustling café next to the cream-yellow walls of the University of Helsinki, Lena predicted, "You are probably going to get a little crazy yourself over there with nothing to do! Do you know that our winters are very long?"

Yet, this fantasy of Karelia as a depressed and depressing cultural wasteland I so often heard mentioned in Helsinki contrasted sharply with the perspective of Karelian locals themselves. Where Lena spoke with some exaggeration that there would be nothing to hold my attention in Ilomantsi, Satu, a native of Joensuu, the capital of northern Karelia, saw stress syndromes as problems particular to city dwellers.

"*Stadilaiset* [literally, "city people" or people of Helsinki]," she said, "run around like chickens with their heads cut off because they have lost a sense of community. If you only care about saving time and saving money and don't care about how people feel, you will obviously suffer from stress and depression!" I ventured to mention some of the comments I had collected from my friends in Helsinki. Satu only laughed. "Why do you think so many of them come here to recharge?" she said. "Just look at the trail of people wanting to leave Helsinki over the summer, and you tell me where Finns go to get better."

Stress and its disorders, according to Satu, affect those in the city where the new economy makes itself felt at full force. Pathogenic stress is a disorder of those who have "lost a sense of community" and must rely on the consumption of private services, such as yoga techniques, for their well-being. Contra my friends in the city who saw residents of Ilomantsi as limited by the environment and the traditional life of a farmer for their choice of workout routines and yoga camps, denizens of Ilomantsi saw the issue differently. They saw Karelia instead as a vibrant community yet to be instrumentalized to the need to save time and money. Freedom and control over one's life rested with the countryside. There is no need to buy time to stretch one's limbs at yoga studios. Time exists in plentiful. None, according to Satu, must run around like headless chickens when there is a community that operates based on its own rhythm.

Pitting the city against the periphery, two conflicting narratives emerge. Each spins an image of the other as the one more vulnerable to mental illness—as the one more likely to break in the face of present-day challenges. However, they both imagine the city and/or the countryside as an effect of the present. Rather than a binary relationship between the city and the periphery, here we see that the relationship between city and periphery is mediated through an idea of the present. It is only against what is current—for example, yoga and time pressure—that a distinct imaginary of the other emerges.

Moreover, talk about mental illness brings the threat of becoming other to oneself to the forefront of thought. In taking my project on burnout, a mental illness, to Finland, "Finns" become subjects of my investigation, an imposition those in Helsinki resist by finding comfort in my taking part of the project to Ilomantsi, the east. It is not "Finns" per se but "those" Finns I am interested in. This tension that emerges when faced with a researcher examining unwelcomed themes cannot then be reduced to the story of the rural-urban divide. The eagerness with which individuals nominated the city or the country as prime candidates for burnout already points to the infectiousness of the anxiety that plagues the question, who is mentally ill, and what does that say about us? As I noted, this is anxiety provoked by the presence of an anthropologist—a figure with supposed claims to an authoritative discourse about and of the other.[7]

I now turn to Jyrki and the matter of shame, something that this project on mental health also provoked. Jyrki worried about his aging mother. Sick, she was granted early retirement from a coat manufacturing company where she had worked for over forty years, but he complained that it was relief she failed to enjoy. "She is so ashamed," he explained to me. He shared with me his concern one day as he asked me if I should like to accompany him on his grocery rounds for his mother. "She cannot leave her house."

Although business consultants and public relations officers for big corporations described loyalty, guilt, and sacrifice as sentiments of the past, Jyrki's mother suffered from a crushing sense of shame. It appeared those on the receiving end of welfare expressed contrasting sentiments from those who held fast to the idea that Finland had long since moved on.

Unlike my friends who spoke of mental illness, especially stress, as part of casual conversation about what distinguishes the city from the countryside, Jyrki, an organizer at a nongovernmental organization for people struggling with mental health, had a more nuanced take. For Jyrki, feeling ashamed about one's inability to work had nothing to do with where one lived or even with shifts in economic demand. Work, as it fed into welfare, had more to do with self-worth and one's status within the collective. He explained his mother's experience after she was given early retirement in the following:

> She didn't want to go to the supermarket in the middle of the day because then people would know that she wasn't working. If you don't work, you are not one of the people and you don't have value. You become part of society by working. Work is very important in Finland, and it's *shameful* if you don't work if you are not over sixty-three.

I asked Jyrki if anyone had said anything to the effect of criticizing his mother for having retired early. "No," he said, rather taken aback. "First, that will be the end of her! And second, she doesn't want to go shopping in the daytime, not because someone said anything but because she doesn't want people to see her."

Seeing my look of surprise, he added, "This does not go for all Finns." Jyrki proposed that the "new" generation of Finns were either getting "weaker" in their morals or were becoming "Americanized." Unlike "the older generation," like his mother, most people nowadays would "welcome" early retirement. The "new" generation of workers was those who could enjoy the benefits of being a citizen of the welfare state without having to feel any shame. Reminiscent of Kirsti's comments about those who feel no need to cover their windows, Finland now had "Americans" within who enjoyed wealth and felt no shame.

Shame comes from one's relationality to an ideal—here, an ideal of what constitutes moral citizenship and an imagined community that upholds it. As studies in chronotopic thinking shows (cf. Bakhtin 1981; Davidson 2007; Glaeser 2000), the language of the now and then that differentiates people into generational categories of the "old" and the "new" allows certain moral qualities found to be lacking in the present to be projected onto another time and space. This utopic space, back then, one that is "not here" and "not now," articulates a position taken against the present.

This position, however, is not merely illusory. That there is shame and not nothing reveals a moral experience that grounds and gives sense to the political economy of exchange. Jyrki's mother feels the weight of this moral framework without having anyone criticize her in its name.

This unprovoked self-censorship by Jyrki's sixty-year-old mother underscores her continued recognition of herself as a subject of a particular moral injunction. This not only sheds light on how informal social structures uphold tacit moral rules concerning work but also how the taken-for-grantedness of this moral directive gets reproduced in the everyday despite the shifts that take place in the realm of work. Despite the laying out of the present as a "new" moment, be it through shifts in the institutions of medicine, economics, and/or welfare, "something" remains in place to shame.

Jean-Paul Sartre (1992) details a famous scene on shame in *Being and Nothingness*. In this setting, he is looking through a keyhole and suddenly hears footsteps approaching. The sound of this approaching person makes Sartre suddenly aware of how he may appear. It is this moment in which he becomes conscious of himself vis-à-vis the other's gaze that he feels his shame, his object-hood.

Shame appears with what the introduction of the footsteps bring with it: an anonymous gaze against which Sartre must contend with his compromised position. Where for Sartre, shame emerges at the moment "I recognize that I am this object that the Other regards and judges" (Miller 2006, 14) and thus inaugurates the social, Jacques-Alan Miller (2006) turns to Jacques Lacan to argue differently. According to Miller, Sartre's focus on the subject's slip into an object is not enough to cause shame and that shame has less to do with judgment than it has to do with jouissance.

Miller contrasts guilt from shame and argues that "guilt is the effect on the subject of an Other that judges, thus of an Other that contains the values that the subject has supposedly transgressed," while shame "is related to an Other prior to the Other that judges" (2006, 13). Shame, Miller argues through Lacan, has more in common with the experience of one's own nudity. Nudity requires no judgment to be shameful. Shame in this reading has more to do with how both the judge and the judged share a relation to nudity as already something shameful.

Transgression thus need not take place: both parties, the one shamed and the one who shames are equally vulnerable to the common condition that binds them to each other—that they are both nude under their clothing. Joan Copjec sees shame as something that wells up beyond our control, like a blush. Contra Sartre, who links shame to the condition of our object-hood, Copjec argues, "to experience shame is to experience oneself not as a despised or degraded object, but to experience oneself as a subject" (2006, 167). In feeling oneself aroused in the most intimate way possible by the thought of an Other (e.g., blush), one feels oneself subjected but awoken to our very subject-hood.

For Lacan, it is through our very subjectedness, our experience of negativity, that the subject comes to experience itself as a subject. The experience of shame emerges as a condition divorced from discourse: for example, no one had to tell Jyrki's mother that she should not have retired early. Jyrki's mother did not have to speak, to justify herself. No such demand arose. Instead, she already experienced the shame, the blush, of having awoken to being a subject out of work. It goes for Kirsti's parents as well. They also did not have anybody telling them that they ought to cover up their furniture. They already knew to hide their goods.

According to Slavoj Žižek, hiding their "goods" despite their own judgment to keep them is the primary condition of real "obedience"—obedience without conviction. Real obedience comes from obeying a rule in spite of oneself. In contrast, "obedience out of conviction is not real obedience because it is already 'mediated' through our subjectivity—that is, we are not really obeying authority but simply following our judgment" (Žižek 1989, 37). The move to cover up what we hold dear, then, upholds one's interiority while preserving the fantasy that maintains the image of a flat society. It is obedience in that it despite doing the opposite (e.g., buying new furniture), you obey the rule by hiding the fact.

The fantasy of both Kirsti's and Jyrki's parents is that of the fantasy of social equanimity and people's collective abidance of the laws of hard work and an a priori moral "obligation" to other citizens. In both cases, they act "as if" they fully believe in the ideology of the social democratic state, while it is only through hiding aberrant actions that they contribute to the social reality of the state.

It is on this point that Émile Durkheim's idea of individual obeisance to the regulative order as set by society falls short. He claims that "man's characteristic privilege is that the bond he accepts is not physical but moral; that is, social" (1951, 252). According to Durkheim, individuals abide by the social regulative order precisely because it comes from an external place, outside of the managerial control of each individual. Individuals are bound to this power by "respect." How are we to make sense of Kirsti's and Jyrki's parents who, while giving "respect" to social order by hiding their actions, nonetheless got what they wanted. The regulative order fails to curb desire.

Žižek's (1989) formulation of real obeisance provides an alternative. For Žižek, obeisance is senseless and purely symbolic in a way that conscious "respect" or "conviction" play no role in the automatism with which the law is obeyed. Law is obeyed because it *is*, and this tautology is the fundament to the idea of Law's (capital *L*) authority (Žižek 1989). Law points to the original suspension in the world of symbolic networks through which subjects must come into "who" they are; it is the taken-for-granted woodwork of the social stage that are never consciously pointed out but are nonetheless essential in keeping the idea of social reality in place.

# Ville

Ville was in between jobs and had a temporary position as a translator of sorts for a Finnish rug company that had ambitions of exporting their products beyond Europe. Introduced through a friend of Jyrki's at a party, Ville asked me to put my linguistic skills to use. He wanted me to not only help him smooth out his English translations of the company's promotional material but also to translate the company website into Japanese—Japan being a big market at the time for all things Finnish.

When we met to officially start this process, he editorialized that "this is what you have to do when only a small number of people speak your language." He seemed also agitated. He flipped through the sheets of paper that needed my examination until he came to one page. Handing me the stack of sheets opened at this offending page, he pointed an angry finger at the last paragraph.

"This part here sounds so strange even in Finnish that I don't see why it isn't already English!" he said. He pointed to a subsection with the heading "History of

Excellence" in which the company laid out what made them uniquely "excellent" and how they wove modern designs out of a traditional recipe of "pure Finnish wool."

Aside from the usual promotional discourse, I found nothing grammatically wrong with it. Not happy with my blank response, Ville pushed the sheets of paper closer to me. "Well, read it!" he said, forcing me to read again. I read again but did not see anything strange—or at least anything that would provoke such a strong response as Ville's.

Not hiding his exasperation, he took the sheets from my hands and proceeded to read the text aloud, in doing so ignoring the fact that he had made me read it several times. "We only provide the materials of the best quality, blah, blah, blah," he read. "Don't you think this is excessive?" he asked. It still read to me like any other promotional material, so I neither agreed nor disagreed. He took my nonresponse as an answer, however.

"Of course, you wouldn't [think this is excessive]!" he said, sitting back on his chair, "We're doing this for *you* guys! We never used to say such things. It's so *American* to talk about how accomplished you are. It's like clap, clap, clap, clap [he clapped his hands with an exaggerated smile]—'I am *so* good!' Finnish people would not do this." He explained that such a statement "in Finland" would sound in contrast as if the company had something to hide: that actually their products were of poor quality and thus in need of a verbal makeover.

The work of translation has a way of bringing difference to the fore. It provokes thinking to coalesce around frozen essences between which the untranslatable emerges (Sakai 2008). As we moved away from the task at hand, he revealed that the reason why he felt so strongly against self-congratulatory statements such as that was because he was forced to make them himself. In his current search for a stable job, he had interviewed at several companies where they had asked him what "positive attributes" he had to offer. As he claimed he had never thought of making such a list before, he told me how he fell silent during the interview. Blanking out in front of his interviewers in response to what seemed to be an important question to be able to answer, he said, "I felt stupid. We don't know how to sell ourselves here in Finland. These are all new things that happened over the past ten years or so."

Based on this experience, he confessed to feeling nervous about all upcoming interviews, as now he anticipated having to "fabricate" something, which, according to Ville, should be self-evident. "They should just look at my résumé and know what kind of skills I have," he exclaimed. "In Finland, this was not always the case where you had to make a stupid list of your positive attributes."

As he complained, a loud group of well-heeled people in tailored business attire thronged into the coffee shop where we worked. They spoke in the exaggerated way one does when showing a foreign guest one wants to impress around town. In English, what seemed to be the leader of the group could be heard reciting an oft-used phrase as he encouraged his guest to procure drinks at the self-service line. "Finland drinks the most amount of coffee in the world!"

Ville did not miss a beat. "Just look at these people walking around like they have something up their backs!" he exclaimed. Now everyone in the group had collected their cups of coffee and was laughing together in polite unison. Another of its member could be heard going on about a trip to Greece he had taken with his family. At this, Ville sighed. "Vacation in Greece! People nowadays walk around like they're so great or something!"

Ville expressed distress at not the imposition of a "foreign" practice of self-appeal but the fact that such a practice now seemed the norm and was demanded of him as part of the routine of everyday life. The "American" was no longer a figure of distaste one could regard from a distance. The "American" surrounded him and threatened to transform him. They did not even have the courtesy of muffling conversation about their vacations to Greece lest others may hear.

Such perceptions of threat were especially significant amongst individuals at the early stages of their careers. Janne, another individual I got to know through a serendipitous encounter, was a college graduate in his late twenties who saw the need to "sell" oneself as an inevitable evil given what he said as the "state of today." Like Ville, he was in the process of applying for jobs, and found particularly onerous the demand to itemize and underscore his accomplishments.

"Now we must all learn the American way of 'selling' ourselves. Finns don't like to speak so grandly about what we can offer. But now the times have changed and we must hurry to speak up or else the job will go to someone else!" Claiming that the practice of "selling ourselves" as a foreign—specifically American—practice not only identifies difference in the everyday but also retrospectively constitutes "Finnishness" as something "not" that. Specifically, against the fabrications of the American mode of self-presentation, Finnishness gained coherence as an "honest" presentation of the self, self put on display without artifice, without, as Ville added, "the shame of self-aggrandizement."

These essentialized notions of Finnishness, however, provide no closure to Ville or to Janne or to any of the individuals who appear in this book. What is contested in the discourse of "today" is a sense of being a part of a community as they knew it. It is only by questioning what we mean by the here and now that the notion of community, of a common sense of being in time, becomes an issue. Being a part of a community, having a common sense of being, however only appears as loss, as this question of community both provokes a turn to national essences as well as to the discomfort that such common being also shifts through time. As both Ville and Janne make clear, the need to sell oneself during job interviews have become part of the everyday. It is they who have become untimely. Finnishness as a chronotope that references a time before such a change then becomes a way for such individuals to demarcate a space for themselves out of time, as well as out of the project of the present that demand they act otherwise.

Janne lamented the state of affairs, but he remarked that honesty may be lost in Finland but not in other parts of the world—especially not in the Far East. He was not alone in this romanticism. In anticipation for the release of the 2006 film *Jadesoturi* (Jade warrior), publicists covered station walls in glossy promotional posters. Coproduced with a Chinese crew, the film resets the *Kalevala* in ancient China (albeit with a white Finnish hero). In this mythic space that is not Finland but more Finnish than contemporary Finland, heroes of the Finnish national epic use kung fu to save their honor and to protect humanity from enslavement.

One night, as Janne and I took a train to see his friend play in a black metal concert, our conversation turned to the posters for *Jadesoturi* that surrounded us. "Asia still has honor," Janne said. "Finns have become dishonest." Yet, it was an Asia he could not place on a map. Janne cared very little what he exactly meant by "Asia."

When he bought a wall hanging with Korean script, he called me over to his house to translate the Japanese on his purchase. Having no knowledge or background in Korean, I was of no use. He wondered whether I had become too Americanized. In another instance, he asked me whether I could help him pick out some Chinese vases at an antique store.

At each such moment, he demonstrated his admiration for "Asia." However, it was one divorced from Asia as it exists as a cultural, linguistic, and territorial entity. But his uninterest in Asia as it exists gave strength to his conviction that it occupied a time and space untouched by the calculative demands of advanced capitalism. If honest and conscientious workers got no recognition in Finland other than as pathologically stressed individuals in need of medical intervention, Asia as a nonplace gave such workers value.

When Janne was not looking for a job, he worked at making his first CD. After much deliberation, he named his band *Koroshiya* or "killer" in Japanese. His music was a mix of heavy metal and rock, and he dressed the part. Janne sported a long chin-beard that fell past his Adam's apple, a long ponytail, and a black trench coat that almost grazed his ankles, not an uncommon ensemble for someone deeply into the dark or gothic variety of heavy metal common in the Nordic region.

The first time we met, I was out drinking with some friends at a bar popular among Finnish musicians and would-be musicians. Janne suddenly came up to my table, stuck his hand down his shirt to pull out a golden pendant head on a chain that said something in Chinese. In a drunk but still gentle voice, he asked very politely if I could translate what it said. It had been a present from his aunt who had traveled to Singapore.

When he was not preparing for a job interview and was not working on his music, he was generous with his time and helped recruit his friends. It is in the context of hanging out with band members and young college graduates without jobs that I collected stories of anxiety and frustrations that came from having a dream without being offered the means to realize it. Common in discussions about job prospects was the sentiment that they will not "sell out." With degrees in engineering and computer science from the University of Helsinki and from Helsinki Polytechnic Stadia, Janne and his friends were qualified for many of the positions they applied for had they presented themselves in a different light—the way their employers wanted them to present themselves.

Janne and his friends saw themselves as trench coat–clad Nordic samurais, true Finns who upheld a code of honor disregarded by a growing class of office people in suits. The difference between China and Japan made no difference to Janne. He expressed his respects for the "ancient Chinese" in the same breath as he professed his love for "Bushido" (loosely translated, the feudal Japanese "code of the warrior class").

Janne explained, "Bushido has all the elements of what made Finns so different from Americans and from other Europeans. I love the code of the warrior and Japanese culture in general because I think the Japanese kept this idea of honor and respect—things that I think Finns are quickly losing." I asked him whether he knew that Japan had long since embraced neoliberal politics. Bushido has the same mythic quality and relevance to modern-day Japan as the world of Kalevala does to Finland. He did not respond.

The allure of the other grows as the concerns of those most proximate begin to grate. Vinay Kamat (2008), writing on health-seeking behaviors in Tanzania, remarked on the extraordinary willingness of certain individuals to travel great distances to seek a healer when healers already existed in their own villages—healers whom others from other villages sought at long distances to meet. This observation led to his discovery of the remarkable allure that distance creates. Local healers who one sees every day, whose marital disarray and personal mishaps remain in plain sight lose the veneer of mystery that healers in more distant villages maintain. Healing and therapy, then, remain dependent on a certain desire of the seeker to find for him- or herself the healer who can play the part of the healer.

Andrew Alan Johnson, writing on Singaporean uses of Thai magic, argues that the perceived efficacy of the amulets of distant others depends on this very mystique. According to Johnson, "One wants not to understand something in order for its to be effective; to follow Mauss's line of thought, magic exists where one can dream about otherness" (2016, 9). Janne dreams about "Asia" as a place where honesty, honor, and truth continue to hold fast on the lives of its people. His notion of Asia animates the very Finnishness that he claims is quickly disappearing from current-day Finland.

"Asians," in Janne's perspective, become allochronous others that provide the point of reference from which to critique Finland in the present. Pertti Anttonen claims that for critique, people turn to "the medieval age in Europe or the present-day Orient, where 'ageless' and 'profound' traditions are felt to speak for a kind of social well-being that Westerners have lost due to their modernization" (2005, 33). In making the "now" a specific moment in history, the present gains articulation as a specific time and space—one dominated by a stance against moral sentiments of shame, honesty, and loyalty. Instead, in the "now," transparency takes the place of such sentiments by putting in place a technique for identifying the best candidate for a job. One must be able to catalog our attributes just as we should be able to list our degrees and qualifications. Mechanized thus, there is neither shame nor embarrassment in highlighting our own value.

Indeed, what came to be known as Finland's "new economy" unfolded under the banner of a post-ideological outlook. Pointing to the call for company loyalty and work for work's sake as ideological products of past welfare politics, economic policymakers demanded reform based on "the belief in the efficiency of free, open and competitive markets as a coordination mechanism of advanced economies and societies" (Heiskala 2007, 85). Honesty for such policymakers referred to peeling off the carpet to reveal Finland as having been always already competitive. It was a sentiment echoed by those frustrated by the likes of Janne and Ville, those who felt comfortable wearing their Burberry scarves and driving their luxury sports cars.

## Liisa

Liisa worked for Nokia. Like many who worked there, she saw the fame of Nokia as synonymous for the fame of the nation and saw her company as responsible for making the world aware of Finland. She was not alone in such a perspective. For instance, *Helsingin Sanomat* (Snellman 2001), Finland's premier newspaper, compared the success of Nokia during the recession of the 1990s with "the miracle of the Winter War" when a small Finnish military force staved off a large convoy of Soviet tanks using guerilla tactics and throwing Molotov cocktails. However, though proud of Nokia's achievement, Liisa was also weary of trumping up the novelty of economic ideas that rose with Nokia.[8]

As a public relations officer for Nokia, Liisa was adamant that I understood "correctly" Finland's place in the global economy. Before we got to know each other, she had agreed to share with me only Nokia's workplace wellness program. It was after she found interest in the aspect of my project that dealt with stress and its effects on economic productivity that she was willing to talk to me more broadly about her life and give me access to a network of individuals in the IT world. She asked to see some of the scholarship (e.g., Honkapohja et al. 1999; Jonung et al. 2009; Kalela et al. 2001) that informed my understanding of Finnish history and the economic context under which Nokia increased its economic and political significance within the nation. She agreed with insights from this body of literature that the 1990s was a major turning point for Finland and that the events that unfolded within this decade did much to recalibrate Finland's place in the global economy as well as its model of Nordic welfare.

With the dissolution of the USSR in 1991, Finland no longer had to sacrifice its freedom of speech or political and economic independence to Moscow; it joined both the EU and the European Monetary Union (EMU) in 1995 and 1999, respectively.[9] This era, according to Liisa, provided Finns with much pride and security. Taking up the euro and becoming a member of the EU provided much needed certainty as to Finland's place within "the West." Indeed, Finland was one of the first waves of countries to join the EMU, and it proved to individuals like Liisa that the nation was "among the civilized and the prosperous." However, she disagreed with the notion that new economic policies entered Finland during this era.

After my repeated usage of the term *new economy* one evening as we sat talking, she quickly stepped in.

> It is not correct to say that Finland had a welfare economy from the '40s to the '90s. Even in the '30s we had a *modern* economy! When I was working in the '80s it was already the case that we didn't have "Big Daddy" taking care of us. We had to think of our future in the workforce ourselves. People understood that they are on their own and that they needed to sell themselves. This is not a *modern* development!

Liisa's usage of the term *modern* carries none of the significance given to it by scholars of temporal experience such as Reinhardt Koselleck (2002). For Koselleck, the modern emerges from the kind of "rejection" of the past as articulated by Finnish economic policymakers during the economic crisis of the 1990s (cf. Kettunen 1998). In breaking with and codifying time as *the past*, modern sensibilities emerge. The current is that which moves into the future by cutting itself away from the past.

Lisa Baraitser (2017, 6) details this current of time as one driven by political and economic shifts that occur together with technological developments that compress time and space in different ways. Such movements create ripples. Time rendered obsolete manifests as shocks, crises, and anxieties that in turn provoke specific aesthetics of the present. As Viivi, at the beginning of this chapter, claims in reference to her financial woes, "It wasn't like this during my mother's time." In the movement of time, space becomes churned up. It becomes open to review.

By "modern," Liisa refers to economic rationalism, the perspective that maximization of profits through workplace efficiency and lean production provide the remedy to political ideology that demand that the state protect that nation against the commodifying effects of capital. What is modern here refers to a supposed post-ideological condition purchased via divorcing the economic from the political (the state). The push for this split has always existed within the more business-friendly political parties. In this sense, Liisa was right. There is nothing "new" in the logics of the new economy; just because they are implemented in the present does not mean that Finland was not part of "the modern economy."[10]

Liisa saw not being a part of this modern form of exchange as a threat to Finland's place not only in Europe but also in the world. "Finns and Europeans in general have a collective conscience, but Asia has *ten* times that of Finland. They are [she paused] like birds. When one bird looks in one direction, they all turn together." When I pressed her to explain, her response was simple. Europeans, according to Liisa, occupied a "profound" position in between Asians and Americans. Asians, trapped in tradition, act like flocks of birds, inhuman in their mechanical solidarity. Americans, Liisa tells me, lack history and therefore fail to consider the weight of "hundreds of years of civilization and culture." "Finns and Europeans" straddle this zone in between lack and too much cultural cohesion, a position, she says, that makes them "profoundly modern."

Finland, in particular, emerges as the most modern nation in this equation. In addition to having to contend with its history of welfare, Finland gains its "profound" quality through its long years of capture in between the influence of Moscow and Western market forces. The character of the modern takes shape through this history of having to constantly balance the East against the West, the past against the present: it is a feat requiring a live and current consciousness capable of carrying the nation through to the present and to the final actualization of its logic—the new economy.

She was not the first to make such an analysis. And as Janne's and Liisa's responses foregrounding my ethnicity indicate, my own status as an Eastern/Asian figure asking about Finland's new economy provoked very specific responses.

Within my first week of making my rounds at the University of Helsinki introducing my project and myself to graduate students and scholars alike, my presence elicited discomfort, even laughter. Jukka Tontti, professor of social psychology, and one who sponsored me during my affiliation at his department, mentioned me in one of his seminars, and his class broke out in laughter. "They could not understand why you would be conducting an anthropological study here in Finland," he explained. "They wanted to know why you were not doing [your project] in your own country." A graduate student from the Department of Anthropology was more direct. Assuming my citizenship to be Japanese, she wondered why I did not study the problem of stress syndromes there. "They are the ones dying from honor," she said. "You will not find that here."

Finland is not the place of the ideologically driven. Those that are placed in rehabilitation centers. On the other hand, Japan is a country long associated with notions of "honor"—one that drives its citizens to their graves. The zone of the modern eschews forms of exchange that make no economic sense. When such relations occur, individuals are diagnosed with a mental illness. They do not remain part of the social fabric as part of the culture of honor. But why should I encounter such resistances, such laughter?

Here, I see my presence as raising the specter of the "East" and of provoking individuals in ways a white ethnographer would not. In her essay "Writing against Culture," Lila Abu-Lughod reminds us "every view is a view from somewhere and every act of speaking a speaking from somewhere" (1996, 468). Knowledge gained from ethnographic examinations, she argues, is situated knowledge, not one gained from "standing apart from the Other" (468). Part of accepting ethnographic knowledge as situated knowledge comes down to seeing oneself as part of what is being examined. It is a point made explicit by Claude Lévi-Strauss (1987, 29) who argues that the ethnographer is always already a part of his observation. I do not have access to thought untainted by my presence. The responses I get are responses not merely to my questions but are responses to me—to what I represent. The present, thus, contains both what is present and what what is present represents.

My questions concerning Finland's economic transformations have the added sting that they come from me—someone supposedly from a less modern place. By asking individuals like Liisa about Finland's "modern" developments from my untimely background, I irritate sensibilities. I appear to be speaking to her from a coeval space.

In fact, the specter of the East is nothing new. The era of colonial expansion in Europe in the nineteenth century did more than increase awareness of the spice lands in the exotic East. It was the era in which travelogues grew as a genre and when Europeans from powerful centers dedicated many a page to Europe's internal others. Finland, with its non-Indo-European language, its stint as a grand duchy of Russia, and its ambivalent place within Scandinavia, suffered the ignominy of being treated as an object of scientific and ethnological curiosity for those who took their Europeanness for granted.

In her book *Finns in the Shadow of the "Aryans": Race Theories and Racism*, Aira Kemiläinen (1998) describes how early twentieth-century monographs by Scandinavian and British ethnologists further damaged Finnish national self-representations by making claims that Finns had Mongoloid genes.

She makes explicit in her book that it is intended for "foreign readers," and to them, she emphasizes the error and racism implicit in equating the Finns with "ugly looking Huns," the Mongolians, and the Japanese because "the Finns are among the blondest populations of the world" (Kemiläinen 1998, 273). Fighting back against this trend, Kemiläinen remarks, "It could be a shock for a small blond girl to read in a textbook that she was a Mongolian" (78).

Jopi Nyman (2000) describes how Finns were often depicted as ugly and as akin to the "Chinese" in the early twentieth-century travelogues and journals written by tourists from Western European countries. Paying attention to the text of Mrs. Alec Tweedie (1898), the author of *Through Finland in Carts*, Nyman shows how she turns the Finns she met in her travels into "passive beings, representatives of a lower race and culture, just like the Muslims" (2000, 66). According to Tweedie, the Finnish saying, "*Se oli niin sallittu*" (It is so ordained) echoed the "fatalism" of the Mohammedan who respond to misfortune with the remark, "It is the will of Allah" (66).

Besides the most obvious problem within this genre of writing in which local inhabitants grace the pages next to native plants and animals that catches the fancy of the European observer, Finnish critics take as self-evident the offensiveness of being compared to the "ugliness" and "passivity" of the "Asiatics" (e.g., Kemiläinen). Of interest here is that there is offense, and there is offense only because of the danger such comparisons pose to the self-determination of the nation.

Individuals like Liisa continue to feel at risk of being orientalized and excluded from the happy club of Europeans beyond the suspicion of individuals driven by an agency not their own. Moreover, this demand to be recognized as part of modern Europe manifest in other ways.

In a section of a website created by the Finnish Ministry for Foreign Affairs titled "Remarkable Features of Finland Plus Some Common Misconceptions," Maarit Ojanen (2006) writes, "Regardless of the fact that we are European, our country is often missing from maps of Europe. Television weather maps are typical of this omission. The capital is called Helsinki, not Helsinsky. People who live in Helsinki, and Finns in general, are offended by this erroneous spelling, because it makes Finnish look like a Slavonic language, which it is not." The National Museum in Helsinki provides a space to air this concern by providing a plaque titled "Ethnic Development" as part of at the permanent exhibit. The plaque states for all to see the following facts: "Genes of Finns are 75% Western (Europoid) and 25% Eastern (Mongoloid), while our culture is Western."

These abstracted and reified notions of Finnish culture, genetics, and the dichotomization of the West and the East are prominent in spaces where Finnish identity is made visible: such as in tourist and business brochures, museums, and sites of comparison. Although the European Commission promises to integrate the region as equal members of the European Community, this creation of a supranational unity ironically puts in motion exclusionary politics that highlights those who deviate from the European standard.

Against those at the center who take their Europeanness for granted, those in the periphery must identify as being European through acceptance of their very displacement: they do not occupy the source of what makes Europe "Europe." As such, coming to identify oneself as being European is never a passive process for those in the periphery of the West but one fraught with friction. Individuals who must prove to others their European membership are subjects caught in between a symbolic category that does not belong to them, yet from which their idea of themselves derive. Thus, unlike postcolonial and subaltern scholars in the non-West who take a critical stance toward all forms of European cultural hegemony (cf. Bhabba 1994; Chakrabarty 2000; Sakai 1997), those exoticized by Europe but imagine themselves a part of this orientalizing power have a stake in keeping alive the existence of "Orientals" more "Oriental" than themselves.

In terms of those who see the new economy of the present as having always already been part of the national past, any attempt to carve the present out from the past threatens to position Finland as occupying a space external to modern sensibilities of exchange.

This disavowal, however, fails to extend beyond discourse. As we see through Kirsti's personal experiences and those of others, the present manifests as an interruption to the everyday as a given and self-evident time and space. Whether in the form of women who flaunt their luxury scarves to neighbors who cover their windows no longer, the everyday is ruptured by difference that forces it open to history. As a moment in history, the everyday or the present manifests as a particular suspension in which one's sense of what is falls under examination.

# Negativity

Extraordinary events that rupture the fabric of the everyday provoke thinking on what ordinarily goes without saying (Blanchot 1993). The everyday opened up as a question of the present, a matter of history, "is no longer the average, statistically established existence of a given society at a given moment; it is a category, a utopia, an Idea" (239). In this review of what is given as the everyday, it loses the very anonymity fundamental to its condition as the everyday. Instead, certain figures and practices emerge to mark the present as a time and space distinct from the past.

The "neighbor" who flaunts wealth, "the Asians" who still have honor, the self-commodifying "American," and or "Finns" as having always already been modern emerges as figures of the here and now who rip the everyday apart. Although these codifications identify the emergent horizon of the present, they paradoxically underscore the everyday as an existence against such determined thinking. Figures and events that come to mark the present by its difference from the past serve as prostheses that nonetheless reference the indeterminacy at the core of what constitutes the everyday.

One poses the everyday as a question when faced with that which challenges what was given. Such challenges to what was given not only convert the sphere of the everyday into happenings of history but also have the effect of making what was given about one's sense of self suspect. The question of the everyday, then, is at once a question about what is given, as well as one that problematizes how we are given to ourselves in a set time and space. Such questions concerning the everyday has the double effect of making clear while making unclear the given circumstances under which we see the everyday more clearly.

In his book *Empiricism and Subjectivity*, Gilles Deleuze reframes Kant's question, "How can the given be given to the subject?" (1991, 110) via Hume to ask instead, "How is the subject (human nature) constituted within the given?"

Placing the emphasis on the creative potential of how subjects become affected by instances of seeing the everyday differently, Deleuze gives primacy to the given as a condition productive of new potentials for becoming other. Where Deleuze sees the openness of the everyday as a driving force for the freedom of social movement, what I saw repeated in my encounters in the field was something less affirmative.

For instance, in Kirsti's story about the decision regarding whether to cover the window to hide the purchase of a new piece of furniture, we see that she locates the decision not in her parents but in the "kind of dynamic [that] goes way back" and in the specific region of eastern Karelia. Moreover, one cannot forget the original context in which she is reminded of her parents' covered windows. She shares this story with an eye toward sharing with me her "resentment" at the women flaunting their Burberry scarves that were trending at the time. In this chain of events, something about the everyday is apprehended as different. A "wedge" (Nielsen 2014) has been made in time in ways that call forth an analysis of the present as "the present." In speaking in the register of "the present," the given and the everyday are lost.

Although she emphasizes her parents' "easternness," her narrative trajectory traces her resentment to the scarves back to this very origin. New forms of intimate enjoyment incite judgment: however, in judging others, one also judges oneself. Acknowledging her resentment of the scarf wearers does two things: Kirsti aligns herself with her parents and the east but also sees herself out of time with the present in which individuals enjoy luxury goods as a given. Moreover, in making these reflections, she herself becomes divided. Under such conditions, nothing remains to ground the self-evident. Her language of the "the present" and of "the new" underscores this form of unraveling in which she cannot just be since she poses the everyday as a question.

In the transition from one condition of the everyday in which it was a given to cover up one's wealth, to another (e.g., where people are considered "old fashioned" or "crazy" to cover up windows just to hide furniture), certain elements fail to gain symbolic translation but are, however, necessary parts of the whole that constitute social "normalcy." The experience of the given that remains untranslated haunts the present as a residual enigma irreducible to history. And in this loss of the self-evident in terms of relationality, codification of national essences, individual character, and utopic rendering of the other prevail.

# UNTIMELY SACRIFICES

Henna died alone in her apartment at the age of fifty-seven. Although the directing managers at the real estate agency where she had worked for the past twenty years kept the details of her death hidden, they informed the office that Henna's death was caused by a heart attack, one in turn caused by stress. As the office went into mourning, many also speculated about why her life was cut short in so violent and sudden a manner.

Death fascinates, and the shock of Henna's abrupt departure turned into wonderment. People wondered why she worked the way she did. "There was *no reason* for her to work so much," said Oskari, an agent who had a desk next to Henna's. Oskari was not alone in asking why.

When actions are perceived to have been taken for "no reason," wonderment has a way of quickly turning into allegations of madness—a suspicion legitimized by the official announcement of her death as a condition brought on by occupational burnout, a mental illness.

But Henna's sanity was not all that was brought under examination after her death. As Martin Heidegger reminds us, thinking about our death is a way of thinking about our relationship to time. Being is time, or so he tells us, and in being, we attempt to grasp the condition of our own intelligibility. There was something of that at work here. Henna's death made no sense, but it also marked the beginning of a need to make sense and to positively identify why we do what we do in the here and now.

Prominent in such discussions was the problem of sacrifice and whether it made sense in the workplace under current political, economic, and social conditions. For instance, Oskari and others pointed to Henna's death as a timely issue stemming from the job precarity, competition, and cutbacks in social welfare that characterized the challenges of late capitalism. According to many, the kind of sacrifices Henna made for others had no place in the workplace today. The sacrificial structure that drove the virtuous circle of Nordic welfare was a thing of the past. Current economic imperatives demanded citizen workers to approach energetic expenditure more instrumentally. One gives the gift of one's energy and time not out of moral political convictions, but only when it makes reasonable sense. With the structure of sacrificial labor made untimely, the sanity of workers like Henna falls under doubt.

Here, we return to address more fully the question, where does history end and where do I begin? Calling Henna an untimely worker from an older era yet to shake the demands of history also makes those who are timely suspect. Are those who act in timely ways not also operating under the self-erasure of becoming a part of the historical present? What does it take to give as an act authored by ourselves when such gifts must also make sense under conditions of timeliness?

In this chapter, I explore timeliness as a condition that requires a certain form of giving in, of opening oneself up to a concept of the times—of self-erasure. Specifically, I ask what such an approach to belonging in time exposes concerning the place of the egological subject.

Different economic regimes come with their own brand of pathogenic fatigue. In this way, emergent fatigue categories and how they render particular relationalities problematic within set time and place become key analytics. Through exploring the particular stakes of timely exchange, I focus on what forms of relationality and exchange are enabled expression at the expense of others.

Occupational burnout emerged together with the awareness among Finnish policymakers that they ought to "update" the welfare mechanisms of the nation if they were to increase the nation's competitive edge in the global economy. Against martyr workers and other untimely forms of workplace exchange, Finnish health experts introduced new techniques of stress management as well as policies that demanded more workplace transparency that would allow workers better control over workplace exchange.

But as Marcel Mauss would argue, we are not always in control over what we give. In attempting to solve social problems, health and political regimes put forward a particular conceptualization of exchange or of how exchange should be. But we must heed these formulations as promises yet to be realized. To buy into this promise would mean to sacrifice—to "give our thoughts," as Émile Durkheim (1995) puts it, to the technical gods in hopes that they will answer our prayers.

In the face of increasing faith placed in technomedical means to manage and to defer death, how does the category of burnout give a particular conceptual shape to relationality? And if we see stress management as a technique that purports to give us timely control over relationality, what emerges as the goal, the destination of such a mode of exchange? To what end do we manage how we spend and save our energetic output? And what happens when we believe we could bring the relations that pass in between individuals under the formulation of managed exchange? In short, I here examine the promise of technomedical thinking that we could control relationality as that—a promise, the very definition of which comes from its lack—a promise is a promise of that which is yet to come.

In the conversations that followed in the wake of Henna's death, I saw how the notion of untimely sacrifice structured the analysis of what moves us to do what we do. In seeing sacrifice as structure, Henna emerges retrospectively as a worker out of joint with the present, someone driven by an older ethos to give. Moreover, identifying Henna as a product of an untimely sacrificial structure allowed individuals to not only *make sense* of *why* she did what she did, but also to distinguish the present as a time and space cut off from such a past in which sacrificial labor mattered. Against such a past, the present emerged as a time and space that allowed individuals to take back control over the forces that move us to give our energy against our self-interests. In this scenario, one makes a gift of sacrifice only, as Oskari put it, when it is "reasonable" for us to do so. And as anthropological studies on time tell us, the trope of the past has a way of not only guiding the present but also of promising time and being as potentially *manageable* conditions.

Making sense of Henna's "unreason" through the structure of sacrificial labor, then, promised a certain hope for the present. It allowed individuals to say that in the present, we see this structure clearly and that we could break out of this cycle driven by the virtuous circle of capital-nation-state. We could, they said, bring sacrificial exchange within the folds of reason.

But sacrifice is that which often defies social reason. It continues to frustrate and to irritate those who attempt to administrate over the force that moves us to expend our energy. It is moreover a question that has plagued industrialists who have long strived to make labor more efficient.

And now back to Oskari.

Oskari had a pet theory. "Henna is what we call a martyr worker. She worked like mad, and for what? And now she is dead." In calling Henna a "martyr worker," he highlighted what he expressed as Henna's "unreason." She had "no reason" to give her time as much as she did to the office.

"She is from an older generation of workers," he said. But this leaves the question, what is the relationship between reason and being from an "older generation," those who are "unreasonable"? What is reason when it cannot transcend its narrow temporal confines?

Oskari added that he was "not surprised" by how Henna had died. Henna's death, in this view, appears as something preordained, something bound to happen, an inevitability given the telos of what constitutes exchange at work today and the unreason of the older generation. These categories, "today," "martyrs," "older generation," provided reasons for actions that interrupt the smooth operation of the everyday. They come to ground why individuals like Henna may give themselves for apparently "no reason," suffering all the pains of sacrifice without any of the recompense.

Many at the agency shared Oskari's perspective that linked Henna's heart attack to an untimely orientation to the present. Lisa, one of the managers at the agency, saw Henna as an inflexible and maladaptive worker. In a private conversation with me, she criticized Henna for having stubbornly clung onto ideals of a past workplace. Although she recognized Henna as someone with great community spirit who was always willing to lend a hand, Lisa claimed that she had let this develop into pathology—Henna refused to stop giving her time and energy when it was necessary for her to stop. Lisa exclaimed that "we live in a faster and harder world" and that agents will do well to better manage their work-life balance. "We must only take on work that we can reasonably handle," she added.

In making her statement on Henna's death to the whole office, Lisa highlighted how "survival" depended on striking the right balance between work and life. Highlighting the dimension of burnout as a condition that stems from, as Finnish researchers put it, "depletion of energetic resources" (Ahola 2007; Shirom 2003), Lisa saw keeping such an account crucial to preventing the depletion of energy. Human energy is finite, in this model, and it must be managed. In closing, she promised the office a workshop on stress management with an occupational health expert.

Death is terminal and beyond intervention. But Lisa turns Henna's death into an occasion to make a point. By turning death into a problem concerning the economics of human energy, Lisa successfully exchanged the terminality of death for a more manageable condition. Death here, under the category of occupational burnout, became something to be *worked* on, and under this framework, what moves individuals to work fell under the scrutiny of medical and economic management.

Health experts from the Finnish Institute of Occupational Health (FIOH) link the cause of lost working hours to stress. FIOH found that businesses most vulnerable to the disorder were those that had undergone the most organizational transformation, whether through adding new technology, cutting the workforce, or introducing new compensation patterns. According to these experts, repeated changes in work had the tendency to create stressful conditions at the workplace and to decrease the likelihood workers would cooperate with each other. Occupational burnout thus marks the tension that arises between what *was* and what *is*. It affects those who fail to, as FIOH put it, update themselves. It marks as untimely all forms of self-expenditure that go against the current of time. It is this wasteful effort that stress management attempts to correct.

Gilles Deleuze calls apparatuses, a term he borrows from Michel Foucault, "machines which make one see and speak" (1992, 160). But machines that shed light also cast shadows. It is a point *not* taken up by Deleuze who focuses on what becomes and thus can be affirmed. Here, in asking what is made visible, the goal is to examine that which is left out of the line of vision. What does the spotlight on sacrifice, an untimely mode of exchange, obfuscate? What passes in between individuals that remain beyond such lines of light?

In taking up this challenge between obfuscation and affirmation, in this chapter, I rethink stress and the positive enunciations it allows us to make on relationality through classic anthropological and recent theoretical takes on the logic of sacrifice.

## Empowerment

Although cases like Henna's do not gain national attention as "death from overwork" (*karōshi*) as they do in Japan (Kitanaka 2011) or China (Luo and Ruiz 2012), Finnish health experts identify death as one of the possible outcomes of occupational burnout.

In stress management workshops, they highlight how chronic exposure to high-stress situations hold individuals in a constant grip of "fight or flight" response that triggers an overproduction of hormones that hardens arterial walls and increase the likelihood of stroke and heart attacks. Experts agree that although cardiac arrest is the most extreme end point of occupational burnout, when taken together with an unhealthy lifestyle can slide into clinical depression or a loss of desire to live.

In response to the rise in complaints of workplace stress, FIOH promoted stress management workshops to many businesses. These focused on what they called a participative method. The workshop, as the name suggests, was to produce a space not for top-down forms of management but rather for a platform for dialogue among employers, workers, and experts. By getting workers and employers to communicate to each other the pressures and concerns at the workplace, the occupational health expert was to help them see how to create a frictionless and more productive workflow. Through identifying and talking about existing problems that contributed to making the workplace a stressful place, experts argued, both workers and employers would be "empowered" and be able to take control over workplace exchanges.

Empowerment was a key concept not only in these workshops but also in rehabilitation programs on occupational burnout. As the disorder was linked to the burning out of the will to work, what the FIOH called the empowerment paradigm was aimed at intervening against this processual attenuation of spirit.

Empowerment in the context of an office-wide workshop had a lot to do with keeping individuals in control over the exchange of labor for compensation or for other recognizable benefits (be they career advancement or social recognition). The concept of empowerment thus went hand in hand with public health campaign promoting a healthy work-life balance. Methodologically, the techniques of empowerment came from getting clients to be "aware" of their limits. Both at the level of the office and at the level of the individual, entities were to note what limitations they have and what capacity they have based on these limitations. A healthy work-life balance was to be reached via making organizational and individual limits transparent. Through such transparency of limited resources and capacities, workers were to make better decisions concerning which tasks and professional services they were capable of doing without overreaching physical, psychological, and/or professional abilities.

According to FIOH, one is limited in the hours one can physically endure as well as how much pressure and unrecognized efforts one can psychologically take. One is also limited in terms of one's professional capacities to handle certain tasks. One cannot simply take on a job as a way to get ahead should one's skills not be adequately up to the task. Thus, empowerment came from keeping an account of oneself as a transparent resource and, based on this knowledge of what we need and what we have to offer, making the best exchange possible for ourselves at the workplace.

Empowerment also demanded a certain lifestyle. In addition to keeping an account of one's energetic resources, experts prescribed getting adequate sleep, exercise, and good nutrition in addition to meditating, yoga, and Pilates as techniques for enhancing mindfulness over one's aforementioned limits as well as potentials. Taking stock of oneself, according to experts, empowers workers to negotiate their salary, worth, and most of all, finding a workplace that would engage, motivate, and allow them to grow. The Delphic maxim "Know thyself" thus takes on a contemporary twist.

This demand to take stock of one's biological and psychological aptitudes is not a phenomenon unique to Finland. Increasingly, overexertion has become cast as the failure of individual workers to take responsibility over their own health. Yet, ethnographies of work have long shown us that work involves much more than what is under contract as work. Moreover, under advanced capitalism's demands to constantly innovate, workers are increasingly expected not only to keep taking on increasingly complex tasks but also to maintain an enthusiastic and positive attitude.

Vicki Smith, writing on the contradictions of US labor reforms, notes that "workers seldom carry out their jobs simply because everything is pre-specified and they are forced to comply. Indeed, quite the opposite: Managers and employers rely upon workers' initiative and consent in order to achieve their goals in postindustrial work organizations" (1996, 167). She further adds that "consent, often generated by workers' perceptions of the legitimacy of the work organization or by their perception of individual or collective gains as they work for capital, may obscure, or at least make more palatable, particularly exploitative or disadvantageous work conditions" (167).

Studies of work and studies of sacrificial gift exchange rarely overlap, but burnout and the investigation of what moves us—what *fires us up* to work—reveals the artificiality of this distinction. Medical, economic, and political projects attempt to exorcise the spirit of sacrifice in exchanges at work. However, the issue of stress reveals work as a domain dependent on the capture of individuals in the dream that one must work, must give, and through this exchange, gain distinction.

Although framed in the technical register of contractual exchange, workplace exchange is more than legal or economic. There is a certain negativity at work in the workplace that refuses to be positively identified, managed, and made productive. There is a state of being on fire, of expenditure, and of the sacrificial at play that resists being captured within the formula of a work-life balance. There is a force that sparks desire and hunger or a search for meaning, redemption, and recognition that pushes individuals beyond themselves regardless of the end results. Such a logic I found exists outside the formulas for productive enterprise. I turn now to Sakari, one of Henna's closest allies, and his friends.

# Sakari

Henna's death ruptured the office. For many, her death legitimatized a suspicion that they worked too hard. For individuals in this camp, Henna's death was evidence that life was not only "harder and faster" but also the reason why new techniques of self-management were necessary. However, there were those for whom her death could not be anything but loss. Her death was not an issue to be worked on; it was not to be made useful, even as a point of protest. It was not to be a prop for promoting techniques for maintaining a good work-life balance. For these individuals, Henna's death left a void no stress management workshop could fill.

Sakari in particular was offended by the casual manner in which coworkers like Oskari speculated about the causes of Henna's death. He rallied Henna's friends from the office one night and gathered them at a pub close by. I joined them.

Kaisa, Henna's first protégé and her "lieutenant" of sorts, was already addressing a small group of agents when I arrived. "Henna was the type of person who is the last one with a bottle at a party and the first one in the office the next morning!" Aki, another agent chimed in.

> She is from that generation of workers who, when asked to do something—it didn't matter what—gave it their all. They are the kind of workers who pride themselves on holding nothing back. But we live in a different time now. Today, you can give it your all, but no one will recognize it. They tell you instead, "Good, do more!" When you tell someone like Henna she can do more . . . well . . .

Choked up, he could not continue. However, we all knew how his sentence would have ended. He merely fell short of stating the obvious. Sakari broke the silence.

"*Perrrrrkele!* [fuck; literally, devil]," he said. He gave "perkele" extra strength by rolling and extending the *r*. The group joined in. "*Perrrrrrkele!*" we all repeated in chorus and drank in Henna's name.

Sakari and his group turned the meetings at the pub into a monthly ritual of loud cursing and heavy drinking. In light of Lisa's calls to reduce alcohol intake and lead a healthy lifestyle, they instead opted to drink more. There at the pub, they put aside all concerns for productivity and embraced the nonproductive aspects of social engagement made possible via collective intoxication.

As is often the case, rituals evolve into something else. Not all meetings directly concerned Henna. Sakari and his friends often encouraged each other to keep up the pace of alcoholic intake and laughed about having to go into work the next day. Not being a heavy drinker, I often fell victim to reproach. When the point was not to hold back from saving oneself for work the next day, any member not drinking enough appeared to be breaking the magic coherence of the group. To be sustained together as a collective, every member had to be intoxicated. There was a palpable pressure to drink in such circumstances, and I realized ironically that I was feeling no small amount of stress in having to keep up with the group. It was in such moments I was forced to reflect on my own question concerning what one "dares" to do or refuse to do.

One night, I saw this competition to outdo each other at annihilation paradoxically transform into a very productive sentiment. Once, Jussi, a regular at these meetings, complained he had a fever all day. It was going on midnight, and

I turned to face Jussi as he downed what might have been his fourth beer. Aki laughed and slapped his back. As I looked on amazed, they, in turn, laughed at my look of shock. Members around the table offered similar stories of having gone into work sick and commended Jussi by getting him another drink.

"That's crazy," I said. And since no one else asked, I asked Jussi whether he should get a glass of water instead and hail a taxi home. At the mention of a taxi, the whole table exploded into laughter. "She said a taxi!" they roared. What I had forgotten in my concern for Jussi's health was the fact that *Stadilaiset*, denizens of Helsinki, rarely took taxis—they rode bikes or took a public tram. My mention of a taxi, a private and luxurious form of transportation, was exactly the kind of excess these *Stadilaiset* found ridiculous. My quick reliance on a taxi also revealed my "American" leanings and my lack of fortitude. Instead of making use of public transport, a system financed by the commons for the commons, here I was pushing Jussi to take an individualized means of transportation to navigate the city. The taxi epitomized both luxury as well as the antisociality of one unwilling to come together as part of the circuit of the city to get from one point to another.

"This is nothing," Jussi said, although he looked noticeably flushed. Kaisa slapped Jussi on the back and told me that it was "a matter of honesty." She said, "Finns would rather work through sickness than have colleagues question how sick we really are. We believe that you have to really deserve a sick day. If you think you can still work, then it probably means that you should go to work." I asked Jussi whether he would go into work tomorrow. The monthly drinking ritual in honor of Henna always took place on a Wednesday, or, as they called it, the "little weekend" (*pikku viikonloppu*).

"Of course," he answered and finished his beer.

I insisted that this made no sense. Why knowingly tax yourself by drinking and going into work when you quite obviously have a fever? What point does that make? Why do this to yourself when you know how the office treated Henna? At the mention of Henna's name, however, there was silence. I felt I had overstepped my welcome as an outsider.

What had I said? Here, I wish to return to the beginning of this chapter to ask what Henna's death allows expression. What different possibilities of relationality did it bring into discussion? How might we understand what passes between individuals, and what are the ways in which individuals attempt to control their exposure to others?

Jean-Luc Nancy (1991) argues that at the core of our attempt to interpret experience is a sacrificial structure that kills the live current between individuals by supplanting it with static ideas. These ideas then structure the very way we relate to ourselves and to the other. Examining sacrifice as a structure that structures relations, Nancy argues that in making sense of why we do what we do, we sacrifice all that remains in excess of this idea. Demanding that death *means* something is one such instance in which we sacrifice the absolute negativity of death for an idea of it. Where Lisa and Timo took Henna's death as an example of what not to do, Sakari and his group of young real estate agents saw it as heroism immortalized. In both cases, death is reclaimed as meaning, something that can be made productive in life. At the same time, there is something lost in these meanings.

It is instructive once again to return to Iiris. Contra those quick to give the name "sacrifice" to self-expenditure for the sake of others, Iiris never used the word to describe what she did. To do so would be to give the act meaning. Instead, as with others who suffered from not being able to explain why they did what they did, a different form of sacrifice unfolds. Iiris does not foreclose her experience through assigning to it what "it" is. Rather, remaining speechless, an affective residue echoes. Something remains to be said, and that something provoked me to write. The sacrifice of speech fascinates, and those like Iiris and Jussi alert us to its allure.

Several months after this Henna's death, Diwa, Sakari's wife, invited me to their home. Sakari had just been released from hospital for appendicitis, and I was invited along with some other of his friends for dinner. When I made it to their house in Kontula, a working-class suburb of Helsinki, Sakari was already on his second can of hard cider and looking for another. Diwa, concerned about his health, had hidden the rest of the six-pack, and Sakari was quick to tell me how happy he was that I had come with a bottle of wine. I caught Diwa's angry glare as I handed him my gift. He put it next to the other bottles that were brought by his other guests, and I realized just then that he intended to drink them all that night. As he finished his cider and started to open one of the bottles of wine, Diwa stated to no one in particular, "You know he only got out of the hospital three days ago?"

Besides the alcohol, the table was laden with special dishes Diwa had prepared for his welcome home party. Sakari's family cherished Diwa, who had grown up in a strict Muslim family, for having pushed Sakari to cut back on his alcohol consumption. That night, however, Sakari seemed intent on drinking to excess. "I am so sick and tired of people telling me to eat right, drink less, exercise, and be healthy!" he said.

Ignoring Diwa, he downed a glass of wine and reached for the bottle to pour himself another. Jussi interjected, lightening the conversation with a joke about a poster that was put up in the office coffee room about discount coupons for a yoga class. As the tension in the room started to lift, the phone rang. It was for Sakari. He promptly left the room and made his way out the patio to the snowy garden outside. Diwa ran after him with a coat.

When they both came back, I gathered from their expression that things were tense. Sakari explained that the office had called and had demanded that he step in and hand over a file and a key to a unit that was to be shown tomorrow. "But it's already 9:00 p.m.!" Diwa exclaimed. "And he has been back from the hospital for only three days! He is still on sick leave!"

"I'm not Henna," he said. But bringing up his friend and mentor he had just lost had a way of bringing up other memories. Instead of leaving the room, he stopped to finish his wine. "I had a grandmother just like her," said Sakari. Here is what he related:

> When she got too sick to be alone, we offered to take her in, but she would have none of it. She said she'd rather go to an [old people's] home. We went to visit her often, but each time we went, she looked worse and worse. We knew she was suffering from something terrible. But each time we'd ask her how things were, she'd only say in this hoarse whisper, "*Perrrrkele!*"

For Sakari, Henna was a reminder of his grandmother's complete commitment to a code of conduct in which one did not rely on others as long as one had the capacity to do things on one's own. One was not to "hold back" on what one could give. Sakari soon left for the office.

"I'm not Henna," he said, but Sakari appeared to be equally vulnerable to the incapacity to hold back. He proved this by announcing that it was imperative that he went into the office immediately, despite being in recovery, on leave, and drunk. He offered a long explanation about having the only keys to a unit that had to be shown very early the next day, and as nobody from the office had volunteered to come pick up the keys, he said he "must drop off the keys this very night."

"I am not Henna," he says, but his actions showed otherwise. He appeared to be possessed by the same untimely force to give. What moves him? "He is not Henna," he says; he joins others in distinguishing the present as a "faster and harder world," and yet he betrays himself by insisting on making a sacrifice.

In an era marked by untimely sacrifices, the voluntary giving of our time and energy "count" only if one makes them in the way that they count. The technology of occupational health treats what passes in between individuals as a quantifiable energetic balance. However, it also covers over the sacrifice—the self-erasure to the logic of the present and of the individual as the manager of quantifiable energetic resources—necessary for this line of vision to work. Individuals must, as Durkheim might put it, not only make sacrifices at the altar of technomedical thinking but also, and more importantly, give it credit, give it their "thought"— be *one* with its logic.

In his study of sacrifice, Durkheim reminds us that gods "cannot do without their worshippers any more than these can do without their gods" (1995, 351).

Gods need, in addition to the oblations worshippers place at their alter, their thoughts. Durkheim, ever the examiner of social function, argues that it is only through receiving the worshipper's thought that gods gain credibility. "Though superior to men," Durkheim says, gods "can live only in the *human consciousness*" (351). And without gods to provide positive credit to thought, man thinks without thinking, sees without really seeing.

Can we not hear echoes of Durkheim's gods in the hollow visions of the machine that is the institution of occupational burnout? Ideas of the present as distinct from the past, the notion that sacrifice could be made untimely—these social truths depend on the very kinds of oblations—the sacrificial gift of one's thoughts—to remain in circulation, to remain within the human consciousness. Durkheim argues "the individual gets from society the best part of himself, all that gives him a distinct character" (1995, 351). In exchange, the individual gives social institutions his thought, his credit that they exist and have an impact.

## Fascination

Henna's death fascinates. Maurice Blanchot defines that which fascinates as having the capacity to "rob us of our power to make sense" (1982, 32). The traumatic stain of Henna's death here pulls others into its orbit. Oskari, for one, sees no sense in it. Calling her "mad," a "martyr," and a worker from an "older generation" provides him the distance necessary to disengage from this fascination. However, it offers him and others no closure.

Despite this, the empowerment paradigm offered a framework and the language necessary to talk about—and to possibly bring under one's control—the unreason of untimely sacrifices under present circumstances. Techniques aimed at self-awareness and stress management make visible workers like Henna as individuals driven by an untimely ethics. Health experts, the media, office managers like Lisa, and workers like Oskari attribute deaths like Henna's to an automaticity devoid of self-authored decisions. Their deaths were ends already decided on from the telos of today.

This retroactive construction of Henna as a worker from an "older generation" who becomes the figure of an untimely "martyr" in today's workplace thus dismisses Henna as an egological subject capable of making her own decisions. In this scenario, she is but a figure of history. And as a figure of the past, her death gains meaning as the end of a way of being, one unsustainable in the present. Stress science and the rehabilitative expertise around it then forge a passage between the past and the present to enable individuals to update themselves. Her death fills, as Ian Hacking (1998) might put it, an "ecological niche" that marks the temporal-spatial contours of a pathology that finds relevance in one context and is lost in another.

In this sense, then, there is *no* figure timelier than martyr workers. They belong to our contemporary moment. Friedrich Nietzsche's usage of the term *untimely* (*unzeitgemäss*) is instructive here. Walter Kaufmann first translated Nietzsche's collection of essays *Unzeitgemässe Betrachtungen* (1873–76) into English as *Untimely Meditations*. However, the term *zeitgemäss* in German has besides being "timely," the following connotations: "in compliance with," "in fashion," "up to date," "appropriate," and "modern" (Breazeale 1997, xliv). Its antonym, *unzeitgemäss*, thus covers not only the sense of being out of sync with the contemporary but also being out of fashion—out of joint with the current moment. Nietzsche added his own spin on this notion of untimeliness as that which refers to the timeless (xlv). Thus, what is made untimely, out of joint, and *not* with the current slides into that which transcends its own time.[1]

Thus, contra Hacking, that which is timeless fills no "ecological niche." It is something beyond our apprehension of the emergent. A martyr, thus, is a timely name for a timeless problem of one's exposure to the demands of the other.

Timeliness, according to George Bataille, requires a particular form of sacrifice. Being *timely*, as in producing in an expected and timely manner, expending one's energy in ways that make sense, requires a certain subordination of oneself to the logic of the present. Seeing oneself through the telos of the economic present, according to Bataille, one renounces one's will to that of the times. Where health experts promise techniques of control over one's relation to time and to the other, *this* in itself according to Bataille does not offer timely presence. In fact, he argues, it does quite the opposite.

Bataille's point is instructive. Technical thinking offered through the medico-economic alliance allows for the possibility that we are in control. The promise of stress management supplements the assumptions of advanced capitalism that our illnesses, failures, and our successes stem from personal choices and the lifestyle we adopt. But here, this egological line of thinking covers over a sacrificial logic. It can only work via subjugating individuals into thinking of themselves as an energetic resource to be spent, saved, and updated as needed—a utile object among others.

A scholar much inspired by ethnographic scholarship on sacrifice, Bataille writes that in order to transform an individual from the degraded existence of a tool whose telos lies beyond its immediate existence, to an existence of immanent presence, he or she must make a sacrifice.

Under medicotechnical management, life appears as a thing to be preserved and to be preserved for the future. Stress management techniques thus do not only defer death; they also defer life. Life is always preserved for a future goal set beyond the present. The present serves the future, a destination health experts promises as reachable via technological thinking.

Often neglected in analyses of Bataille is his take on time. God, according to Bataille, stands against the fear of death, of the loss of control over one's engagement with others, of the not knowing of what has been communicated and exchanged. God then is an expression of the fear of a lack of control over oneself and of being rendered into a mere "thing" whose meaning exists beyond itself. God also stands for what is named and codified as the timely and the present. And for Bataille, following Nietzsche, God is that which must be sacrificed.

What Bataille means here is that we must sacrifice this attempt to take control over time and over the promised management over death. Timely existence, then, in this perspective can only take place when we relinquish our hold on the future and free ourselves from being subjugated to its ends.

This release, according to Bataille takes the form of what he calls a privileged instant, a moment of release that ruptures the straitjacket of reasoned thought and allows for "convulsive communication of what is ordinarily stifled" (1992, 242). Among such forms of communication, he lists laughter, inebriation, and eroticism, all forms of relationality that emerge when one sacrifices the self that ordinarily calculates, controls, and manages. Thus, where Henri Hubert and Marcel Mauss focus on the productive aspects of sacrifice as a ritual that enables communication between collectives and their gods, Bataille reads sacrifice differently. The "essential phase" of sacrifice for Bataille lies in the destructive phase and not in the process of the ritual wherein the destroyed object or victim is used as a symbol to negotiate with gods. Bataille sees in destruction the capacity to fascinate and to restore to individuals a lost value, a sense of totality that the register of negotiation and reason splits apart. It is such waste, the threat of unproductive expenditure, that is at stake in making the here and now visible through the lens of occupational burnout. It is this lens that we must break in order to experience the present as it is not made visible by the machines of light, not in order to become new, which is another capture within another line of light, but so that we may experience the intimacy that is not for a set purpose.

So let us return to *perkele*. The word itself is appropriate—it was the name of a pagan god that was turned into a curse when Finland Christianized. *Perkele*, Sakari says, when he cannot say anything else concerning Henna's death. In this nonstatement, we might hear echoes of Bataille's unreason—the unproductive expenditure that is done not *for* anything or anyone. But although I follow Bataille some distance, I cannot see the liberation that sacrifice gives for Sakari and others. I see, instead of a release, a retreat. I see in *perkele* and in the curses spoken and unspoken by my interlocutors, a falling-silent, an acknowledgment of unreason, yes, but without its attendant liberation. Occupational burnout promises that what exhausts us could be named and domesticated; yet a promise is that—a promise.

Henna dies, and the office sees her death as a case of burnout. Burnout promises a certain line of vision. It, however, also points to its own limits and to the enigma of what moves us to give.

## Real Relationships

A month later, Sakari and Diwa invited me back to their house. Diwa handed me a gold gilded box of dried dates from Pakistan as I sat at the table. She had remembered I had liked them from the last time I was invited. Like the dates, the couple spared no expenses in the dinner that followed. Despite being the only guest, the table was covered in plates of food enough to feed five.

"This is nothing," Diwa, said. "We are friends. You must treat this as your own home."

"There is no holding back," said Sakari as he poured me a glass of wine. "You must feel at home here, and I will fire up the sauna after dinner."

Drinking in Diwa's presence, however, had a different effect from drinking together with the regular members at the monthly pub ritual. With Diwa looking on and counting how many glasses Sakari had consumed, the conversation over dinner turned again to the problem of health, productivity, and how Henna had died.

This time, Sakari reframed drinking as a matter of honesty. Diwa audibly sighed. "How is drinking a matter of honesty, Sakari?" I asked. Diwa followed. "Yes, *kultsi* [sweetie], how is drinking a matter of honesty? Was it for honesty's sake that you came home one night with your nose broken and you didn't even know how it happened?"

Things took an unexpected turn. I had wanted to express solidarity with Diwa. I had no idea that what I had presumed would be a conversation about ideas concerning drinking would turn into a discussion about Sakari's broken nose. Looking more closely at his face, I could see his nose slightly swollen at the base. Seeing me looking at him, he waved me away, muttering, "It's nothing. . . . I probably fell down." It was, however, apparent that something more than the idea of honesty was at stake here—something beyond what language could communicate. What has a broken nose and drinking got to do with honesty?

Registering my shock, Diwa seemed encouraged. "Daena," she said, "he stays out regardless of the week of the day; he stays out and drinks and he doesn't even care that he has to go into work the next day! He works and drinks, and he works and drinks! He has learned nothing from the workshop [on stress management]."

With Diwa and me interrogating him about his nose, Sakari lost his patience. "This is the problem!" Sakari almost yelled. He continued,

> Today, people just work and work and that's all they care about. They don't have the time or can't be bothered to *make* time to establish real relationships with each other at work—or even outside of work. They are happy to stab each other in the back. We don't care about being *real* with each other anymore, and when you say drinking together isn't important, that is the kind of perspective you are promoting!

As if to underscore his point, he opened a can of hard cider and, much to Diwa's dismay, chugged it. When he emptied the can, he went back to the fridge to get another can of cider and placed a can in front of me as well. Without looking, I could feel Diwa turn to look at me.

At stake for Sakari is the loss of "real" relationships, one necessary for a contest of respect—one also, according to his perspective, linked to "honesty." Today, according to Sakari, "people just work and work and that's all they care about." This "they" only care about instrumentalized relationships, and under such conditions of relationality, Sakari adds, people are comfortable about "stabbing each other in the back." In that case, Sakari's broken nose points to a different kind of relationality. What is "real" here appears to be the fact that he does not know how it happened, but there has been "real" contact made—a contact made not for the promotion of a career or for productivity. It was a contact made in a register beyond such relationality founded on capitalist reasoning.

Working for the sake of work, for Sakari, brings about an almost Hobbesian state of nature in which individuals promote their own interest in competition with others. However, what of respect generated through such competition? Could that also be considered a product of the real?

Rather than answer me directly, Sakari suddenly brought up his Russian neighbors. "You know we Finns hate the Russians," he said, "but my neighbors, they are Russians, and they are good people. In fact, they are *very* good people. Over there [in Russia], they still know how to respect each other. They are honest." And "respecting each other" included a lot of drinking. "They are old, but they are hard drinkers," Sakari continued. "They stay up with me at nights, and we just watch the snow and drink and tell stories. We all have to get up and catch the train in the morning, but we sit in the snow with our jackets in the garden and drink [he laughs]."

Midway through telling me about his Russian neighbors, Sakari suddenly shifted his attention to Diwa and asked her to "tell her story." "You never want to talk about real things," he scolded. "We are all friends here, and that means you can talk. I think this comes from a lack of alcohol on your part. Alcohol allows you to talk about all the things that bother you. It can bring you closer to others."

By "real things," Sakari wanted Diwa to talk about the violence and hardship she experienced as a young woman growing up in the Pashtun region of Pakistan. She did not drink and frowned openly at her husband who kept pushing her to drink. "I don't need to drink to talk about my past," she said defiant.

"But you can be real only when you are totally and disgustingly drunk!" he said. Sakari did not just want Diwa to talk about her past. He wanted her to share that part of her life in a very distinct way—a path opened only through intoxication. What he wanted was for the speaker to let go of all inhibitions and social decorum and talk about "real" issues, "real" thoughts that fail to find expression in well-calculated speech. He told me how much he enjoyed getting drunk and talking with his Russian neighbors now that Henna was gone. His group of friends at the office, according to Sakari, did not measure up.

Suddenly, he pointed to the garden. "Look!" he said. I followed his finger and looked. His garden, covered in snow, still revealed a small lump where sat what seemed to be a rounded concrete block. "It's a stone hedgehog!" he said. "I look at that thing and I like to think that I 'jailed' it there. It is jailed, and I am free! When I drink, I feel even more open and communicative. I want to talk and get to know people. This is real. When you talk about dumb shit, scary shit, dark shit. And it was something that used to happen even at work. Not anymore."

This real relationality depends on the erasure of a calculating self. It was something Sakari found in inebriated conversations around which a coming together could be experienced that had none of the characteristics of office small talk. What he wanted in what he called "real" conversations were a sense of self-exposure not mediated by social reason. Like laughter, he wanted stories to pour out in the moment of engagement; he wanted people to tell stories not intended for future use—for example, networking. Sakari missed that in Henna and sought it in his neighbors.

"Finland is now among the most competitive countries in the world," he said, his eyes reddening from drink. "[The Russians] still have something real in them." In comparison to Russia, where, as Sakari says, "they *still* have something real," the competitive world cares not for anything that does not involve the calculation of productivity. But in placing "the Russians" behind Finland in terms of economic competitiveness, Sakari can both condescend to as well as turn to Russia as a place of difference, a place yet to be subsumed under the logics of competitive capitalism.

# The Disease of Prestige and Industry

*Oho!* a popular tabloid features Pepe Willberg, a singer, with the caption, "Depression took my ability to work" (*Masennus vei työkykyni*) (Häkli, 2006). The article itself, however, assures the readers that he is "now back to work again" (*nyt jaksan taas*). In the same issue, Viivi, once a host for entertainment news says, "I burned out" (*Olin palaa loppuun*). In another tabloid, *Apu* (Nykänen, 2006), Tanja Saarela, former model and then-minister of culture in 2006, appears with her dog with the heading, "Recovering" (*Toipumassa*). The article describes how she struggles daily with stress and depression but how walking with her dog in the forest helped her overcome her condition. "Depression melts away in the forest," she says.

In this genre of writing related to burnout, recovery plays a key feature, not falling speechless. Celebrities talk about "burning out" as part of their stressful lifestyle of a public figure. They are stressed in part because they are in demand. Being burned out, then, signifies for their popularity, a valuable asset that makes them who they are—celebrities. Thus, celebrities, far from failing to make sense of why they work so much, can pinpoint exactly why. Theirs is not a tale of not making sense. Theirs is a story with closure. They see society changing, and they struggle, but they recover in the end. Their photographs that accompany their interviews attest to their resilience. They smile bravely, even radiantly, buoyed by the challenges they have managed to overcome.

In fact, this genre of writing makes no reference to the official diagnostic category, occupational burnout (*työuupumus*). Instead, the idea of burnout and its status as a new hazard grounds celebrities as workers of today who also suffer but as those who pull through. Placed next to martyr workers, celebrities show well-being is something to be fought for. Whether it is through walking the dog in the forest, like Tanja Saarela, or spending time with the family, like Pepe Willberg, stories about burnout by celebrities highlight individual ingenuity shining out against all odds.

The easy crossover of occupational burnout into its idiomatic usage as burnout gives it a life outside of the clinic as well as within. But the achievement of those who make the passage to become successful workers of the new economy cannot be measured without those who fall under the care of the Finnish health institutions. It is against the backdrop of those taking medication, getting counseling, and retreating from society that the true valor of workers who survive can be recognized.

Celebrities with burnout not only confirm their social prestige and popularity but also that they have the capacity to convert the negativity of their energetic expenditure into an experience under their control. Like Pepe and Tanja who overcome their respective struggles with stress despite feeling burned out, these stories set the tone for the heroes to come.

Burning out articulates both the anxieties of the present as well as the fantasy of a capitalist subject capable of self-revitalization—a feat all the more celebratory given the risk. In celebrating celebrities who burn out and yet manage to return to work, we come to author our gods ourselves. The celebrated, then, are those with the capacity to overcome and to master, not those who must work at themselves to recover.

Occupational burnout as a conceptual edifice orders the risks and fantasies that emerge in times of social transformation. Indeed, medical ideas of exhaustion have long provided a framework for understanding new technological and industrial demands that make their mark on the individual. Medicine, as Anna Schaffner (2016) argues in her book on exhaustion, draws on the world outside of medicine, just as everyday stories draw on medicine for coherence. When dealing with conditions with multiple valences such as burnout, fatigue, and stress, it becomes even harder to keep the clinic outside of the idiom and vice versa. In fact, according to Laura Bear, "an important role for institutions becomes the normative mediation between conflicting representations, technologies, and rhythms in time" (2014, 7). The institution developed around occupational burnout, then, provides a "time map" that directs individuals in their visualization of what it takes to navigate in the here and now (7).

But in claiming occupational burnout as a new hazard, a product of the here and now, Finnish health experts at once affirm the present in its singularity while simultaneously placing it within a national history without which there can be no concept of the new. In determining what is "new" and timely, one does not in fact open a new horizon of time. Rather, one "hand[s] on what has been handed down . . . repeat repetitions" (Hamacher 1997, 38). In his analysis of the condition of the here and now, for instance, Werner Hamacher is particular. He claims that those who speak in terms of the new, and the here and now, "do not pierce the generality but corroborates it" (38). Moreover, he argues, those who use this formula "speak and they do not speak—and it is the impossible connection between these two, which articulates itself in every *now* and every *here*; the impossible connection between that enthralling and its breaking, between the repetition and its interruption, between the connection and the break" (39; emphases original).

In naming occupational burnout as a new hazard, a problem of the here and now, Finnish health experts create a passage from the past to the present. But as Hamacher argues, this inauguration of the present takes place by a paradoxical disavowal of the very singularity of the very moment in creation. The present comes into being only insofar as it is considered alongside the past. The here and now is what repeats. It is that which is "handed down" from what precedes it.

And as something that stems from something else, it loses its status as a singular moment.

Experts fall within the category of those who "speak and do not speak." They do not speak as such; their affirmation of the *new* presents itself as an echo of the past. The formulation of occupational burnout as the disorder of the untimely itself points to this temporal difficulty. The claim of a here and now thus simultaneously disavows this space its singularity as its emergence always depends on the past. Occupational burnout names this impossible space between what continues by ending.

In fact, the difficulty of the "here and now" marks the history of fatigue. The ends and beginnings of technological and industrial regimes reveals how every economic "here and now" brings with it its own brand of exhaustion.

For instance, in the nineteenth century, when steam first powered industry and the newly invented telegraph and the telephone sped up communication, the public was well receptive to George Beard (1881) when he spoke of the dangers of "nervous bankruptcy" and "nervous exhaustion" or neurasthenia that could ensue.

The fast pace of life fatigued both man and machine. Where mechanical fatigue could be patched up, the strain of technological innovation on the workforce proved harder to heal. Against those who complained of "hopelessness before the task at hand," "insomnia," "habitual mental depression," "lack of nerve strength," "swelling of the lymph nodes," and "fatigue" (Abbey and Garfinkel 1991), Beard (1881) argued that the symptoms manifested a nervousness specific to the recent advancements in "American civilization." Beard gave neurasthenia the appellation "American nervousness," thus making explicit the links between technological, industrial, and social change to shifts in the experience of exhaustion. In doing so, Beard made exhaustion a part of the story of American industrial and labor history.

Occupational burnout is thus not unique in inaugurating the end of one epoch and the birth of another. According to Beard, neurasthenia marks the tipping point at which "American civilization" has advanced to the point of "overloading the circuits" (1881, 96) and that technology has become "tyrants of trade" (105). Although the range of symptoms proved a challenge for Beard to produce a coherent theory of neurasthenia (Abbey and Garfinkel 1991), Beard borrowed from both ideas of electrical currents and thermodynamics that were in vogue during his time to develop a model for how we come to "bankrupt" our nerves. The nervous system, like electrical currents, requires a battery. Without proper management, according to Beard, we could "overload" these circuits and expend what finite energetic resources we have at our disposal.

Beard also built on another theory that was dominant during his time—social Darwinism. Neurasthenia only affected the most refined and the upper classes, those individuals involved with doing "brain work": the businessmen, the writers, and the industrialists (Beard 1881). Beard considered it absurd that "savages" and the lower classes need worry about their nerves. For one, they were considered not refined enough and thus insensitive to the pressures of the urban environment. Second, these groups were considered irrelevant to the pressures of industrialization since "nervous bankruptcy" only mattered to those in capitalist and "civilized" centers where circuits of industry, technology, and capital fused with the nervous system.

Indeed, the notion of "bankruptcy" itself gave currency to the capitalist logic that human energy could be saved and spent just like money. This economy of nervous energy gave "civilized" and "modern" individuals not only the lingua franca to put into words a world changed by rapid industrialization (Harding and Stewart 2003, 260) but also gave them recognition as valuable individuals with a direct hand in this grand march forward. The notion of neurasthenia, then, put into motion the ideal Victorian figure: an individual with great intellect and sensitivity who suffers from nerves but who because of these nervous traits have the capacity to wire together man, machine, and time for the benefit of market expansion.

If neurasthenia was considered an illness of advanced civilization, occupational burnout, too, presents itself as the disorder that affects only those nation-states involved in advanced capitalism. Part of the appeal of occupational burnout in Finland, then, must also include the perspective that it allowed for those who bemoaned the ostensibly "outdated" status of the nation to legitimize the nation's membership in timely market exchange.

Going back to neurasthenia, following its success in the United States, neurasthenia gained legitimacy as a clinical category in other countries with the spread of capitalist forces. However, this widespread usage also led to its decline. With increasing medical experts expressing skepticism toward this condition as a catch-all "garbage bin" of ailments among the lay population, it started to lose its overall coherence (Wessely 1990). Ultimately, neurasthenia fell out of use completely with the medical establishment when the supposition of the disease's physical origins came under attack (47).

Sigmund Freud in particular removed neurasthenia from physical medicine altogether by recategorizing the symptoms formerly identified with neurasthenia as psychiatric symptoms. Under Freud, symptoms of fatigue formerly identified as a part of neurasthenia became signs of "anxiety neurosis" and "hysteria." Such a categorical transformation (from physical to psychiatric) came with social consequences as it peeled off the veneer of neurasthenia as the disease of the highly civilized. The discourse of nerves reframed as part of an understanding of an individual rendered hysterical as opposed to the nervous conditions of an entrepreneur under pressure of the technological advances of the times lost its luster.

If neurasthenia was a defining nervous condition for industrialized nations in the late nineteenth century, by the mid-twentieth century stress took over as the disease of civilization.

I have already touched on this shift in the introduction. Allow me to elaborate on this point here.

Like neurasthenia, stress referred to a nonspecific reaction to external pressure—a nonspecificity that made it hard for Hans Selye, the man who would then go on to make the category famous, to legitimize as a diagnostic condition. This nonspecificity of stress, however, became key to shifting the attention from specific disease categories to a more generalized understanding of human well-being.

In the 1950s, Selye was the first to get the medical, the industrial, and the military world aware of the consequences of wear and tear on the body and the psyche and to how excessive demand on the person affected work performance (Davies 2015; Viner 1999). Where Beard turned to nerves as the key idiom of neurasthenia, Selye built on a more advanced knowledge of human neurology to add that it was not only nerves at issue in stress but also hormones (1956, 3). Taking the neurological and the endocrinal together, Selye built on earlier studies by Walter Cannon on the effect of the "fight or flight" mechanism on homeostasis to explore how external shocks affect the production of hormones that regulate human defense mechanisms (Jackson 2013).

Selye found that the energy needed in this response to environmental change and traumatic shocks existed in finite amounts. This energy, "adaptation energy," when depleted, Selye discovered, attenuated the organism's capacity to resist external strain and pressure. Selye's laboratory animals in this weakened state died, and those that survived sustained other injuries such as ulcers, insomnia, reduced immunological resistance to disease, and high blood pressure (Jackson 2013).

Selye was the first to identify these nonspecific reactions to external pressures and how these reactions themselves carried deleterious health effects (Viner 1999). Where disease till then referred to the effect of a specific external agent, Selye overturned this concept. Stress was a subtractive disease. Stress results from the loss of an organism's ability to maintain homeostasis against environmental change—a loss that concerned not just laboratory rats but humans as well.

By reframing what constitutes disease, Selye complicated the relationship between the inside and the outside, the organism and the pathogen. Stress, or general adaptation syndrome (GAS), as he first called it, highlights the human dimension of disease, especially the dimension that involves man's ease or dis-ease at which he or she adapts to social, political, and industrial change. Disease, in this formulation, points not to a specific condition as such but to a general maladjustment, a glitch in man's inability to keep up with the times—one that appears to exist in man's very biology. It is no longer an external pathogen that must be eradicated. The pathogenic force lies within the human him- or herself. It is here that the hermetic self of the capitalist subject emerges as an object of technomedical intervention.

Selye's breakthrough came in the identification of the problem that gets in the way of man's ability to work at his or her peak. Maladaptiveness, according to Selye, creates a psychic and physiological "by-product"—stress. This negative effect, according to Selye, need not only stem from overstimulation. He argued that humans suffer equally from being understimulated—for example, from the drudgery of repetitive factory work. There is a balance, an economy of human excitement and energetic expenditure. Selye argued that social functioning could be optimized via exercising this balance between saving and expending human energetic expenditure at the collective level.

Although Selye began his endocrinal research using laboratory animals in the 1930s, his work on GAS only started to gain traction in the late 1940s when the military-industrial complex picked up on the notion of human adaptability as a possible path toward better operational efficiency. Military psychiatrists and industrialists saw in stress a promise to control combat fatigue and human limits to labor.

Industrialists in the United States in particular emphasized Selye's argument that life under pressure was a "natural" state of man's biological existence and underlined the dangers of boredom and inactivity (Viner 1999). Adapting to and keeping up with the tempo of work set by technological innovation became mantras of this era and with the language of stress at their hands, workers had more than back pains and ergonomic issues to express their concern. When Richard S. Lazarus introduced the notion of "coping" into the relationship between adaptation and disease as developed by Selye in the 1970s, the stage was set for a new philosophy of self-help and self-regulation (Jackson 2013, 19).

Like neurasthenia before it, the concept of stress gained general appeal at a moment of industrial and technological transformation that required individuals to keep up with the speed of production. Stress was not only a modular concept appropriated by the military-industrial complex to produce the *homo faber* of their needs. Selye himself translated his ideas on neuronal and endocrinal adaptation into a social philosophy.

Just as homeostasis is maintained within the individual body through man's "harmonious conduct of the organs," Selye reasoned that man's harmonious relationships with other men could come from maintaining a balance between self-sacrifice and self-interest (1974, 64). Selye saw stress as arising out of a "permanent fight between altruistic and egoistic tendencies" (1956, 281). Against this tension, he promoted what he called his "philosophy of gratitude" (281).

In it, Selye proposed that individuals exercise "altruistic egoism," or what he described as "interpersonal altruism" (1956, 281). According to this philosophy, when egotistical actions also serve to promote the interests of the society, the egotist becomes essential to his neighbors to the point of inducing "gratitude." Both society and individual reach a state of equilibrium in such a case, as individuals freely pursue their interests while also serving the needs of the society.

This philosophy complemented the spirit of capital in Selye's day and was much welcomed by industrialists and medical experts in the military intent on maximizing operational efficiency without sacrificing national support. Like Bear's concept of neurasthenia before him, Selye's notion of stress soon gained recognition beyond the United States.

This general concern with optimization of the social collective, especially the workforce, became a new field in medicine in the 1960s called occupational health (Davies 2015). Building on stress science that shows a link between the pressures of a rapidly changing technoindustrial society and diminished human well-being, occupational health experts set out to examine new avenues of intervention and techniques of self-management.

Yet, even though the field of occupational health paved the way for an interdisciplinary investigation of the connections between human physiological and psychological stability, and technoindustrial transformation, it continues to reproduce the concerns with human energy use that began with Beard's link between nervous overloading and technological development. From the age of nerves to the age of stress, the question remains: How can the workforce keep up with an ever-faster mode of production without overexpending its energetic resources? What technomedical interventions do we need to keep abreast of capital expansion?

The needs of capital emerge as unquestioned givens in both notions of nerves and stress. The problem resides not in a faster and harder life but in the workforce that fails to keep up. The disorder while making visible the pressures of social transformation on the individual simultaneously pushes the apparatus to intervene on those who fail.

Since the rise of stress as the disease of advanced civilizations, we have seen new stress disorders gain social relevance. If burnout gained the attention of the health community in the late 1970s in the United States, it was chronic fatigue syndrome that gained notoriety as "yuppie flu" during the economic upheavals of the 1980s (Cathébras 1994). Each of these stress disorders echo elements of neurasthenia and neurosis to the point where Pascal Cathébras calls them "modern avatars of fatigue [*avatars modernes de la fatigue*]" (1991).

Taking these divergent notions of fatigue together, Cathébras argues that more than push for the legitimacy and specificity of these disorders, we ought to examine the politics and social contexts behind the production of new fatigue categories. It is a move supported by others such as Anne Case and Angus Déaton, economists who see stress disorders and the general rise in morbidity among those in stressful social, economic, and political conditions as a result of despair. Case and Deaton call deaths resulting from "drug overdoses, suicides, and alcohol-related mortality . . . as 'deaths of despair'" (2017, 398). Like neurasthenia in the time of Beard, these conditions arise out of a certain sense of hopelessness with the times we find ourselves—times as set by institutional, industrial, technological demand.

Case and Deaton's study is foregrounded by the Whitehall Study in the United Kingdom. In this study, British epidemiologists discovered a clear link between stress, occurrence of cardiac disease, and decreased well-being among British civil servants who occupied lower positions in the occupational hierarchy than among those in higher positions. Those with low job control and access to information, they found, were more likely to suffer "higher blood pressure, higher plasma glucose, smok[e] more, and repor[t] less leisure-time physical activity" (Marmot et al. 1978, 244) than those who had more status and more influence over their work.

Fatigue categories fall within disorders and diseases that arise out of the very structure of capital and the politics of welfare that distribute despair unevenly. Yet, we cannot deny that each of the categories of stress and fatigue arise out of the specific and very local institutional-industrial makeup of the nation-state with its own particular health systems and economic histories. Fatigue categories are thus regionally specific, and not every industrialized country will have signs of a particular disorder despite scientific evidence linking a disorder to shared changes in the demands of work. Fatigue categories are "sensitive to cultural and ideological motives" and thus products of specific time and space (Cathébras 1994, 261).

For instance, although burnout is listed in the International Statistical Classification of Diseases and Related Health Problems (ICD-10), a classification inventory published by the World Health Organization, not all countries use burnout as a category to refer to symptoms identifiable as burnout. The Netherlands prefers to use the term *work-related neurasthenia* (Friberg 2009) and Japan uses *death from overwork* (*karōshi*) over burnout (Schaufeli and Enzmann 1998); France does not recognize burnout at all and instead has its own category, "spasmophilia" (*spasmophilie*) (Cathébras 1994).

These unique fatigue categories allow both physicians and patients to call attention to distress in temporally and spatially meaningful ways. However, although fatigue categories may be "transient," to use Ian Hacking's terminology to denote mental illness that "appears at a time, in a place, and later fades away" (1998, 1), and thus regionally specific to the institutional contexts in which they emerge, they have in common despair, hopelessness, and exhaustion that stem from the experience of social transformation—in short, they have in common history.

## The Press, Impressions, Death

In physics, stress refers to force applied to a material object that weighs down (e.g., gravity) or adds pressure on the surface causing deformation. In turn, strain, or the deformation caused thereof, generates a proportional internal energy, or *restoring force*, which counteracts stress by pushing the material back into its original state.

Hooke's law, as it is known in physics, depicts this theory of applied external force in relation to the production of counteractive internal energy. Robert Hooke, a British physicist, first published the formula in 1678 "as the extension, so the force" (*ut tensio, sic vis*).

Imagine a wire spring. When we apply a certain amount of force to stretch that spring outward, it also generates a force that snaps the spring back into its original shape. It is a process that, too, must take into account the innate elasticity of the material. Things do not simply collapse under stress; they spring back. But when they are not entirely restored, this is fatigue.

Stress scientists borrow much from this history of stress long recorded in physics as a backdrop to how physiological mechanisms work under pressure. There is an economy of energy relevant to both physics and the biology of homeostasis. The resonance between the two was not lost to Selye. He compared his theory of stress to the natural sciences and reframed the poetics and experience of stress—for example, the racing pulse, the pounding heart, and the sweat of nervous anxiety—as an independent energy-based mechanism that could be measured, controlled, and restored (Viner 1999).

In thus housing the formulation of how cells and organs operate under stress within the archive of physics, Selye also gave his musings on social stability the status of natural science. Selye's concept of stress relates external pressure (e.g., sociotechnical transformation) to internal mechanisms to create a seamless circuit, one that includes the human as part of the technoindustrial productive complex. In this vulgar materialist reading, the human element comes to matter only insomuch as he or she is capable of maintaining his or her own energy to withstand pressure. In this way, the notion of stress parallels Hooke's theory of the extended spring ready to pull itself back to its stable form. The human, in this formulation, as a mere spring in the machinery of capital, becomes a means to an end other than to him- or herself. Moreover, as part of a productive circuit, the human is denuded of all human attributes such as desire, fear, anxiety, depression; the human's quickened pulse, the knots and butterflies in his or her stomach, his or her nights without sleep matter only as they affect the human as a medium, a spring, a cog in the greater machinery of the social apparatus.

Stress science thus provides a technomedical promise that we may remain productive no matter how fast or hard life becomes just so long as we work within the laws of physics—stress and strain are natural forces that are productive, so long as one can resist or resolve the issue of fatigue. And with self-management techniques, we were to realize the right energetic balance ourselves.

This promise that we can tinker with the mechanics of energy is a promise against untimeliness. The possibility that we may tinker with the physics and economics of energy provides a safeguard against falling out of the demands of time, of not adapting, and of not being able to snap back into shape when our internal spring is pulled. It thus promises a certain timelessness, a condition without limits or end, an infinitude projected into the future unencumbered by anything that may negate this power to tinker.

However, this formulation of energy as a blanket force that works uniformly in machines as it does for human beings could not have made the impression that it did on the public without another history of stress—that of the printing press. Without print media and an external substrate on which ideas concerning organic and societal stability could be circulated publicly, Selye's formulations would have had limited currency.

The press not only impresses ideas onto the public but is also an apparatus that operates through stress. It takes the application of pressure, or stress, for the print to make its impressions on paper. What history of stress, finitude, and energy could we have had had Selye chosen to archive his ideas of stress within the history of the printing press?

The archive, Jacques Derrida argues, consigns by assigning a *"topo-nomology"*—a place and name—to ideas. It aims to "coordinate a single corpus, in a system or a synchrony in which all elements articulate the unity of an ideal configuration" (1995, 3). The stress archive gathers scientific documents, media reports, industrial reports, and personal discourse together around a certain understanding of the experience of being under pressure at the current moment. And in "gathering together" and giving impressions a privileged domicile within the official records, the archive directs the future of what constitutes archivable material. It thus not only makes visible *what* could be recorded but also *where* it would fall within the official record (e.g., physics). Selye's original institutionalization of stress, energy, and stability continues to impress itself on us through the medium of the archive.

Rather than the language of the printing press, where stress makes an indelible mark, the clinical discourse of stress and burnout relies on the register of energy and balance. The archive, according to Derrida,

> names at once the *commencement* and the *commandment*. This name apparently coordinates two principles in one: the principle according to nature or history, *there* where things *commence*—physical, historical, or ontological principle—but also the principle according to the law, *there* where men and gods *command*, *there* where authority, social order are exercised, *in this place* from which *order* is given—nomological principle. (1995, 1; emphases original)

The archive names things into being. It is where facts, events, history begin and also begets the authority and power over that which has yet to emerge. It is, as Derrida puts it, "at once *commencement* and *commandment*." The archive thus manifests whatever power is present. It represents the state of the *now* in how documents gain order and become institutionalized within this public space.

The archive thus has its own force separate from the documents that it shelters. As Derrida highlights in his essay on the archive, "There is no political power without control of the archive, if not of memory" (1995, 4). Without in some way having a say in how we order and classify exhaustion—for example, as part of the physics of force or as part of the poetics of labor that grounds revolutions—there can be no institutionalization of fatigue. Fatigue and death, such as that of Henna, becomes properly public when it falls within an archive of stress, and as part of the impression left by Walter B. Cannon and then by Selye. The very fact that some individuals "deplete energetic resources" alone do not produce a context for talking about stress, or of death from making untimely martyrdom. How we talk about stress and fatigue come from Selye and biologists who made a conscious choice to set a very specific course for how later generations would archive what might be otherwise singular moments of exhaustion set apart from industrial history. It is to this choice to which the politics of the archive refers and to the context in which disparate ideas gain consignation as a single coherent corpus. It is also in the politics involved in the very establishment of the archive that its very weakness, its fever, lies. But we get ahead of ourselves.

We return to the problem of choice. Speaking of choice here is apt. For instance, Selye's predecessor, Cannon, the father of homeostasis and the "fight or flight" response, chose to turn to the anthropological archive instead of physics. In "'Voodoo' Death" (1942), an article published by the *American Anthropologist*, Cannon elucidates how the neurophysiological-behavioral pattern involved in the fight-or-flight response can be triggered by certain social contexts. He concludes that the social has within it a certain force that can even kill its members.

Out of the anthropological records on voodoo death, William Brown's (1845) account of "death induced by ghostly power" makes an impression on Cannon. Brown describes how a Maori woman who was told that she had eaten a fruit from a tabooed place exclaimed how she had violated the sanctity of the chief and that his spirit would kill her (Cannon 1942, 170). The next day she was dead.

Through Edward Tregear (1890), Cannon learns that taboo (*tapu*) is "an awful weapon" (cited in Cannon 1942, 170). It is an awesome power Tregear witnesses himself: "'I have seen a strong young man die' he declares 'the same day he was *tapued*; the victims die under it as though their strength ran out as water'" (170). Based on such accounts, Cannon himself remarks that death comes about through the "fatal power of the imagination working through unmitigated terror" (170).

What is this power that kills through impressing itself into our imaginations? What is a force that kills through being thought?

Returning to Durkheim's notion of sacrifice is instructive here. Durkheim writes of sacrifice as a form of self-erasure, the act of giving the gods the ultimate sacrifice of "our thoughts." Gods live only insofar as we give them our thoughts, give them credit, and give them a space within our minds. It is this credibility that gives them their power to impress themselves on us. The categories—god, taboo, and burnout—thus have no force of their own unless we give them some real estate within our minds. Moreover, it is a relationality authored by us, the community, though we forget our own hand in this. We name what gods come into being, and yet through forgetting their origins, we give in to their awesome power.

The traditional anthropological formulations of voodoo death follow this logic of the social. One's demise stems from the force of the social. The social truth of voodoo presses down on the individual until he or she succumbs under it. As in Cannon's account, an enemy points at you with a bone or a stick, curses you, and you die. The curse takes over you. It erases your physical existence, but the bone amasses more power through this archive of death, thus in a sense retaining your memory (cf. Siegel 2006). Here, history and the archive take over the real of death.

In giving credit to social facts, one enhances the "awful weaponry" society attributes to what it holds sacred. As we author gods, we also author diseases. How we identify a disease relies not only on the scientific knowledge available at the time but also on political and economic incentives that shape how such knowledge gain institutionalization. Stress came to matter at a specific point in industrial history; so did occupational burnout in Finland. Allan Young (1980), for example, does not discredit the physiology of exhaustion; however, he sees the advent of stress science as a product of a mode of production that dominated a particular era. Stress as a general syndrome fails to gain much credit on its own as a primary diagnosis. However, as a total social fact, it comes to archive the experience of job precarity, the uncertainty of social transformation, and heightened sense of competitiveness under advanced capitalism.

These accounts place the source of violence in the social (Lévi-Strauss 1987). However, they do not ask why individuals give their thoughts at all. What is this experience of giving one's thought? And in giving away thought, can we still speak of any "one" as such? What is one without the interiority of thought? In giving one's thought, one also reaches the limit of thought as something to be had, something one can own. Sacrifice points to the impossibility of maintaining one's own interiority; it points instead to one's rupture. In giving one's thought, one bleeds out. It is sometimes a fatal condition as we see from Tregear's "strong young man" whose "strength ran out as water." Sakari, Iiris, and Henna might concur that this fatality continues.

As Bataille (1986) argues, anthropological accounts elucidate *how* sacrifices work but not *why* they work. He locates this secret in the very negativity of social force. Should we take social force as something unavowable, as something outside of the realm of language and of conceptualization, we can take a different take on what it means to give "it" thought. What is an "it" we cannot identify? How do we give "it" anything? In the face of an unavowable "it," an "it" that nonetheless fascinates, we lose our capacity to be the author of our own actions. We do not give our thoughts, but we *give in* to that which resists domestication within an archive. We sacrifice not because we give but because we lose ourselves to that which remains beyond ourselves. We lose ourselves to that which fascinates, to a force we do not fully comprehend.

The difference between giving and giving in is the difference between having an "I" from not having a "place" from which to speak. In giving, the worshipper continues to say "I," as in "I am cursed." In giving in, the worshipper gives up saying "I." In relinquishing to say "I," the worshipper also lets go of him- or herself as the subject who gives. In breaking the bond with him- or herself thus, the worshipper loses his or her private existence. In giving in, the worshipper is turned inside out. The worshipper becomes part of the exchange. The gift always carries within it a part of the giver. In giving in, one bleeds out to become part of the outside; and in thus becoming conscious of one's lack of interiority, horror sets in. One becomes speechless lest we buy into what counts as timely social fact. It is a condition we see with Iiris, Sakari, and so many others I came into contact with.

Thus, contra long-standing anthropological tradition that locates the awesome violence of voodoo death in the force of the social, Henna, Sakari, and Iiris reveal something else at work. They speak to this horror of being for which no formulation can give the clarity of social reality.

For instance, Sakari feels the pressure to go into the office so he may return the keys for a unit that is to be shown early the next morning despite knowing he has the right to refuse. He is on sick leave after all. However, the demand weighs on him. His supervisor points to Sakari with the bone, as it were, and Sakari wavers. Something drives him; what, he cannot explain. It starts a conflict between him and Diwa.

Diwa presents another type of pressure. Her demand, however, comes from a place of care. Against Diwa's direct concern for his well-being, Sakari maintains his capacity to say "I." "I am so sick and tired of people telling me to eat right, drink less, exercise, and be healthy!" he says. It is against the pressure from the office that he can only say "I" in the negative, as in "I am not Henna." He is not Henna, but he nonetheless fails to answer my direct question. He cannot answer why he would think twice about going into the office to return the key during his sick leave. He had just been returned from the hospital for major surgery after all.

Should we follow the tradition of anthropological takes on voodoo death, Sakari's actions would be easily explained. He is a martyr worker, and he is driven to work because he succumbs under the weight of history. His office marks him by calling on him and he feels compelled to obey. He may in the end follow Henna to his grave. However, we see that he does not claim these formulations as his own. He falls silent instead in answer to my question "Why do you do it?"

Sakari gives his thought to the god that is the Nordic welfare, but this god is not *perkele*, the pre-Christian Finnish god. In his untimely sacrifices, none answers his call. But he continues to be moved. He repeats his sacrifices past the point of efficacy. No exchange takes place; yet he cannot stop. How are we to make sense of this excess? What continues to move him when the god of Nordic welfare has long since fallen into oblivion? How is it that new gods have yet to make their impression on him?

There is something at work in excess of social facts, formulations, techniques, and or beliefs that make us give ourselves. To be so convinced, there would be no speechlessness concerning what moves us. There is rather, as James Siegel puts it, "a violence that inheres in the social and turns against it" (2006, 2). More specifically, he describes this violence as one that "serves no social purpose and stem not from social reality but from points where no definition of social reality can take place—where, therefore, phantasy, and, often, violence occur, a violence that does not serve to construct new social forms or restore old ones" (1).

This violence resists being reduced to language and thus evades the exchange of symbols and meanings. It resists conceptualizations and thus serves no timely purpose. Its timeless force lies in this very anti-utile no sense that is nonetheless fundamental to communication. Following Bataille, Derrida asks, "What if what cannot be assimilated, the absolute indigestible, played a fundamental role in the system?" (1986, 151). No communication, no community, and no form of being in common can take place without this absolute negativity that says nothing but nonetheless drives us to give, makes us forget ourselves. That which moves us, then, is not what is positively identifiable: it is that which remains "unemployed," free of purpose, and thus that which continues to push us to reach beyond ourselves for meaning (Bataille 1988). It is the negativity, the space, without which no positive identification would be possible.

In our attempts to know, for example, why individuals would work to the point of pathogenic exhaustion, we communicate in order to gather information and to appropriate knowledge. However, against this purposive form of exchange, there is yet another.

Paradoxically, it is what lies in excess of social formulation that constitutes communication. Alphonso Lingis, following Bataille, argues that communication refers to the "contact of an individual with what is and remains beyond him" (2009, 121). What moves us to give is not something that originates within us but that which draws us out of ourselves. In reaching out, in being moved, inspired, captured by the world, and only through the loss of ourselves as the unmoved mover could we even get a sense of who we might be. Why we do what we do, then, comes from letting go of this very question. Only in letting go of asking why can we begin to sense what moves us to give. Like laughter and the uncontrolled discharges of erotic energy, what moves us to give is that which remains beyond what we know as "it." The force that moves us is mute. Its silence is what gives it force.

There is thus a limit to the productive power of the archive to document and to authorize. As Derrida puts it, it contains within it a self-destructive force.

The archive "shelters" within itself the memory of how it came to be. It is the memory of its initial inscription—its commencement, the memory of how it came to have this place, this name. The archive shelters this originary moment and also shelters itself from it. It must forget the memory of its own institution lest it loses the force necessary to keep itself together. Unless we forget that *we* author gods, gods lose their charismatic divinity. The truth of stress must remain outside of the industrial history through which it gained acceptance. The very condition for us to know, for us to know why we do anything, then, lies in this very capacity to forget that we author the very reason why we do what we do. Should we not forget how we began, the very authority of our laws also loses its power.

At the very basic level, we must forget that when we give, receive, and return a gift, what moves us is a "polite fiction" at best. Without forgetting this basic fact, we would lose our capacity to speak from the position of "I." As Derrida argues, the archive is not what is. It is but a repository of what we *think* is but not the thing itself. The original, that "thing" itself, fails to be captured as text. It is that which always haunts the archive. The politics of the archive exist in this very gap between the original and the record of the original. The sickness of the archive, or archive fever, rests in our attempt to establish the point of origin, the origin from which we are moved, the primal origin that drives us to the point of fatigue, of death and sacrifice.

# PÄÄSKYNPESÄ

The staff at Pääskynpesä (literally, "Swallow's Nest"), a rehabilitation center that doubles as a resort hotel, told me I could not miss it. They were right. It is an imposing glass-and-concrete structure set into a hillside; its gray angles reflected in the water of Lake Ilomantsi. In a town with a population size of 6,057 on the Russian border in Finnish northern Karelia, it, along with the water tower turned wine terrace, is a defining feature of the town.

Ilomantsi suffered heavily from Soviet attacks during World War II, and the village center had been rebuilt in sparse but clean rows of gray concrete blocks flanked by birch trees, urban design that contrasted sharply with the ornate wooden Orthodox church located at the edge of town. Even in the middle of the day, the town center was largely quiet.

My first visit to Pääskynpesä was in early March 2007, and Lake Ilomantsi was completely frozen over. The rehabilitation center was an island of warmth in the white landscape, and steam on the glass walls that separated the pool from the lobby added to the feeling. In contrast to the aged people in wheelchairs sitting motionless in front of the large window overlooking the lake, children ran in and out, coming from the pool. Adding to my first impression of action and inaction, age and youth, was the contrast between silence and the occasional raucous caused by two slot machines that clanged every so often in the most alarming manner.

The staff at the front desk kindly explained to me this queer juxtaposition of silence and clamor. The rehabilitation center doubled as a resort hotel (*loma-hotelli*), meaning it serviced the local residents with recreational needs as well as its clients. The two slot machines that flanked the public restrooms were, according to this staff, a regular feature of many public spaces in Finland since the money from slot machines funded many of the nation's welfare and health programs. In addition to the pool, the center also provided outdoor recreational equipment such as snowshoes, kayaks, Nordic skis, tents, and so forth. The front desk also wanted to tell me that the center held weekly entertainment featuring local artists and organized dances. He gave me a flyer for the center's upcoming musical event that roughly translates as "The Heavy Price of Peace" (*Musiikkinäytelmä: "Raskas Rauha"*). It featured "wartime songs and stories" (*sota-ajan lauluja ja tarinoita*) followed by folk dancing. He then took me on a quick tour of the facilities.

As *Musiikkinäytelmä* would indicate, Pääskynpesä was not always a resort hotel. It used to be a hospital for World War II veterans. Bordering Russian Karelia, Ilomantsi played a crucial role for Finland during the war offensives against the Soviet Union and many from the town died in that struggle. The travails of that era live on in the present.

"Don't linger in the forest after dark," I was warned during my first trip to Ilomantsi when I stayed with a farming family on the outskirts of town. "Why?" I asked my worried hosts. They hesitated. One of their little girls, however, piped up in a very clear voice. "There are ghosts of Russian and Finnish soldiers who died during the war."

Peace is heavy, indeed. The poster for the musical event, *"Raskas Rauha,"* literally, "Heavy Peace," brought back such memories of having walked about the forest with the warning by the little girl not to stay out too late. The forests here carried that heaviness of blood and sacrifice. Trenches dug during the war still marked the forest floor and the numerous shelters dug into the ground, though covered in green moss today, testified to the intensity of the fighting that once took place. Ilomantsi was just such a place haunted by memory no forest or moss could quite cover over.

Converted into a resort hotel, Pääskynpesä boasted a vast natural preserve and hiking trail that traversed old battlegrounds and trenches made during World War II. Although it used to provide much needed physical therapy for war veterans and people with severe disabilities, with Finland's war generation on the decline, rehabilitation centers like Pääskynpesä have come to broaden the scope of their therapeutic programs to open the door to individuals with eating disorders, burnout, and depression, among others. This was why I was there.

Inside the center, social workers, psychologists, and other clinical personnel had their own individual offices on the second floor, while the physical therapists shared an office with other activity supervisors on the ground floor in between the lobby and the cafeteria. Mixed in with individual offices on the second floor were classrooms, entertainment rooms with televisions, a pool table, a smoking room, and a communal computer. In a small section were rooms kept expressly for Finland's aging war veterans and patients requiring intensive medical attention. Hotel guests and clients for courses such as burnout stayed on the third floor, as did I. The third floor had a common television room, a common reading room, and a little room for child day care.

In this chapter, I detail what constitutes the goals and objectives of rehabilitation for individuals with burnout in Finland. Through my time spent with clients who came to Pääskynpesä that spring in 2007, I explore the daily rhythm of life for those placed within such centers to examine not only how the center gathers and consigns on clients certain ways of being but also how such order unleashes its own disorder. Following clients at Pääskynpesä and at other such facilities, I found that falling speechless was not a condition that went away with rehabilitation. Rather, I discovered that the loss of one's capacity to gather oneself together around the coherence of concepts, words, and language went hand in hand with the capacity to see oneself through the lens of burnout.

But first, I provide the legal and political context through which resort hotels came to occupy a node in the rehabilitative apparatus. It must be noted how Finland's institutional responses to occupational burnout differs to the ones in the United States. Where treatments for mental health issues tend to take individualized form in the United States, in Finland, the state apparatus sees occupational burnout as a structural problem stemming from recent transformations in organizational and workplace demand. Occupational burnout in Finland thus demands a systematic response to occupational burnout not as privatized therapy but as collective rehabilitation that requires the engagement of both worker and employer groups.

Legal and juridical amendments made during the early 2000s reflect this notion of rehabilitation as a collective and structural endeavor. Although the constitution of Finland (731/1999) decrees that "public authorities shall assume responsibility for the protection of the labor force" (Ministry of Social Affairs and Health 2006, 13), several key revisions and amendments to occupational health law were made to render the legal structures more timely.

Following demands by the Central Organization of Finnish Trade Unions (Suomen Ammattiliittojen Keskusjärjestö or SAK) that employer groups pay more attention to the physical and psychological consequences of a more "hectic" and more technologically demanding workplace, the government made amendments to occupational health law.[1] Chief among them is the Act on Occupational Health Services (OHS) revised in 2001 (1383/2001). Brought front and center in this revision is the responsibility of employers to promote the "work ability and functional capacity" of employees. To meet this demand, the act mandates all employers to provide preventative health "services" to their employees. On a similar note, the Occupational Safety and Health Act of 2002 decrees that employers must voluntarily "identify the hazards and risk factors related to the work or working conditions, eliminate or remedy them, and assess the effects of the remaining risks to employees' health and safety." In 2004, the Occupational Health Act was amended again to make the provision of occupational rehabilitation a statutory obligation. This act, which encouraged both employers and employees to patronize rehabilitation services, was meant to prevent conditions such as burnout from developing into a more serious disease (e.g., depression) and/or worse, death.

Adding to the attention already placed on the importance of occupational health, the Finnish government passed yet another law in 2006, the Act on Occupational Safety and Health Enforcement and Cooperation on Workplace Safety and Health (44/2006). This act underscored the points made in the previous two acts by providing legal structures that ensured that employers followed through with their obligations for maintaining occupational health.

These legal responses taken by the state apparatus to the demands by SAK reveal more than how policymakers see workplace issues as simultaneously political issues as well as a legal one. The numerous amendments and revisions made to Finland's occupational health laws show how the notion of "today's" workplace and the risks associated with it become woven into legal structures. They in fact not only serve to acknowledge the existence of the "new economy" but also gives institutional life to the "new" economic model.

These amendments and revisions articulated what constituted timely responses and responsibilities to the occupational health risks at hand. In doing so, they legally rewrote the very notion of health and sickness. Under these changes made to the occupational health acts, health gained visibility through the notion of well-being, and sickness came to encompass all manner of disability that took away from one's ability to maintain one's capacity to work. The amendments recognized the hardships of a more "hectic" workplace as raised by SAK; they also created pathways for intervening on such disabilities in ways that allow employers to render the workforce into timely workers. The technomedical apparatus cares for well-being, but this care must also bring economic benefit to the nation-state. The virtuous circle has always been a productive one. The new economy merely advances this productive virtue by siphoning collective resources into the promotion of well-being and of positive feelings as economic catalysts.

The Finnish Social Insurance Institute (KELA) encouraged this move to rethink what constitutes disability (Niemelä and Salminen 2006). Simo Mannila et al. (2005) argue that a view of "disability" that specifically considered reduced working capacity as "impairment" diverges from the "classic" sense of disability, by which they refer to deafness, blindness, and other physiological challenges. KELA specifies reduced working capacity, or "work impairment" (*työkyvyttö-*

*myys*), as a way to call attention to the potential risk of such a disability linking up with more serious conditions that may cause premature retirement—a further loss to national economic competitiveness.

Here, the amendments made to occupational health acts make visible what is necessary to function in a more "hectic" workplace as health services in the form of rehabilitation, stress workshops, and/or other "general preventative health services" such as yoga and mindfulness retreats. Such provisions not only bridge the divide between timely belonging, health, and work capacity but also articulate what it takes to be part of a productive member of society in the here and now. Health services that are to be provided by private employers are not at all private matters. Although private employers must provide these services, they are not alone in footing the bill. KELA refunds up to 50 percent of the costs. Capital-nation-state works hand in hand to ensure its triadic survival.

# Rehabilitation

Rehabilitation programs for work impairment boomed in the mid-2000s.[2] KELA offered to buy programs that met their approval as part of their nationwide registry and menu of programs from which local KELA officers could send individuals for therapy. In turn, ailing rehabilitation centers were quick to develop programs in line with KELA's so as to obtain much needed business.

Converted resort hotels that once served as hospitals for World War II veterans such as Pääskynpesä welcomed such prospects. Pääskynpesä developed their Exhaustion in Work-Life Rehabilitation course (*Työelämässä uupuneet kuntoutuskurssi*) under such circumstances when old regional hospitals needed to keep up with changing needs of the nation.

Pääskynpesä started its first program for people with burnout in 2004. Although the program must pass KELA's accreditation process, rehabilitation centers dotted across the Finnish landscape are allowed some leeway in modifying the treatment in ways that take advantage of the uniqueness of the location or of the equipment available at the center itself. It was not enough that they followed KELA's standards. Each center needed to add a unique value to their program so as to add variety to KELA's growing list of rehabilitative options for workers.

Once sold, KELA reviewed the program every four years for possible contract renewal. This review process added pressure on rehabilitative center staff to continue to innovate and to make their product ever attractive. This pressure made my entry into the center all the more reasonable to those who initially did not see a purpose to my role there but reconsidered the advantages of having me there if it meant that I could possibly offer recommendations for how to improve the program at the center. With that in mind, I was given a generous discounted rate and access to the program, except for private psychological counseling sessions.

Although most rehabilitation centers were also located in quiet forested surroundings, Pääskynpesä emphasized its surroundings as unique features of its therapeutic package: a "Day in the Forest" (*Luontokuntoutus*) as well as a "Day of Silence." Both these activities sought to give clients a chance to take advantage of the vast forest and lake territory of Ilomantsi and Iljala, an outpost of the Orthodox Church (Church of Saint Elijah).

Riding the bus from the regional capital of Joensuu, the reason for these unique features became obvious. Ilomantsi, Finland's most eastern province, was not only a site where nineteenth-century folklorists situated national heritage—the land of *kantele* and runes—but also Finland's point of contact with Russian Karelia, a region of Russia culturally similar to Finland but largely Orthodox. As such, Ilomantsi not only had one of the largest population of Russian immigrants but also long stretches of empty forests that were once battlefields. Both these features left Ilomantsi a legacy of Russian influences as well as collective national archives of war. Pääskynpesä incorporated both forest and Orthodox religious spaces into its rehabilitative program as its unique contribution that nonetheless spoke to all Finns.

Pääskynpesä's course, like all KELA's programs for burnout, ran for a total of ten days with ten members per course and a shorter follow-up session of seven days in the following summer. People attending the course were referred to as clients (*asiakas*). Such clients were able to choose where they sought rehabilitation and were encouraged by rehabilitative experts to *own* their treatment by seeing themselves as clients and not as patients. Experts also hoped that ownership of the program by clients would spark a process of change that would lead to personal empowerment. Thus, the sense of ownership of the rehabilitative program, based on KELA's empowerment paradigm, was to lead to ownership of oneself—one that was to allow individuals to take timely control over their productive achievements (cf. Mannila et al. 2005).

But change does not come easily. It takes time. It also requires a certain space for change to take place. The rehabilitation center provides such a place for time and space necessary for change. And as change here refers to purposive and timely change—that is, change for the purpose of regaining productive capacity in the here and now—clients were to inhabit fully this place at the center. They not only took part in the activities as stipulated by the program but also ate and slept at the center away from their home and families for the duration of the program.[3]

Rehabilitative experts saw the center as a training ground for the future. Rehabilitation, they told me, is not a cure. It is more a process that directs the path to a desired future, one that allows clients to be productive and empowered through their productive membership in society. At the center, experts taught clients new skills that would allow them to cope in a "faster and harder" world. There, they also taught clients how to unlearn old habits. For this to happen, in addition to separating clients from their everyday by obligating them to stay at the center, programs for burnout often provided activities that attempted to foster a sense of group cohesion among the members. Physically cut off, surrounded by a lake and dense forest, clients spent their days forging new connections with each other within a time and space authored to make them withstand the pressures of time. Thus, rehabilitation encompassed much more than techniques aimed at developing individual self-awareness. The center provided the place necessary for individuals to relate to others in a controlled environment. The center, therefore, not only directed individual processes of self-reflection but also directed the channels of communication in between each client member.

But in setting time and space apart from the everyday thus, what is it that takes place? What forms of communication and sense of community unfold?

Although KELA states its goals clearly as in getting clients to become timely citizens capable of weathering the stresses of the day, time is not altogether something that could be appropriated for productive ends. Even though rehabilitative programs "spatialize" time as time belonging to rehabilitative ends (Nancy 1993, 150), time does not belong, time is not to be thus possessed, time fails to be appropriated. Time merely flows.

In other words, the notion that we can set a block of time apart for use as rehabilitative space is but a conceptual fiction. Time remains in excess of such medicotechnical attempts to spatialize time as an immobilized block. In setting time apart as a particular space for specific activities to take place, we sacrifice the constantly flowing and living aspects of time. In appropriating time by suspending it as a time and space for rehabilitation, we kill time. Sacrificed here are not the working hours that would be given over for rehabilitative purposes but rather, the notion of time and of being as conditions irreducible to an end other than their own. Thus, sacrificed is the very notion of a point beyond productive life. Clients must make sacrifices—give their thoughts, as Émile Durkheim tells us—to this god of productivity if they are to regain a place of themselves in the present.

In this dead space of time at the rehabilitation center, no guarantee could be made for anything to take place, let alone desired change. It is a time and space haunted by that which has been sacrificed. However, this negativity also provokes. It has a force of its own, though not one identifiable as any one particular force. In other words, it has no name. It does not operate in the name of rehabilitation, or of resistance, or as escape. It is negativity of time, space, and of being erased, killed, and supplanted by conceptual categories that nonetheless carry an effect. It is a force in excess of named force but a force also because it is not named. It is alive. It is what passes in between individuals that escapes immobilization as this or that power. It is the space of negativity without which no name can be distinguished.

It is such a happening that I wish to focus on here. Where medical anthropology has traditionally focused on the force and unintended effects of the medical apparatus—for instance, what *it* allows and disallows, what resistances and potentials *it* opens, what rights, what identities, and what politics *it* mobilizes (cf. Kleinman 1980; Petryna 2002; Whyte 2009)—here, I attend to force in excess, that which remains to be named.

There is what Benjamin Noys (2012) calls a persistence of the negative. It is a turn away from affirmation, from the effect of the positively identifiable. This is a turn I wish to make in this chapter.

Here, I examine the force negativity carries—a negation that escapes conceptualization and thus the confinement of timely technological understanding. Through the medium of ethnographic writing, I document such moments of the negative—moments for which laughter, tears, insomnia, and connections with another—would lose all power should it be sacrificed for the clarity of language.

Taking part in the group activities at the center, I was provoked into rethinking the point of ethnographic writing. Moments that moved me to take notes were not specific events at which people clearly articulated their feelings, their plans, or their future desires. Moments that compelled me to pick up pen and pad were those that made no sense to me. In these moments of noncomprehension, something happened in this block of time set apart for rehabilitation. I say *something*, as it leaves open the possibility that not every exchange stems from the postulates of rehabilitation or of resistances to rehabilitation.

These moments of noncomprehension for which ordinary attempts to document and to record fail are precisely the moments at which the enigma of the negative, the force of time that flows on its own ruptures the polite fiction that we know what we communicate at all.

Ethnographic writing here, then, emerges at the limits of reason—at the limits of that which can be affirmed. I do not "speak for" another (cf. Fassin 2014). Writing on the reverse side of affirmation neither discloses nor grasps for certain the ethnographic as "the ethnographic." Nothing is given, nothing is certain as the given (*datum*) of ethnographic writing. Writing ethnographically here involves a nonassumption of what moves one to write. In such an orientation to writing, it is impossible to speak for another since what moves that other is itself not positively identifiable. Writing, in this sense, emerges through this mutually uncanny negativity, one that cannot be sublated under the framework of rehabilitation while it emerges in its shadow.

# The Program

I arrived a few days before the official start of the program. By the time the first clients arrived, I had been there long enough to forget how it felt like to step into the center for the first time. However, I was able to see this moment in the faces and deliberate movements of clients who made their way to the center.

The clients were also easy to pick out by the clothes they wore. In contrast to long-term patients who wore nightgowns in the lobby and also in contrast to the locals who came to use the pool or the slot machine, clients appeared urban and professional in their suits and colorful silk scarves.

I also remarked in my field notes that despite their reason for being there, the clients on the whole were rather bright-eyed and alert in the manner in which they made inquiries as to their rooms at the front desk. I also caught this sense of alertness—something I did not expect from individuals suffering from burnout—in my first formal introduction to the group.

Miia, the resident psychologist, asked me to join in after she had her first group session with the group. As I entered the room toward the end of the session, it felt to me as if I were crashing a staff meeting of sorts. In front of bright faces, I was given some time to explain my project to the clients and to ask if anyone would be interested in sitting with me for formal interviews. They were all asked to sign a waiver stating that my presence at the center and participation in some of their group activities did not disturb the rehabilitative process. Of the twelve participants, only four signed up for the formal interviews, but all signed the waiver. It told me, then, that not many found being interviewed by me on a one-on-one basis completely appetizing but were willing to let me join them for meals, group activities, and related social activities meant for fun.

After the group gave me their approval to join, Miia gave me a formal schedule of activities for the following ten days. Looking over the sheets of paper in my own room, I saw how early the days were to begin at the center.

Indeed, the daily schedule at the rehabilitation center was unexpectedly hard. Despite the title of the course, "Exhausted" (*Uupuneet*), the schedule presented rehabilitation as another kind of work. Activities began at 8:00 a.m. sharp every day except for Sunday and ended at 4:00 p.m. Although not quite a full workday, I was tired by the time the last daily activity ended.

By the third day, the enthusiasm of the first two days dwindled. Whereas in the beginning, members ate together as a group at the larger tables, by the third day, they had started to have breakfast at their own. Spending so much time together during the day made eating breakfast a valuable time to be alone and to collect one's thoughts. With no pressure to be together at a set time, eating alone also purchased more time to sleep in. I quickly joined others in identifying quiet corner tables to eat my porridge alone.

From 8:00 a.m., sessions ran for about forty-five minutes to an hour. Although the repertoire of activities did not change much, each day brought new combinations of activities. For instance, if day one began with physical therapy followed by group counseling, the next day might begin with the counseling session, which would be followed by physical exercise or nutritional counseling. These activities reflected the diversity in the staff who made up the rehabilitative team of experts.

Within the ten-day period, clients met with a physician, psychologist, physiotherapists, a public health nurse, a social worker, a nutritionist, and a leisure instructor or "free-time" leader (*vapaa-ajanohjaaja*). Of these experts, the physiotherapist had the most contact with clients, meeting with them nineteen times, and Miia met with groups or individuals a total of nine times. The rest of the professionals met with the group once, except the social worker, who met with the clients twice.

The physician provided the initial health check to make sure that no one would hurt themselves through participating in physiotherapy and to proscribe what exercise a client should avoid. Although I had no access to private psychotherapy sessions between Miia and individual clients, the staff openly encouraged me to attend most of the physical therapy sessions. They claimed that these sessions included exercises everyone should perform on a daily basis.

Activities included stretching, creative breathing exercises, demonstrations on how to solve ergonomic issues at work, and meditative relaxation. In addition to these activities meant to encourage "relaxation," more physically taxing exercises involved water aerobics, mid-range walks, and aerobic-type exercises (e.g., skip rope, dancing, running in place to music).

These diverse activities again stem from the objectives and goals of rehabilitation as determined by the standards set by KELA. Although KELA does not dictate the exact menu of the exercise program, it nonetheless provides training pamphlets and folders through which individual physiotherapists must pick and choose the appropriate exercises for his or her group.

Relaxation exercises required work. They demanded clients to listen to their body and to be aware of their breathing, body positions, and existing tension within the body. As much of KELA's objectives revolved around self-awareness and mindfulness of one's physical and psychological limits to stress, relaxation exercises played a key role in getting clients to begin thinking along the lines of thresholds and limits.

There are echoes of Hans Selye here. Even though experts readily acknowledge the social determinants of burnout, the rehabilitative technique rests on this supposed accessibility of the original problem—a cause that rests within the individual. Here, the cause of tension and stress, the problem of repeated exposure to pressure and depletion of energetic resources is located in the individual's misrecognition of his or her physical limits. They must "listen" to the strain and stress of the body if they are to save themselves. The problem is ostensibly accessible and open to techniques that would make the body more productive.

I was to experience for myself what "listening" to the body meant. Taru ran my first participation in a physiotherapy session. As we all respectively finished our breakfast at the cafeteria and slowly gathered at the gymnasium, Taru was already in stretched position on a mat with closed eyes. As we entered, Taru slowly got up and told us to spread out.

The March cold outside left frosty traces on the windows and made the gymnasium with its bright wooden floor feel that much warmer. We began with gentle aerobics in the form of a folk dance to warm up. Under Taru's command, we grasped each other's wrists and forearm until we took up pretzel-like hand positions. Once we were properly twisted into each other, Taru asked us to kick our legs up in unison in time with Taru's hand clapping. This was impossible. We already had no control of our upper torso, so entangled that we were, and to kick our legs up in unison to Taru's quick claps made us only topple over.

As we each collapsed into each other, the initial tension in the room also fell apart. Laughter crept on us. The more I tried not to laugh when I saw that Pekka, one of the first members to fall into a heap, was still trying to kick his legs up in time to Taru's claps even as he lay pinned to the floor with Onni lying on top of him, the more I had to laugh.

Taru was intentionally pushing the ridiculous. As people began to relax enough to laugh, Taru showed us how to stretch our necks, our shoulders, and our backs—the parts of our bodies most inclined to hurt in office work. After several rounds of stretches, Taru turned on a CD player and told us to get stretch mats for ourselves.

The CD was of a Chinese flute and strings. Once Taru saw we all had our mats, she told us to close our eyes and breathe deeply. "Breath in through one foot, pull it through the leg, and then pass it out through the other leg and out through the other foot," she said. We had now reached the official "relaxation" aspect of physiotherapy. She told us during our deep-breathing exercises that we were listening to something called "Tao Art."

A sense of togetherness different from that from group counseling sessions developed. In contrast to the support and positive encouragement clients often gave each other at group counseling sessions, physiotherapy sessions brought forth much good-natured teasing.

For example, Taru expressed her continued disappointment at my folk-dancing capabilities. She would make an explicit effort to teach me how to loop my arms through the twisted knots of the other group members' arms and get other members to make suggestions.

Each such teaching moment, however, made the loops and arm holds more complicated and much harder for me to kick my legs in any shape or form, let alone in unison with the others. I ended up just losing my step or falling back on Taru's foot or letting my neighbor take the full force of my weight. Once Taru had to duck through the links of arms to keep from getting hit on the head by my badly looped arm. The repeated times at which this happened made the whole group laugh and mess up even more. At such a point, Taru would point at me and grimace to the group's delight.

Whereas breakfasts were solitary affairs, dinners were more social. After the second day, members started to make small groups together for dinner. I joined a group that readily made me some space at their table and then continued on with them to the sauna attached to the swimming pool. The sauna was then followed by long stretches of time in the lobby.

The lobby was a welcome respite from the directed activities. The lobby had an extensive bar and attracted many clients to it. Even after the official time for lights to be turned off at the center, clients preferred to sit together in the lobby rather than go to their individual rooms or use the entertainment room on the third floor.

Insomnia is a common symptom of burnout, and it seemed it was the case at the center as well. Nights were long at the center, especially given northern Karelia's latitude. I often passed members quietly sitting alone or in small groups in the lobby long after I had swum in the pool and sat in the sauna for a good amount of time and had made myself ready to go to bed.

Besides my desire to join clients, the lobby drew me to it for other reasons as well. Even though the room I was given was clean and the bed comfortably padded with a therapeutic mattress, the past history of the rehabilitation center as a regional hospital still left its trace. It was almost as if I felt it in the air, a memory I did not have, and yet one I could feel pressing in me.

My naked feet felt pink and fleshy against the cold linoleum floor of sterile hospital floors. The white walls, white sheets, and fluorescent lighting also reminded me that this was a *medical* space. And although my window looked out onto dramatic views of the lake and forest beyond, it was so dark at night that the window felt less as an opening to an outside but a black mirror that pushed my gaze back in. Looking out, I could only see my face lit up by the bright fluorescent light of my room. Even after closing the curtain, I often found myself unable to sleep. It was at such moments that the desire to join the silence down in the lobby became the strongest. It was then that seeking the intimacy of strangers made the most sense.

Going down to the lobby after lights-out at the center was an awkward task. The blue glow of the snow outside provided enough light for me to see, but it was still hard to identify people's faces and to figure out the island of groups that had formed. In the cover of the night, people spoke of what they missed from home, how they missed their kids, doubts they carried, and their thoughts about the return home.

Unlike in the more formalized interviews I had with them through the week and unlike the environment of the group therapy sessions, these faceless conversations in the gloom were free flowing. Connected by the blanket of darkness, voices melted more easily together. One conversation will start in one island of couches to be taken up in yet another corner of the lobby. When you cannot see faces, it appears people care less whether you have been invited to speak.

And yet, it was still hard for me to jump into their midst. One night, as I minced my way slowly down to the lobby, Kylli saw me fidgeting in the gloom clearly unsure as to where to put myself. Without hesitation, she waved me over to her island of couches and pushed Onni who was sitting next to her off the seat. He seemed surprised, but when he saw me, he gallantly invited me to his seat.

As I thanked him and took over Onni's seat, he got up and walked behind Kylli's chair. From that position, he proceeded to massage her back. In between vigorous rubs from behind, Kylli told me that I was embarking on a "brave journey."

"You've come all the way to Finland," she said. "I mean, not even Helsinki, but here"—she rolled her eyes and pointed at her surroundings—"here, in this little town!" She laughed. She told me that she was one of the few who signed up for the formal interviews and that she looked forward to "telling the world that Finland had reached a crisis." Suddenly, however, I saw her mouth contort and she was crying. In between big gasps of air in between sobs, she repeated, "Finland has reached a crisis. It has been going on for a long time, but now we have reached a real crisis." Onni handed her his own glass of Gin Lonkero (a gin-based cocktail that comes in a can) for her to drink and rushed to get her some tissues. Given that the lobby bar had long since closed for the night, it was a generous gesture. He had given her his last drink of what seemed to become a long night.

Kylli calmed down after several other members came over from nearby chairs to pat her on the arm or bring over more boxes of tissue paper. I felt the eyes of some group members who turned toward me disapprovingly over what had transpired. Or rather, in the dark, I could not exactly read what expression those had who faced me, but I felt my own self-conscious presence at the root of what had happened. I got ready to make some remark as an excuse to leave. I did not want to intrude any more on the clients' time away from Pääskynpesä's staff and official activities. Kylli, however, held me back.

Without much context, she started telling me about why she "ended up"—as she put it—at the rehabilitation center. "I needed to communicate with different school officials so that I could put these kids from my school into different schools, fulfill their needs. . . . I needed to use the computer. But I don't like computers and computers don't like me!" she said. She laughed. This made those sitting around her laugh as well. I asked her if she could start at the beginning. This is her story:

> I work with children who need special education, and it was my job to find them a place in regular schools once they were ready to move on. In Finland, we have a law for special kids, but then the law goes in loops [she made spirals in the air with her finger]. It was all shit! [*paska*!].
>
> We had a system of evaluation, but when you do it, you just put roses, roses, roses, roses. You say, "This is rosy, and everything is *rosy*!" You do this because you know you are not allowed to state what the problem is in the evaluations and so you say that everything is "rosy," and you end up feeling guilty inside. I say we have reached a crisis in Finland because schools don't want to take my kids [the special education students from her school] *anymore*. They say they don't have room: I know it's about money. But I had to keep saying in the evaluations that everything was *rosy*.

She paused. When she began again, her voice was more subdued. "If you are sick and or you are missing a leg, then you have a real problem and people accept it. But if you are just *tired*, nobody says, 'Why don't you go home and sleep?'" Kylli then addressed the group who was listening along with me. "We come from different places, different occupations, but I think we all have something in common. We feel shame [*häpeä*]. Shame because we are supposed to be working. We are nothing if we don't have work."

Onni, who had not stopped massaging Kylli's back, chimed in. Facing me, he asked, "Don't you know of people who give a lot more than what they need to give at work in Japan?" I answered that such themes were common in workplace studies conducted in Japan. Onni then pressed for more comparisons between Finland and Japan despite the fact that I had never said I did research in Japan on this theme. "You should know," he pushed. "It should be the same."

This was a common theme with Onni. Conversations with him often revolved around Japan. "Why are you not doing this research in Japan?" he liked to ask. "Why can I not do this in Finland?" I would respond. Things seemed to be heading in this predictable path until Kylli saved me.

Patting Onni's hand that rested on her should, Kylli expressed how much she felt "at home" at Pääskynpesä. "I belong here," she said, still patting Onni's hand, "despite what my husband might think," she added.

"I have been feeling so exhausted [*uupunut*] for so long that now I think that I have always kind of wanted to be here." Looking around the room, she claimed that even though this was only the third day she was spending with the group, she already felt as though she had spent "real time" with them. No one said anything in response but felt the tension in the air around us notably high again.

Around me, I felt motion. These were quick movements of individuals taking flight. People dispersed as quickly as they came to Kylli's aid. In contrast, I saw Onni nodding his head in agreement.

He said that he had also felt some sense of shame as he found it hard to think of himself as someone with a "mental illness." But he admitted that the idea of getting rehabilitation intrigued him and that now meeting others who shared many of the complaints he himself had held against his workplace, he already felt halfway vindicated. Vindicated about what?

"I thought it was me," he said. "I thought that I was wrong. I didn't know why it was that the more I tried to do well at work, the more things turned out for the worst. I couldn't explain why I felt like things were going down. Here, you learn the words to explain how you feel."

Kylli reached over and gave him a big hug. Helmi, another member of the group, reached over also and gave him a vigorous pat on the back. The flat of her hand hitting the bulk of his back made muffled thumps.

What accounts for such physical contact among a group of people who had known each other for only three days? It was not only alcohol that made the members more physically intimate. The group members hugged and kissed each other in ways that were over the top in comparison to the standards of social decorum I had otherwise seen in Finland. It seemed as it were among "family" that such things could happen, and even then, the amount of physical interaction among group members vastly outweighed similar expressions of intimacy I saw among families of friends back in Helsinki.

"It's not like we lost a leg," Kylli said. Could this intimacy grow only among those who share this shame? Against a public who would not or could not understand, and thus cannot belong to this space of the lobby, some other relationality emerges. Against those who are obviously in need of care—those who lost a leg— the clients have only themselves to shield themselves from the gaze of those who see them as "only tired"—untimely individuals who must learn to adapt to today's workplace.[4]

Whereas the night was full of hushed discussions, the mornings brought tight-lipped members. As I found one member one day smoking by herself in the smoking room half-asleep and nonresponsive to my question as to where to find the others in the group, I asked Ulla, the secretary of the rehabilitative unit who handled relationships with KELA, about the challenging schedule and whether it was counterintuitive that a therapeutic course for burnout—a syndrome known for its high level of exhaustion—to be so rigorous.

"We follow the KELA standard and do what it requires. And yes, it requires a lot," she replied. I asked her what happens if people failed to keep up. She replied that the rehabilitation process begins with an initial interview set up between a nurse, a physician, and a physiotherapist who will then plan a program together with the client so that the client will not have to take part in every group activity if she or he does not feel up to it. In a further response to my question of whether such diversity in individual regimen raises a concern over the coherence of the rehabilitative process, she replied, "Well, no, because there is more burnout. The newspapers say all the time that it is so busy at work that this kind of rehab is really needed. That is why KELA decided to offer this kind of rehab."

According to Ulla, coherence and/or the strict adherence to the program by attendants do not challenge the benefits of rehabilitation for burnout, as the increased pace at work calls for intervention of any sort—even intervention that allows those on the receiving end some leeway. But this open-endedness of the program allowed for those with heavier depression to fall by the wayside. Although the attendant psychologist, Miia, commented that such a loss was inevitable in any treatment program, I noticed that those like Tuulikki, the smoking woman, fell not only out of the program but also out of the sense of social togetherness that had developed among the participants in the informal spaces of the center. In my rounds at night in the lobby, I never saw Tuulikki, and I rarely saw her at social events.

"Rehabilitation is not a cure," Miia liked to remind me. "The goal here is to help clients sort through their life and to give them the information they need to cope on their own or to seek more intensive and individualized help." It was indeed Miia who described to the group how burnout differed from having "lost one's leg." In the first group counseling session, Miia started the discussion by stating how the public will find it harder to understand the sufferings of those with burnout. "It's not like you lost a leg!" she joked.

It was also on this first day that Miia made sure to tell clients that burnout does not qualify as a primary disease category. It is but a "factor that affects health" according to the International Statistical Classification of Diseases and Related Health Problems (ICD)–10. It is a risk, not an established and present problem self-evident to all.

How does one rehabilitate risk? Moreover, how does one work on a condition that is not a "real" condition in itself insofar as it is not considered a primary diagnostic category but a condition that would lead to one? Are we not in some ways all living with elements of this risk?

KELA's answer lay in the promotion of healthy habits. Rehabilitation, then, follows this general framework to direct clients to improve their control over their health by choosing a lifestyle, dietary regimen, and social outlook that would make them better—here read, healthier—consumers. It not only explains the inclusion of a nutritionist in the team of experts present at the rehabilitation center, but it also explains how at these diverse experts had a common goal of getting clients to take on what they considered to be healthy habits—for instance, going to the gym, taking a walk, eating a balanced meal, and so on. Moreover, experts at the center never forced or pressured the clients to do activities they did not want to do. As clients, they were given the choice to participate or not in the activities offered. Sometimes these decisions fell on the presiding general physician who would allow a client to sit out of certain physically taxing activities. Other times, clients themselves chose to opt out.

Rehabilitative experts I met, not only at Pääskynpesä but also at other places, rewarded such clients. "We want clients to know their limits, and they are telling us that they feel too exhausted or are feeling not up to participating in a task. We want that," said Jenni, a psychologist at Kaisankoti, a rehabilitation center close to Helsinki. Like Miia at Pääskynpesä, Jenni also gave wide berth to what counts as a rehabilitative experience and allowed individual clients to choose, to be in control, and to be consumers of the activities offered.

Yet despite this relative freedom given to them by the experts themselves, clients spoke nightly of shame. "They are supposed to be working," said Kylli. It appears that despite KELA's empowerment paradigm, choosing and taking control over one's health does not erase shame. Here, there is a tension between being clients with a choice and being "sick." Moreover, it also points to the complicated discourse of burnout as both a mental illness and as a mere "factor that affects health"—not a primary diagnosis—a risk that *leads to* more serious conditions.

"It's not like we lost a leg." Kylli and Onni speak of shame, and they feel the eyes of society all the more keenly because they know that their condition is not self-evident as having lost one's leg. Even official documents on occupational burnout underline the significance of the disorder as an antecedent condition to "more serious conditions" such as clinical depression and cardiovascular disease that may cause premature retirement (cf. Ahola 2007). Burnout thus is a potential, a threat of bad tidings yet to come, not its realization—something we believe we can solve through our technomedical acumen. The national attention on burnout as the new hazard of the new economy must be considered together with the attempt by public health and labor officials to identify possible causes of lost working hours and to root out the risk as soon as possible. Burnout thus manifests this desire for control of the future. It gives form to the god of technological thinking and to its altar to which we then make sacrifices. We spend our thoughts and energy on how to contain the growth of burnout, how to stop others from dying from work, like Henna, because and only because we believe we have a way of tinkering with the cause—of changing the course of action. This belief, I argue, is none other than the manifestation of technological thinking. It is a belief that there is a cause we can identify; it is a belief that we can then work on this cause and shape the world to suit our needs. It is, thus, that timely needs and technological thinking go hand in hand and, along with it, the politics of how we ought to be.

James Ferguson reveals in his study of interventions by international agencies how the identification of risk factors leads to an expansion of areas experts believe the locals ought to be "educated" (1994, 65). The identification of the potential failures of a local group, for him, a local group of farmers in Lesotho, increases the faith experts have in the abilities of international agencies to solve problems through technical means—methods the locals ostensibly lack.

Here, the risks presented by burnout come together with prescriptions on how to relax, eat well, and to set realistic goals that take into account the pressures of today's workplace. As Ferguson argues, pointing to individual lack and potential failure (e.g., that a burnt-out worker became such through not wisely following sensible prescriptions on relaxation) allows experts and knowledge producers to increase their sphere of control and to also bring others to give in to their expert authority.

However, giving our thoughts to technological thinking does not dispel our anxiety about how things really are. This is especially the case when the problem is less visible than—for instance, like losing a leg. Should we lose a leg, the problem becomes evident to all as a mechanical issue. We would need a prosthesis to make up for the loss as well as physical therapy. Some amount of psychological counseling may be called for as well for us to get over the trauma of this lost limb. As most such cases of injury result from accidents, we may not even feel responsible for the loss. Even had the loss occurred through gross personal negligence, we may rest assured that the public would have a hard time deciding whether we caused the loss or not. In short, unlike in cases of burnout where clients unanimously expressed "shame" and worried about how they would be seen by others on their return, those who lose a leg—or so psychological experts at the rehabilitation centers tell their clients—would not carry this burden of legitimacy.

Experts also echo this anxiety concerning the status of burnout. I see this in the way the literature of burnout often highlights it as an antecedent condition to disorders linked to rates of premature retirement in Finland and also as a new hazard—a timely issue. There appears to be no self-evidence in its significance; otherwise, there would be no need for such supplements. The archive for burnout thus grows.

The need to speak for burnout—starting with Selye who had to sell his ideas to military and industrial leaders before he was able to get medical credit for his ideas—itself manifests a certain perversion, what Jacques Derrida calls archive fever (1995). Derrida, who sees the archive as representing the now and of operating under the power most dominant in the space of the now, argues that its self-evident authority relies on its capacity to do away with, or "forget," as Derrida puts it, that it names the very thing its records into being. The *mal*, the fever, of the archive rests on this very predicament that the archive is the place of origin as well as the place through which things get named, produced.

As such, the original, the "thing" referenced by the name, acts as a phantom limb cut off and supplanted by the prosthesis that is the archive. Derrida has the following to say about this idiom, "archive fever":

> Listening to the French idiom, and in it the attribute *en mal de*, to be *en mal d'archive* can mean something else than to suffer from a sickness, from a trouble or from what the noun *mal* might name. It is to burn with a passion. It is never to rest, interminably, from searching for the archive right where it slips away. It is to run after the archive, even if there's too much of it, right where something in it anarchives itself. It is to have a compulsive, repetitive, and nostalgic desire for the archive, an irrepressible desire to return to the origin, a homesickness, a nostalgia for the return to the most archaic place of absolute commencement. No desire, no passion, no drive, no compulsion, indeed no repetition compulsion, no "*mal-de*" can arise for a person who is not already, in one way or another, *en mal d'archive*. (1995, 91)

This focus on Derrida's notion of *mal* is relevant for us here in our discussion of burnout and rehabilitation as the rehabitation of timely habits. In his thoughts on the archive and what it does, Derrida turns his attention to its Greek origins, *arkheion*, a word that originally referred to "a house, a domicile, and address, the residence of the superior magistrates, the *archons*, those who commanded" (1995, 2). The archive is thus a place, a *topos*, as well as the space through which those who command name and record. The archive thus speaks to the power necessary to gather together and to consign a synchrony of meaning to that which it brings under its "*topo-nomology*." The archive, one can say, makes one see and speak through its apparatus. It has the power to articulate that which remains unsaid, to positively identify that which without it would remain silent. This is the traumatic point in Derrida's notion of the archive that stands in contrast to that of Michel Foucault's. For Foucault, the archive is "first the law of what can be said, the system which governs the appearance of statements as unique events" (1972, 129). Instead of Foucault's notion of the archive as bringing things into being, for Derrida, the archive involves that which is lost. The archive involves the search for that phantom element for which more archival work becomes necessary. And, as I have said, it is this lost and secret element that requires it to update itself, to keep stating "now" as the true moment of revelation, a moment that would free us from the ideological holds of the past.

Staying close to the notion of the archive as *arkheion*, a residence—or a place—the archive according to Derrida, becomes clear as a place of consignation, a place in which the power to mark, to name, and to order takes place. It is, as he says, "*there* where men and gods *command, there* where authority, social order are exercised, *in this place* from which *order* is given—nomological principle" (1995, 1; emphases original).

The power of the archive thus could be said to be limited within the place of the archive—*there*, where it all takes place. Its *mal*, its sickness, its ill, manifests when the *archon*, the experts, the magistrates, and so forth attempt to do away with this very limit, when they attempt to establish the archive as speaking for a place beyond its space of consignation.

There is what John Caputo observes as "the illness, the disorder, the crisis, the evil (*le mal*) that besets a culture that depends on archives," especially, Caputo argues, those that forget the "distance between the original and the trace" (1997, 264). The archive reads traces left by life as it unfolds. Or rather, it consigns a specific reading. This power to direct how one reads the world is its authority as well as its sickness. It cannot itself legitimize its readings as such legitimacy can only take place within the residence of the archive. It can only claim its legitimacy. It thus must continue to make claim, never to rest. It also makes this claim by inserting itself as having the official word on what is most timely—here, stress, exchange, and burnout.

What is it that gets recorded? What is it that we archive? And how does it relate to memory and/or the production of memory as an experience?

We must here recall that Kylli expressed that "we have shame." It was something expressed by many clients who attended such rehabilitation programs. Thus, contrary to how the popular media describes those who fall ill as "martyr workers," individuals who thoroughly believe in and are willing to stake their lives on what they do, confessions of shame belie contradiction or at least an internal division. Here, the rehabilitative discourse adds to the archive on burnout by comparing clients to individuals who have lost a leg. Through the archive, clients are told to read their condition as both illness and as not a self-evident illness. The condition is bad but not terminal as in the absolute loss of a leg. Burnout can be worked on. Moreover, they are told that burnout is a condition that could be prevented through making healthy lifestyle choices. The archive on burnout thus places the responsibility back on the clients themselves. Rehabilitation, and its specific emphasis on "empowerment," positions clients as themselves holding the key to the way out, the "cure."

But identifying the client as the empowered source does not lead to opening the path for clients themselves to take control over what happened or of their future. There is a discrepancy between living memory and what gets archived as such. As Derrida reminds us, there is a difference between mnēmē, experience stored within us, and hypomnema, experience stored in an externalized place, an archive, as public memory. Bearing the archive in mind when revisiting how and why one got sick thus requires a certain sacrifice of one's own experience.

But what is an experience? In other words, experience may not be something to be sacrificed or stored in an archive. Clients here provoke thought on experience as something that always escapes the clutches of archivization. Contra techniques of the archive that attempt to freeze living experience in place as something that could be and should be positively identified and categorized, clients tell a different story. There is something unspeakable about experience. In experiencing, we have to concede that we already sacrifice the words to make sense of what passes in between us and the world. In witnessing clients who fall speechless, I am provoked into thinking back to George Bataille who highlights communication as an opening—a "wound"—a laceration that falls out of the purview of sense and thus ought to be considered as part of the "nonknowledge"—the negativity that nonetheless adds essential authenticity to the words we use in the everyday.

In thinking about the relationship between memory, experience, and the archive, Derrida turns to Sigmund Freud. Freud compared techniques through which we impress thoughts onto an external substrate—for example, ink on paper, chalk on slate, and "the mystic writing pad" (der Wunderblock). Most of all, he saw the psychic apparatus represented in the mechanics of the mystic writing pad.

The mystic writing pad is a toy that allows the writer to make infinite number of traces without having to get a new pad. Its mystical power lies in its capacity to be used over and over again among others. It is made of "a slab of dark brown resin or wax" on which sits wax paper covered by celluloid top cover. The dark resin becomes visible where the stylus makes an imprint allowing you to write or to draw on the surface.

The celluloid top cover protects the wax paper from being punctured by the stylus should you add too much pressure when you write. Lifting the wax paper off the slab, thereby severing the contact between the resin substrate and the wax paper, erases the surface for you to begin anew. This device thus allows for multiple impressions in contrast to a pen and paper that will require ever more paper to receive new thoughts.

Chalk and slate work in similar ways to the mystic writing pad in that they allow for multiple impressions to be made but for several significant differences. For one, the mystic writing pad includes a celluloid top cover that protects the substrate from harm. In the case of the chalk and slate, there is no such layer that mediates the pressure of the chalk from hitting the slate substrate at a force that might break the tip of the chalk or scratch the slate.

For Freud who saw the mystic writing pad as an analogue to how the psychic apparatus gains consciousness of the world, the celluloid layer played a parallel role to our defensive mechanism that "diminish[es] the strength of excitations coming in, and of a surface behind it which receives the stimuli" (1991, 210).

Second, and more significantly, the process of erasure in the mystic writing pad is not as complete as in the case of the chalk and slate. While lifting the wax paper provides a clean new surface on which to write on, permanent imprints remain in the resin or wax that acts as the substrate. Third, following on point two, where writing on a slate remain on the surface, writing, in the case of the mystic pad, involves much more than the symbols that appears on top. There is another layer. Writing, in the case of the mystic writing pad, is a two-tiered affair: it is at once accessible and also inaccessible. What is imprinted into the substrate does not get erased completely; imprints remain in the substrate though not visible on the surface.

Following Freud and seeing the mystic writing pad as an analogue to the psychic apparatus, experience, it appears, leaves traces. They cannot be erased even through new experiences. Moreover, memories can also not be so easily decoded or reproduced as memories are made at the moment of its imprint. Given this very temporal quality of experience, memories become illegible just as they make their imprint on the substrate, the unconscious. Memories thus gain the spectral quality of dreams—affectively significant experiences that evaporate on the tongue. Dreams and memories resist being put into words. What memory is this that is present and yet irreducible to the words made available to us in the present? What of the experience of such negativity?

Derrida takes Freud's discovery further to link it to the archive. These timeless and repetitive mechanics of inscription, documentation, and registration carry with it a certain violence of exclusion as the dominant archive stamp over all others. Yet, new impressions do not erase what was there before, though new documents may alter how we read the old. A new principle of consignation always carries traces of what it erases. There is, according to Derrida, an autodestructive element to the archive that parallels mnematic apparatuses we use. There is a tension between retention and reception. Just as there is a limit to how much the surface of the mystic pad can receive until one must erase it to gain a new surface, there is a limit to how much of the information imprinted would be retained after its destruction. Although we are capable of receiving more and more new information, like the mystic pad, we cannot hold them in time unless we make some sacrifices. We must let go and erase ourselves in order to keep up with the times—or so the archive demands. But again, this erasure is in no way complete, nor is the archive so "new."

Back to Onni.

Although inventories for burnout (like the Maslach Burnout Inventory) provide the most updated archive on stress disorders, they are nonetheless substitutes for the phantom limb, something essential that has been cut off. Onni, like many other clients, expressed that the rehabilitative program gave him the "tools to talk" about what happened. However, it was not uncommon for him to fall silent when I asked him directly why he kept working the way he did to the point of exhaustion. The exact moment of inscription, the moment at which he felt the pressure of the social to give his time, remains beyond his grasp. Looking back at the moment of his sacrifice, he cannot put into words why he did so despite the new words given to him by the rehabilitative experts.

It was at such times that he brought up Japan as a country supposedly used to such issues. "You should know," he would say. "Don't *you* come from that country where they have that problem?"

The disconnect between experience, memory, and language calls for quick fixes. Here, where Onni falls silent, he regains speech through turning to a codified knowledge of the other—"the overworked Japanese." In Onni's demand that "[I] should know," I heard instead, "this conversation is over." And invariably, when he brought up Japan, it also marked the end of our discussion. Turning to a codified discourse ossified communication.

However, even though the framework of burnout falls short in some instances, it also allowed Onni and others like him to consign under its sign their various misgivings about the workplace today. The archive of the new hazard, burnout, provides a *"prosthetic substitute"* (Derrida 1995, 95) that enables clients to make socially significant their conditions of suffering on the one hand and to provide interested parties (e.g., public health officials, employer groups, health experts, etc.) potential for control and rehabilitation on the other hand. Through burnout, the risks and meaning of the present gain material representation through the figure of the clients. Through burnout, the past takes on a new character as a condition to be overcome. The archive of burnout serves a prosthetic function in that it articulates the risks of today, thereby foreclosing the need to examine a more fundamental violence—the trauma inherent in the social—one that silences and provides no words of closure.

As Claude Lévi-Strauss argues in his *Introduction to the Work of Marcel Mauss* (1987), a social fact is not a social fact unless it manifests as an embodied individual experience. Lévi-Strauss, underlying the importance of the concept as developed by Mauss, further emphasizes that social facts only have force as such when individuals come to apprehend it as part of their everyday existence. In this sense, it is not enough that social facts be articulated through juridical, economic, or political institutions. Their force rests not in their manifold articulations and/ or iterations. The force of the social manifests in individual experience, in one's thought processes, in the way one feels shame, presumes guilt, and in what one expects of oneself and of others. Social facts structure what passes in between individuals. It is only "in the individual" that the force of social institutions be revealed and being a member of society requires that one gives one's thoughts to its "polite fictions."

Where Mauss focuses on the thing that is exchanged, the symbol of one's sacrifice, Lévi-Strauss reveals that the sacrifice takes place at a more fundamental level. The sacrifice—the force of the social—makes its imprint even prior to the symbolic. It is enough that we *feel* we ought to give. And herein lies the core of the horror of the social.

The archive protects against seeing this horror head-on. It diverts the attention from the inherent violence of the social by inscribing the present as a time-space under threat. It is not that we are always already operating under a will not of our own: the burnout archive tells us that control is harder to take *now* when the world feels faster and more competitive. We need only update the way we engage with others to get back in control of our energetic output.

The focus then becomes one of righting the wrongs—especially of the workers—of the current era. This function of the archive is also part of its mechanical and timeless power to articulate what *is* at the exclusion of others. It provides a prosthesis that disavows the possibility of a more timeless violence and in doing so pushes the interests of the times.

However, as we see here, the state of being burned out does not speak for itself. Archive fever must also point to this anxious state. It is not as if you "lost a leg." Onni and other clients like him must depend on the archive for their social legitimacy even as health experts hold public lectures to spread the awareness of burnout. The archive on burnout, it appears, must also rely on other supplements—the history of stress. The fever circulates, as it finds no closure. It is never the self-identical to the thing it records. The archive is itself a place of consignation and not the thing itself that is being archived. The archive, or the *archon*, is a place marked for the purpose of recording, ordering, and documenting what is external to it. Moreover, it only communicates within itself. It is thus a place driven by desire that is also its trauma. The archival drive to gather documents and artifacts together simultaneously distances the one who consigns from that which it attempts to capture and to codify. The archive's topo-nomology runs parallel to the world as it unfolds. In its clutches, life dies; memories turn into illegible imprints. Experience turns to ash under the bright blaze of archontic desire to distinguish it as a specific event within the archive.

The more one is on fire about burnout, burnout, the thing itself, remains silent. Burnout is that thing that takes place in the archive, like a specter that only comes alive in the telling. This archontic principle—the more you speak, the less the thing speaks—gives rise to specific anxieties. Slavoj Žižek's joke about the "fool" who thought "he was a grain of corn" provides a great analogy here:

> After some time in a mental hospital, [the fool] was finally cured: now he knew that he was not a grain but a man. So they let him out; but soon afterwards he came running back, saying: "I met a hen and I was afraid she would eat me." The doctors tried to calm him: "But what are you afraid of? Now you know that you are not a grain but a man." The fool answered: "Yes, of course, I know that, but does the hen know that I am no longer a grain?" (1989, 35)

In the absence of a condition that speaks for itself, clients of burnout must struggle with the fear that "the hen" may not know that they are legitimately sick and not to be eaten. It is thus indeed hard to leave the refuge of the archive and of the space of rehabilitation.

## Learning to Relax: A Day in the Forest (*Luontoretki-päivä*)

On the seventh day of the program, I joined the group for *luontoretki-päivä*. Aino and Tapio, the two physiotherapists who also served as the group's *vapaa-ajanohjaaja*, the "free-time leaders," translated the special program to me as "a day in the *forest*," rather than the literal translation of "nature tour day," the significance of which I understood later.

We met Aino and Tapio at nine o'clock sharp in the basement where the center kept all its equipment. Our two expedition leaders were already busily gathering snow gear, snowshoes, and food by the time the group made its way down from the cafeteria. As I made my way down along with the others, Aino and Tapio came over to shake my hand. No sooner had they introduced themselves, they immediately addressed the group and launched into a short introduction to Tetriniemi, the private nature preserve owned by Pääskynpesä, where we were to hike that day. After that, the group broke into action.

Some clients went to gather heavy winter clothing and shoes, while some others went to help Aino pick up plates and beverages for the trip. In this sudden whirlwind of action, I was left wondering what to do when Tapio came by and handed me some skiwear that somehow fit me perfectly well. He also saw my socks peeking over my sneakers and told me briskly but kindly to get thicker socks if I did not want to get blisters or icy toes.

I was slowly catching up to the others. We were to snowshoe one of the trails in the nature preserve behind the rehabilitation center, and it was to be a serious excursion with a campfire, lunch outdoors, and some drinks. Excited, I ran back to my room to fetch some warmer socks whereupon I bumped into Pekka. He was late. In my elated state, I recalled a pleasant conversation we had just had the previous night and called out to him. I found out too late that he was not in the mood to talk. He only grunted in response and brushed past me in a hurry. Reading his face then, I saw that his eyes looked bloodshot and that he looked like he had not slept in days.

As I got back to the basement from fetching my socks from my room, I saw Pekka again. Tapio was offering him a warmer jacket, but Pekka flatly refused. Tapio gently persuaded him to take it, and I saw Pekka slowly let himself be persuaded. He took the jacket without looking at Tapio, who nonetheless kept looking directly at him. Seeing Tapio's gentle and persuasive manner, I kicked myself for addressing Pekka out of my own sense of joy. A hike in the forest was not the same thing for everyone there.

As I got ready to put on the warm winter gear that was prepared for me, I noticed that others had been helping Aino pack food and other items into the van all along. In fact, I noticed that people were quite knowledgeable about what should be happening, and I did not hear either Aino or Tapio making explicit pleas for help.

In the hustle and bustle of this stage of preparations, I was more in the way than Pekka, who, tired as he looked, was carrying armfuls of plastic cups into one of the vans parked outside. Seeing this, I tried to look for something to do, something to pick up, anything to do to pitch in. But I found my efforts anticipated at each turn. Because I saw Pekka with the cups, I asked Aino where the plates were and whether I could bring them to the car. No. Terhi, another client, had already packed the plates. The same went for every other item I thought we may need.

Social pressure creeps up when you least expect it. I experienced a certain anxiety knowing that I was not contributing to the cause when others seemed to know exactly what to do. I had only helped myself by fetching my own thick socks, socks others had already donned without being told. I vaguely remembered one of my earlier Finnish-language lessons in which the instructor joked how Finnish either commands what is to be done or expects that the other party understands exactly what you want him or her to do and to carry it out without being asked. "My mother was exactly like this!" the instructor reminisced. "She expected us children to do what she wanted done, and she also did not tell us what she wanted. She said she wasn't asking for anything complicated. If I am cooking dinner, it should be self-evident that the table must be laid."

It was no coincidence I thought back to my Finnish-language instructor's mother. Without any one person directing or managing the operation, necessary items were wrapped up, carried, and placed in one of the three cars that were made ready for the trip. It did not end there. When nothing remained to be packed, the group suddenly divided into two and got into the two vehicles that remained empty. I saw Pekka and Onni each pick up a set of car keys from the basement, and while I was still wondering what was going on, everyone had found a seat in one of the vans.

I was left looking foolish until Aino and Tapio called me over to their van and saved me. Their van was stacked high with all the equipment. While Aino and Tapio sat up front with Tapio in the driving seat, I sat in the back next to containers of food that jiggled dangerously whenever Tapio went over a rocky patch. The road to the nature preserve got even bumpier and the containers started to rattle against each other despite my efforts to keep them in place. I reached over and picked up the offending container and held it in my lap instead. Silence. Aino looked over her shoulder to see how it was that the containers had stopped rattling. She saw me sitting with the big container in my lap and smiled. It was the first time that day I felt remotely useful.

On the way to Tetriniemi, I asked them about the significance of this excursion in the context of rehabilitation. "Well, it is for people to relax and to be quiet and to think about themselves," said Tapio. Tetriniemi, the vast stretch of forest, was to provide clients with much needed quiet. Tapio added, "We are a small country. There are only a few of us and we like to be alone. We need space!"

But given that clients were already spaced—set aside—from their family, friends, and their workplace by attending Pääskynpesä, it seemed unusual that they would require more space and more quiet. I asked Aino to explain.

"We Finns come from the forest. It's like we fell off the trees! The forest is a place where we feel most at home. Once we get there, you will see for yourself. We don't have to explain to our clients. It is self-evident for us that going to the forest is therapeutic."

Tetriniemi joined up with Petkeljärvi, a national park. If the trees that flanked the roads on the way seemed still and quiet, the forest of Tetriniemi was quieter still. We got to the forest first and waited in the car awhile for the others to arrive.

As we waited, my thoughts drifted to the history of this park. Ilomantsi played a major role in Finland's battle against the USSR during World War II, and although snow covered the traces of this legacy, I could not help thinking about the deep trenches I saw before the snow.

Park rangers had restored some of the bunkers and horse shelters that were used during that time, and I remembered with much disquiet what an old war veteran from Pääskynpesä's musical event (*musiikkinäytelmä*), "The Heavy Price of Peace," told me. As the rehabilitation center lobby filled with music from the '40s, an old man came up to shake my hand. He was a survivor of World War II he said. He wanted to tell me about his experiences during that era and asked me what battlefields I have visited in Finland. I mentioned that I had plans to hike through Tetriniemi. He then gave me this warning: "Soldiers who don't know they are dead still roam the forests. If you go hiking, be careful. You might see them."

Finland coined the name Molotov cocktail (*Molotovin koktaili*) during the Winter War (1939–40) as a provocation to the Soviet foreign minister Vyacheslav Molotov. As Soviet tanks rolled across the border into Finnish territory, Finland strategically took to guerilla tactics. Against the giant tanks of the Soviet army, the Finnish army put on skis and white camouflage to gain stealth and speed on their side. Although outnumbered by Soviet troops, this Finnish tactic won out, and they were able to cut up the Soviet forces into small groups for easier handling.

Over 25,904 Finnish soldiers died or went missing during the Winter War (Kurenmaa and Lentilä 2005), and even though they did not give the USSR an easy victory, Finland lost the war. The end of the Winter War resulted in 11 percent of national territory having to be ceded to the USSR and grounds for another major battle, the Continuation War (1941–44).

The legacy of these wars lives on. On Independence Day, December 7, families get together to watch an annual broadcast of the annual ball held at the Presidential Palace in Helsinki as well as another favorite, *The Unknown Soldier* (*Tuntematon Sotilas*), a film based on the book by Väinö Linna published under the same name in 1954. The film, set in a snowy Karelian forest, depicts how Finns from different provinces came together to fight off an invading army. As in Linna's book, the film also plays up the different regional dialects and vernacular to showcase who "we" are that sacrificed their lives for the nation.

In Helsinki, I was invited by a friend to join this event, and I got to watch this annual broadcast with my friend and her family. Although some members of the family moved into the kitchen saying, "We see this film every year," others stayed with me to watch. The father, Jouko, sat next to me and told me that he saw this film growing up but that he never tired of seeing it. He then pointed at his nephew and asked me if I had seen the T-shirt his nephew was wearing.

Indeed, I had. His nephew had on a black T-shirt with the white-and-blue Finnish flag. The flag had silhouetted on it a gun-toting soldier. Under this image, it read, "Thank you" (*Kiitos*) in big letters. It was an identifiable shirt since people wore it around town even when it was not Independence Day.

I wish to return to the significance of Finland's memories of war and of the forest in chapter 4, but here I return to the Day in Nature.

As I drifted off in my own thoughts, movement of people from the other vans called me back to the issue at hand. Headed by Aino, several of the participants were already helping to unload the snowshoes, ski poles, and food. This time, I was close enough to the equipment to take part in the action. From my hands, the snowshoes went to Onni and then to Kai and then to Helmi who arranged them in a neat pile by the cabin nearby.

Tapio put on his snowshoes first and said that we were going to walk for about a kilometer with some of the food. As I reconnected with the group, they seemed to have perked up in the car and I saw many smiling faces.

Kylli and Onni in usual fashion were up to mischief. The minute things were packed away, they started a snowball fight. Kylli got Onni with a snowball in the back. Onni got Kylli in the front. Kylli then rushed at Onni and the two fell in a pile in the snow. Oona, one of the older members of the group, called out to the two that they were going to be left behind. Kylli giggled. She then put on her snowshoes and scuttled up to Oona who was waiting for her and gave Oona a big hug.

It was a clear bright day. It was so bright that the sky looked even bluer. "Do you know that this is our national flag?" asked Oona, pointed at the snow and then at the sky.

Some people hummed. Some broke away from the little line of people that had formed behind Tapio to wander into the thick snow. Some, like Pekka, remained inscrutable but engrossed in the hike, nonetheless. I noticed one member missing from the group, Tuulikki.

Tuulikki often sat alone and smoked instead of joining activities. She often simply did not respond when I spoke to her or even tried to engage her. Her absence was, however, almost expected as she was often missing from activities that required intense physical exercise.

But on such a fine day, my thoughts suddenly went to Tuulikki. What was she doing alone in the center? Smoking? Depressed? Surely, this would be something that she could benefit from. "We don't believe in a one-shoe-fits-all approach to rehabilitation," Miia, the psychologist, had told me. But what was Tuulikki getting out of her rehabilitative experience? Was it enough that she was getting some form of care? Was it enough that she could take the time to retreat from her everyday? Even just for the ten days of the program? What is this release that we want from society? What release is it that we get from the forest?

Tapio looked back now and again to make sure that we were all following him. In single file behind Tapio, we crossed a frozen lake and up an esker. We then walked some distance until we finally came upon a big wooden lean-to. Up close, I saw it had a little metal stove and a chimney. There was a wooden bench and a place to make a fire.

As I made these observations and jotted them down in my notepad, people were already pulling out plastic sheets and parceling them out on the bench to sit on. Some others took out the carton of cookies and other sweets. Tapio put down three big thermos of warm blueberry juice, and Terhi pulled out the plastic cups and poured them out. As one person picked up an activity, some other person followed it through to completion. From setting up plastic seats to pulling out the warm juice to filling up individual cups, the various hands made the distinct activity into one seamless action. It felt like the basement from the morning all over again.

People invited each other to sit on the bench, and soon the group was nicely ensconced, each with a warm cup of blueberry juice in hand. I hesitated. I did not know exactly where to put myself. Then I saw Pekka and Onni leave the lean-to without saying anything. Not quite comfortable to sit down just yet, I decided to follow Onni and Pekka toward the more heavily wooded area. I did not follow them long until I realized that they had gotten up to get wood from the shed. All this happened again without anyone having asked them to do so.

How did Pekka and Onni know what to do on this excursion planned by those at the rehabilitation center in a site unknown to them? How did Pekka and Onni know where to get the firewood? How did they know that time was right for a fire just then? I marveled at my own presumptions about what being a client entailed. I had assumed from the beginning that the two rehabilitative experts, the providers of service, would be doing most or all of the heavy lifting. That was not the case. Instead, I found that Aino and Tapio had only to start unpacking or lifting objects and the clients took over. Here, Pekka and Onni took it upon themselves to get firewood. And when we returned, Pekka and Onni laden with wood, and I following lamely behind, Tapio said not a word but gestured as to where the fire should be made.

As Pekka and Onni took to building the fire, I felt my heart pounding. I saw how faces lifted from steaming cups of blueberry juice to welcome us back to the lean-to. I noticed also that I was the only one not coming back with any wood. I had a notepad in one hand, and between Pekka and Onni, the wood that was pre-chopped in the shed was cleared out. I felt a sudden sense of paranoia that caught me by surprise. "I am just in the way!" I wrote in my notepad. My own archive from that day also reads I feel "inadequate, inefficient and stressed: something that might get me diagnosed with burnout if I were to continue in this way!"

Voluntary action for the good of the collective went well recognized and well received at the lean-to. Older participants who were already on their second and third drinks made gentle remarks at the quality of the wood and how well Pekka and Onni stacked the wood.

While the fire was being made, Aino and Helmi prepared the grill and opened the packages of sausages to be put on it. As I settled down on the corner of a bench by the fire, Kylli came up to me and handed me a warm cup of blueberry juice. She poured another cup and handed it to Tapio.

The fire started to flare, and the damp wood started to smolder. Pekka picked up some wood and left the fire with an axe. After a short while, he came back with neat bits of kindling with beautifully feathered edges. They were so pretty that I gave a shout when Pekka threw them into the fire. "Wait!" I said. "They're too pretty to be thrown into the fire just like that!" The group burst out laughing.

Kylli held my hand and told me gently that Pekka had to throw the pretty feathered logs into the fire so that our bonfire will light up more efficiently. Tapio, smiling, offered me an axe saying, "Try making more pretty wood to burn." I declined.

This episode, however, opened the space to talk about difference—the difference between those who see the feathered kindling as something extraordinary and those who see it as what it is, something to kindle the fire with.

Helmi, who had once traveled to Arizona before, joked that "everyone in Finland can chop wood and make 'pretty' firewood. It's what we do on most weekends instead of going to the shopping center or to the café." Pekka added more seriously, "You need to be able to make a fire and know your trees if you want a good sauna. [Finnish] people like to go to their cottages [mökki] over the weekend to enjoy going back to nature."

Pekka showed me how he had made the intricate curls on the edges of the wood to give it that feathered look. Conversation moved on to preference for wood and the types of trees that smelled nice in saunas.

As Pekka and I got ready to sit down, we noticed that the bench and all of the seats inside the lean-to were taken. Others also noticed this problem. One of the older ladies nudged her neighbor while looking at me, and then the nudge continued until two clean seats were made, and from somewhere a hand passed me two plastic cushions.

When the meal of hot berry juice and hot dogs was over, Aino put some snow in the kettle and hung it over the fire to make some coffee. The kettle soon started to sizzle and, at this, Tapio got up. With coffee bag in hand, he began the day's discussion. Facing us on the bench, he asked us each to share with the group our particular "landscapes of the mind" (mielen maisemat), landscapes that we turn to or conjure when we need peace and comfort.

Oona laughed and spoke first. Oona's landscape was the scene from her living room window. At sunset, she said, she could look out onto the lake that faced her house and see it glow a brilliant red. We all closed our eyes a minute to digest this scene.

Helmi spoke next. Helmi described a winter landscape of forests covered in thick snow. Onni joked that we must all be in Helmi's mind since we were at that very moment sitting in such a forest covered in snow. Helmi protested. Her forest was not the forest of our present situation. Her forest-scape involved being in a forest where one has forgotten that one is in a forest. One is the forest.

Then it was Kylli's turn. "I love everything about nature! But I love sunshine most of all," she said. She got this far, but she suddenly broke down crying. Squeezed in tight next to Kylli on the bench, I could feel every sob she made. With my arm sandwiched between Helmi and Kylli, I could only look on as Kylli struggled to continue. It brought back unpleasant memories of the night in the lobby when I asked a question that made her cry.

It went on like that for a while: Kylli struggling to speak and the rest of us looking on. People started to speak to fill the silence. Terhi spoke about how she also loved the summer sunlight. Helmi gripped Kylli's shoulders from the right and Oona reached behind my back to stroke Kylli's shoulders from the left. Thus held, Kylli half-cried, half-laughed, and held out her hands when Tapio offered her some hot coffee from the kettle. Aino added, looking specifically at me, that "people recall landscapes that are close to them, but these scenes are something recognizable by all Finns."

Everybody had something to say on the topic and it took a while for everyone to describe his or her favorite scene. Despite Onni's previous attempt at humor, the conversation continued in a serious tone. Looking around, I saw people listening with bowed heads looking into the fire. There were occasional nods and grunts of agreement.

Unlike in the sessions inside the rehabilitation center, clients were less prone to private conversations while others spoke. It was one of the observations I made earlier on in my field notes. In the group sessions with the psychologist, should someone's story go on too long, the others in the group tended to start their own private conversations. None of that happened around the fire. And if they, like Onni, did joke, they included or attempted to involve everyone sitting around the fire.

Physically, the group sat quite still unless someone added more snow to the kettle or wood to the fire. Surrounded by the cold and feeling comforted by the heat of twelve bodies sitting inside the lean-to and with the knowledge that someone always had an eye on the firewood, something warm to drink, and something to talk about, it was easy to fall into a comfortable lull.

Aino and Tapio offered no analysis of the landscapes. They let anyone speak who wanted to speak and allowed those who did not want to speak to remain silent. Clients were thus allowed to offer as many landscapes as they pleased. The point was not to examine but to feel the memory of a place that gives comfort. When people started on the second cup of coffee, Aino pulled out a loaf of *pulla* (dessert bread with cardamom) and some cookies from another container of food. As it was a big *pulla*, about the length of a long chopping board, Aino joked that we all needed to pitch in and eat the bread since it would be heavy to carry back to the center.

When it was time to pack up and be on the move again, Aino noticed that some slices of *pulla* still remained. "Who hasn't eaten *pulla* yet?" she asked the group. Pekka volunteered that he had not eaten any *pulla*. Aino encouraged him to have some by pouring him the remaining coffee as a chaser. Suddenly, Pekka snapped. "Coffee is better alone without any *pulla!*" he said angrily. Aino replied that she had not meant to force him, but Pekka only insisted again that coffee is better without any *pulla*. He proceeded to pack the slices of *pulla* back into its container. He downed the cup of coffee Aino had poured for him and put on his snowshoes. On his way out of the lean-to, he repeated now for the third time that coffee was better without any *pulla*.

This small outbreak chilled a little of the warmth from the fire. The clients dispersed to each bundle up again in skiwear and to pick up the bundles we needed to take back to the van through the deep snow.

We returned the way we came (or so I thought). Along the way, Tapio pointed out different trees and called out their Finnish names to me. This was a welcome treat. During the session, some clients spoke about specific trees that carried meaning to them and we had a long discussion about what that particular species of tree would be in English. Here, Tapio jumped ahead of the group, pointing out each tree that had made its appearance in our conversations.

"*Kataja!*" he exclaimed, and he pointed at a juniper tree with his ski pole. He made good use of his long limbs to jump skillfully through the thick snow to get closer to the tree. "Finnish people are said to be like the *kataja* because these trees do not break.[5] You can push them and bend them down, but they will always spring back!" He demonstrated this by pushing down on a sapling with his pole. The sapling almost touched the ground from the pressure applied by Tapio. It sprung back upon release.

Our last stop was at a *kota*, a wooden Sami building resembling a tepee. As the *kota* was close to the cars, we each dropped off our snowshoes in the trunk along the way. As we all walked toward the *kota*, Onni was already chopping more wood for the new fire to be made. Kylli saw him hard at work and threw several snowballs at him. Onni made a mock growl and put the axe down as if to throw some snow back her way. She giggled coquettishly and hid behind me, using me like a shield. I was pulled this way and that to dodge Onni's snowballs that never really came our way. Other clients watched this play and smiled. But as we entered the *kota*, the mood of the group changed yet again.

While Onni and Tapio made another fire, Aino pulled out a metal grill. There was to be more food. On the grill, Aino laid out a salmon bread wrapped in foil, some *karjalanpiirakat* (Karelian rice pasties), and a big pot of coffee. The dark walls of the *kota* brightened from the fire, and we were soon sitting amid the smell of sizzling fish fat.

Hungry again, despite having eaten at the lean-to, we all lined up to fill our plates. Although the *kota* kept the wind out, there was a dankness within that could not be immediately erased by our fire, and we sat there for a while quietly warming ourselves on the hot fish and crusty pasties. Sitting thus in the smoke, the steam and our breath showing white in the little structure, we were allowed to relax a little before heading back to the rehabilitation center.

As in the informal lobby sessions, the interactions between group members here exhibited distinct familial overtones. Kylli and Onni continued to be intimate. It took a while for the *kota* to warm. Meanwhile, the chill and the smoke in the *kota* made Kylli cough. Onni showed great concern.

He constantly checked the fire. He moved Kylli away from the direction of smoke. He checked the quality of air around where Kylli sat. When Kylli continued to cough, Onni gave her his jacket and squeezed her thus wrapped in his arms. Onni, however, was not the only one concerned about Kylli. Kylli appeared to be the "baby" of the group. Oona came by to give Kylli a woolly blanket. Others gave Kylli a warmer cup of coffee to hold. At each such gesture, Onni nodded in approval. Aino and Tapio looked on.

Group members, including the older members of the group, pitched their voices slightly higher and childlike when they asked Tapio for more coffee. In response, Tapio, despite his younger age compared to many in the group, acted like a father and Aino a mother. Tapio poured coffee and cut the fish bread while Aino laid the table and made cooing voices to jokes made at her expense. Onni was in high spirits. He was never still: if he was not fussing over Kylli, he was chopping wood.

Conversation revolved around the weather and different types of foods and different ways of eating potatoes. Summer potatoes are to be roasted and sprinkled with freshly picked dill and sea salt, Terhi offered. Summer potatoes are better roasted with a stick of butter, said Pekka. How about boiling the summer potatoes? another voice quipped from somewhere in the smoke.

There was more food to be grilled and warmed on the fire. As things cooked, Kylli resumed coughing, and one of the older men in the group lent her his cap. Aino praised the gesture as generous and thoughtful. Seeing Kylli hesitate, Oona encouraged Kylli to put it on. Kylli put the hat on. The man's fur cap was far too large. It fell past her ears and made her look even smaller. Onni whispered something in her ear, and she squeezed his nose with her fingers and gave it a tug. Her gold wedding ring flashed on her finger as she did so. I vaguely thought of Kylli's husband back in her hometown in Joensuu.

After the meal, Tapio told the group to go out for a stroll. "Go and relax. Walk around and dream," he said. The group scattered, but no one moved too far. I saw clients eyeing Tapio and Aino cleaning up inside the *kota*. When Tapio came out of the structure, the group suddenly sprang into motion. They started stacking up the empty containers of food and equipment. Tapio had not said a word; as earlier, hands just moved until nothing remained to be packed.

We all got back in the same van as we came. I sat in my seat again next to the equipment in the back of Tapio and Aino's van. Once we got out of the snow, Tapio and Aino both wanted to know about my impressions of the event. Instead, I asked them if they could articulate the exact rehabilitative goals of the "Day in Nature." I also asked them whether the concept of the "mental landscape" (*mielimaisema*) was a widely known one, as I was rather confused at how readily people could respond to their demand for one.

"The importance of nature is self-evident [*itse selva*] for Finns. We just know," said Aino. When something is that self-evident, she said, it becomes even harder to explain to "foreigners" the exact benefits of being in the forest. "Nature is our private battery! It is a place where we go to recharge ourselves," Aino explained. "It is better to scream in nature than at work or at your customers," she said, laughing.

Tapio jumped in. "Yes! You can scream at the rocks, you can run around like a madman, you can do anything there [in the forest]. It is a place to be alone from the world and to be free of all [social] restrictions. It's a place where you can do what you want and not be seen."

"Is it kind of like in the sauna?" I asked, remembering hearing something similar said about the sauna.

"Yes, you can cry openly in the sauna and you can cry in nature, too. You see Kylli was crying today. Nature is that kind of place," Tapio said. "I hope you now understand what we mean."

The conceptualization of what is a self-evident good—something accepted as part of collective common sense—opens onto national self-analyses. "We" find it self-evident that the forest is such and such a place. And as it is that this "we" refers to Finnish citizens, the forest appears as a natural place to go to "recharge our batteries."

However, this conceptualization of "we-ness" depends on a polite fiction that "we" voluntarily ascribe to—or sacrifice our thoughts to—this concept of a "we" that finds expression thus. This overcoherence of what this "we" stands for parallels the issues found when occupational burnout dictates the terms by which individuals are to be timely productive citizens. In shedding light on what "we" need and who "we" are in time and place, the force of what remains to be seen makes itself felt.

# THE QUESTION OF "FINNISHNESS"

AINO: The importance of nature is self-evident [*itseselvä*] in Finland. We just know. Nature is our private battery! It is a place where we go to recharge ourselves. It is better to scream in nature than at work or at your customers.

TAPIO: Yes, you can scream at the rocks, you can run around like a madman, you can do anything there [in the forest]. It is a place to be alone from the world to be free of all restrictions—a place where you can do what you want and not be seen.

In this chapter, I examine Aino and Tapio's reference to nature as a particularly marked space. As Aino and Tapio's comments above suggest, the space of the forest provides a counterpoint to the expectations and obligations of the social. Although none of the exercises and excursions such as "Day in the Forest" were described to me as treatments (or for rehabilitation as a whole for that matter), many of the staff I talked to at Pääskynpesä as well as the clients themselves attested to the curative powers of the space many referred to generically as "the forest" (*metsä*). Aino, for example, describes the forest as a place to "recharge" and describes this power as having national significance. She claims that the benefits of the forest are "self-evident *in Finland.*" For Tapio, the forest provides a place where you can "run around like a *mad*man." Here, I explore this separation of the "forest" as a space distinct from that of the social and how such a distinction contributes to the idea of the social. Specifically, I question what this separation of the forest from the social can say about the imagined relationship of the individual to the social. I start with a brief genealogy of the creation of the forest as a matter of national significance.

## From Territory to Nation: Making New Boundaries through "Nature"

Finland's history is bound with that of its neighbors, as the country did not exist as such until the twentieth century. Before 1809, Finland had been an integral part of the Swedish Empire (Alapuro 1988, 19; Klinge 2003; Singleton 1998), but the Treaty of Tilsit in 1807 signed between Alexander I of Russia and Napoleon of France wrested Finland and the Baltic region away from Swedish control as a way for Napoleon to persuade Sweden into joining the trade embargo against England.[1] When Czar Alexander I declared Finland an imperial grand duchy in 1809, "Finns"—for the first time conceived of as such—were not only freed from the heavy taxes and damage to human life and property incurred from being Sweden's frontier with Russia during wartime but also granted some degree of independence. Alexander I gave the grand duchy religious, economic, and governmental freedom. Although this was a common Russian policy for dealing with outlying regions at the time, Alexander I invested heavily in keeping the new territory satisfied and peaceful, as Alexander I wanted Finland as a neutral buffer against Sweden. As a show of good faith, Alexander I increased the territory of the grand duchy by "returning" Swedish territories previously annexed by Russia to the grand duchy of Finland. He further limited Swedish influence by relocating the capital of the new Finnish province from the former Swedish provincial capital of Turku, which lay close to the Gulf of Bothnia, to Helsinki, a region much closer to Saint Petersburg. He also reorganized the Finnish political structure by diluting the power of the Swedish nobility through giving more centralized power to the administration. Although convening the diet—the duchy's representative legislative body—was made dependent on the Russian monarch, the lassitude of the Russian metropole in the domestic affairs of Finland gave Finnish bureaucratic administration more political power.

Alexander I's hand in restructuring the power base of the Swedish elites prompted early nationalists to pay attention to internal tensions (Alapuro 1988). As Alexander I's reforms diminished the power of the mainly Swedish upper classes in the context of the four-estate system,[2] the Swedish upper classes became increasingly placed under pressure of Finnish-speaking intellectuals in the struggle for power. However, unlike the case in Romania, where Romanian elites "appealed to or allied themselves with stronger external powers against their tyrannical overlords" (Verdery 1991, 30–31), the elites of Finland did not align themselves with either Sweden or Russia. Instead, they deemphasized their class status and placed themselves at the forefront in constructing an idea of a "Finnish" *Volk* that *included* themselves as one among the masses (Alapuro 1988, 91; Anttonnen 2005, 144).

Risto Alapuro (1989) explains the specific conditions of early struggles over class and language as stemming from the particularity of Scandinavian class structure that Finland inherited from Sweden. Unlike in continental Europe, free peasants formed the dominant land-owning class at the time, and the upper classes depended on meeting their demands and showing solidarity with the masses if they were to stay in power. Second, Alapuro (1989) claims that the aforementioned Russian reforms encouraged social mobility of the Finnish peasant classes which further contributed to the shaky position of the Swedish upper classes in Finland. Aira Kemiläinen shows as further evidence of the intermingling of the so-called Swedish nobility with Finnish intellectuals of peasant backgrounds that by the end of the nineteenth century, the upper estates came to be known merely as "'the educated class' (comparable with 'civilized people,' '*bildningsborgerskap*' in Swedish)" (1998, 108). Third, Finnish independence from Sweden came as a "gift" from Czar Alexander I and therefore took away the need for intellectuals to engage in armed struggle to come into power (Anttonen 2005, 170). Instead, Finnish intellectuals faced the task of legitimizing the status of Finland as having "innate" and natural qualities of a unique and distinct nation. The social position and legitimacy of the "educated class" stemmed from having taken the task of defining the origin and character of the nation on themselves. As Anthony Smith (1999) argues, "the intellectual is the interpreter, *par excellence*, of historical memories and ethnic myths. By tracing a distinguished pedigree for his nation, he also enhances the position of his circle and activity; he is no longer an ambiguous 'marginal' on the fringes of society, but a leader of the advancing column of the reawakened nation" (84). Similar to the process described by Katherine Verdery (1991) in Romania, where intellectuals secured their authoritative position in universities and within the social sphere by transforming the discourses of the nation as an "object" requiring the attention of their expertise (Verdery 1991, 1999), so did Finnish intellectuals secure their position in the nation via universities and in politics as archaeologists, archivists, and translators of "native" idioms.

However, instead of alluding to "historicopolitical" imaginings of Finland, as for example in the case of Poland (Walicki 1999, 271), Finnish intellectuals had to come up with the nation's political and historic past separate from that of

Sweden. Unlike its neighbors, Finland lacked what Smith (1999) calls an organic history that linked the existence of the nation to a noble bloodline. With no royal family tree or a history of serfs to tether "blood" to territory or to origins, Finnish national awakening took shape along the lines of what Smith characterizes as one based on "cultural affinity and ideological 'fit' with the presumed ancestors" (58).

Turning to myths of a "golden age" of heroism and virtue borrowed from the rune singers from the Karelian region not only provided the "ideological 'fit'" but also, as Pertti Anttonen (2005) argues, masked the heterogeneity of the internal population. Uniting through imagining the nation's mythic predecessors masked the fact that the early nationalists spoke a different language from the majority of the nascent *Volk* in the nineteenth century.

Finnish intellectuals borrowed heavily from the German nationalist movements from the eighteenth century. One of their initial tasks was to create a primordial idea of the nation built on a unique language, folklore, and geographic setting. Finnish intellectuals turned to provinces perceived of as being relatively free from Swedish influence, especially the eastern-most province of Karelia, to search for oral poems, proverbs, and songs for the realization of "Finland" as a nation with a coherent ethnic, geographic, and linguistic boundary. Although such a construction would seem to deny Swedish-speaking intellectuals a place in the new nation, they instead cast themselves as the midwives of this new nation, refusing to cast themselves as intellectuals but instead as "originating" from "the people" (Anttonen 2005, 148). Even though the language of the elites contradicted the notion of a primordially "Finnish" nation, significantly, the Swedish-speaking elites placed themselves in the position to speak for the masses "asleep" (to the notion of nationhood) and unable to speak for themselves. In addition to identifying themselves thus as "the people" and not as antagonistic elites, Swedish-speaking Fennomans wrote themselves into the national narrative via their "discoveries" and ability to catalog "the people's culture." If "Finnishness" could not by definition come from the Swedish-speaking group, the Swedish-speaking elites legitimized their place within the nation through the creation and ownership of everyday peasant life and oral poetry they reified as academic knowledge.

The national archive thus developed from this perceived lack within the intellectuals themselves. As Anttonen (2005) argues, the elites could not become the symbols of "the people" through a reference to the past: they instead represented its future. Creating national history and researching Finnish prehistory via ethnological research of neighboring Finno-Ugric tribes negated the Swedish-speaking elites as primordial *Volk* of the nation but also reinstated them as the true nationalists. Without them, there would be no national history or future.

# The Empty Vase: *Kalevala*, Forests, and Origins

Finnish national discourse begins with the recognition of loss. For instance, nationalist discourse of ethnological research and of the *discovery* of the nation suggest that the Finnish national spirit, its integrity, its sentiments, and poetry are lost to the present until excavated, exhumed, and rediscovered.[3] The nation in a sense "awakens" as a concept already stained with this absence. The obsession of nationalist intellectuals to locate the genes, the linguistic origins, the birthplace, and so on of the people circles around this absent center within the concept of the nation.

Jacques Lacan's (1992, 120) analogy of the vase provides an illustrative example:

> It [a vase] creates the void and thereby introduces the possibility of filling it. Emptiness and fullness are introduced into a world that by itself knows not of them. It is on the basis of this fabricated signifier, this vase, that emptiness and fullness as such enter the world, neither more nor less, and with the same sense.
>
> This is the moment to point to the fallacious opposition between what is called concrete and what is called figurative. If the vase may be filled, it is because in the first place in its essence it is empty. And it is exactly in the same sense that speech and discourse may be full or empty.

In creating the vase, this tool, we bring into reality the potential for fullness and emptiness "into a world that by itself knows not of them."

In the nineteenth century, the relationship between Russia and Finland began to sour as the Finnish nationalist movement gained steam. In what was perhaps the most significant move in the creation of Finland's national narrative, Elias Lönnrot (1989) set out to compile the most comprehensive collection of folklore in the province of Karelia: the grand epic of Finland—the *Kalevala*. Anttonen (2005) argues that the choice of Karelia as the hunting ground for such an undertaking stems from territorial anxieties over Finland's easternmost province. Although Karelia exemplifies a region with the least Swedish influence, it also represents a region with a long history of territorial battles with neighboring Russia. Territorial battles with Russia under the reign of Sweden often involved fighting over the region of Karelia, and thus, even after Finland's separation from Sweden, Karelia represented a sacral spot in the national imaginary. Thus, mythologizing Karelian poetry via transforming it into a national epic consolidates the place of Karelians as an integral part of Finland's ethnic totality as well as the territory as the heartland of national romantic aspirations. Treating the *Kalevala* as "national history" served to discursively reverse the sequence of events leading up to the birth of the Finnish state by obscuring the *making* of national history. Casting Karelians as the quintessential Finns was in part a realpolitik attempt to delegitimize Russian claims to the region on the basis of religion (Karelia is largely Orthodox) or recent history.

William Wilson argues that "the nationalists saw in the *Kalevala* not only a record of a noble, heroic past but also the model after which they were to pattern the future of their country" (1976, 42). The ideological construction of Karelia as a place of heritage brought the region of Karelia deeper into the core of Finnish national imaginary. As such, the region became a place of pilgrimage for nationalists—during the (late nineteenth century, early twentieth century), it became common practice for individuals from the city areas of Helsinki to travel to Karelia in search of what they believed to be the "fundamental character of Finnish culture" and the "former Finnish Golden Age" (Anttonen 2005; Klinge 1984; Wilson 1976) and what Sihvo calls "romantic illusion" (1989, 61).

If Karelians, living remote from urban areas and Swedish influences and existing in a posited allochronus time became the repository of national myths, Finland's forests and lakes also became a "resource" for poets and painters. Painters such as Akseli Gallen-Kallela and musicians such as Jean Sibelius further made the idea of Finland as a nation available for domestic and international consumption through the image of its natural environment. These artists' works inspired the nationalist movement in the later nineteenth century.

Aside from the grand national trope of Finland's forests and lakes, a more tangible everyday orientation toward the concept of Finland's "forest" developed with the publication of Aleksis Kivi's book *The Seven Brothers* (*Seitsemän Veljestä*) (1991). Aleksis Kivi, originally with the Swedish name of Alexis Stenvall, was the first writer to publish a novel in Finnish instead of in Swedish, which was until that point the language of the academy, politics, and of the arts. His novel, which was published less than thirty years after the publication of the *Kalevala* (a short version in 1835 and the official publication in 1849) proved Finnish as a language viable for the production of "culture"—and not just as a resource *for* culture. Not long after its publication, *The Seven Brothers*—each of the brothers said to represent a facet of the people—became one of the "best-known and most revered work of Finnish literature" (Impola 1991, iii) after the *Kalevala*.

In his novel, Kivi brings to life the conflicting relationship between the individual and society through the adventures of seven orphaned brothers. They experience repeated conflicts and setbacks in dealing with the village community: when told that they must learn how to read and write to be confirmed by the Lutheran church, they escape into the forest. However, even in their "freedom" from the village, their thoughts return to the life they left behind. Their reconciliation with the people from the village comes through their transformation into literate and hardworking men. If the requirement to observe the social rules of the community drove them into the forest, the terror and solitude of expansive time unregulated by social convention drove them back to the village.

Although focusing on landscapes and "ancient" legends avoids the issue of contemporary internal linguistic and cultural heterogeneity (besides the Swedish speakers, the Samis in the north speak their own language, as do Karelians), the emphasis on things "natural" also stems from Finland's peripheral status vis-à-vis the European region as a whole.[4] Early nationalists took as a matter of concern the perceptions of Finland among those who came to visit and European intellectuals abroad (Mead 1989). The characterization of themselves as the "northern frontiers of settlement in Europe" and as a people who live in "isolation separated by vast amounts of lakes and forests" (Mead 1968, 26) must be considered as perspectives that came not only from a need for self-definition but also from the recognition of Finnish elites themselves of their peripheral and peripheralized status vis-à-vis European centers of power.

Finland's geographical location and its relatively smaller fame in the annals of continental European history often gave elites of Paris and London an image of Finland as the last European frontier, inhabited by polar bears, reindeer, and "Mongoloid" people (Kemiläinen 1998; Mead 1973). The fetishization of themselves as "the forest people" comes with ambivalence, as it implies both a lack of artifice as well as primitiveness, both the appeal toward national essences invoked by the Fennomans in addition to the unflattering characterizations of "Finns" by other European scholars. As Finnish nationalists appealed toward "forest" essences as a defining feature of "Finnishness," they were subsequently faced with the specter of being "Mongoloid" in a racial hierarchy that placed nonwhite groups as being closer to nature than, using the race terminology of the times, "Aryan" groups. By casting Finland as the home of Europe's "noble savages," Finnish nationalists faced the task of walking a fine line between pushing for national uniqueness while not overly fashioning themselves as mere "savages."

Thus, although the trope of the "forest Finns" still lives on, as exemplified by its use by Iiris and others I came to know through fieldwork, the continual question of Finland's place in the European "imagined community" (Anderson 1991) creates anxiety, an anxiety often reflected in the continual repetition that "Finns are European" and a denial of any cultural or genetic connection to Eastern Europe or Central Asia.[5] In a section of a website created by the Finnish Ministry for Foreign Affairs titled "Guide to Finnish Customs and Manners" (Ojanen 2006), Olli Alho from the Finnish Broadcasting Company states that "Finnish customs and manners are clearly European."[6] Finns are "clearly European," but constantly forced to reflect upon their Europeanness. For example, when Finland put in a bid to host the European Food Safety Authority (EFSA) in the early 2000s, they were shocked by the response by the Prime Minister of Italy, Silvio Berlusconi. Berlusconi, who had also put a bid in for the Authority for Parma, clearly favored the Italian city over the Finnish. Against the Finnish bid, Berlusconi reportedly yelled that he had to "endure" Finnish food while in Finland, and that "There is absolutely no comparison between culatello (specialty ham) from Parma and smoked reindeer" (BBC 2005). While my interlocuters laughed at Berlusconi who is known for his colorful statements, his exoticization of Finnish food as mostly "reindeer" meat hit a nerve. Viivi was particularly irate. "We are just as European as Berlusconi," she said.

These reified notions of Finnish culture, genetics, and the dichotomization of the West and the East are prominent in spaces where "Finland" assumes a space of difference such as in tourist and business brochures, museums, as well as in scholarly journals and edited volumes on Finnish economy, politics, and history meant for an international audience. Thus, even though Finland joined the Nordic Council in 1956 and the European Union (EU) in 1995, the recurrence of the assertion that "we are indeed European" point to an assumption or a fear that Finland would not be seen as such. Claims about identity often go hand in hand with those elements felt to be most challenged or contingent and therefore uncertain. Although the supranational ideology of the EU integration process headed by the European Commission attempts to naturalize and standardize a common sense of belonging in the European Community (EC), this creation of normativity ironically apprehends a sense of deviation and particularity. Although the Europeanization process projects an image of a common "European" "community" with new borders, I argue that this image is viewed in distinctly different ways between those who can trace their European genealogy through the map of Europe and by those at the peripheries of Europe. For those nations such as Finland, who lost its place on the map of Europe during its status as a grand duchy within the Russian Empire and, although located on the "right" side of the Iron Curtain, was politically subordinate to the Soviet Union during the Cold War, being European is not taken for granted.

Although those at the "core" of Europe take their very way of life as something synonymous with the standards and ideals of European civilization, those at the periphery must recognize these ideals through recognizing simultaneously that they themselves are not the providers of an ideal Europeanness. As Ulf Hannerz argues, the process of global and regional integration is never egalitarian and that "with regard to cultural flow, the periphery, out there in a distant territory, is more the taker than the giver of meaning and meaningful form" (1997, 107). Ieng Ang further notes that although there is a pan-European movement, the idea that some members are always "more European" than others "undergirds the power politics which is currently being undertaken to launch 'Europe' as a renewed world power into the twenty-first century" (1998, 98).

These repeated assertions of presumed "Western" superiority and "Eastern" inferiority and physical lowliness not only confirm an imagined racial hierarchy but also speak to the subjectivities, specifically to the ambivalences of belonging for those in the peripheries. In my archival research, I came across scholarly articles with little to do with issues of national identity that made detours in the specific arguments just to make a point about Finnish Europeanness or exceptionality. In an edited book on the history of the Finnish national economy, authors often compare the Finnish economy to that of "Western Europe." In a chapter titled "Foreign Trade and Transport," Yrjö Kaukiainen (2006, 127) concludes of Finland, "A remote and sparsely populated northern corner of Europe" as having engaged in an unflagging relationship of trade and commerce with "the developed 'core' areas, that is, western Europe" (159). This connection and unflagging engagement with the "West" thus differentiate Finland from other Finno-Ugric states such as Estonia. Even in clinical and medical journals on burnout (Ahola et al. 2005), authors specifically place Finland with other "Western countries" despite the equal prevalence of burnout in countries outside of this "western" imaginary such as Japan and Taiwan (Maslach et al. 2001).

The categorization of Finland as a specific place in need of a caveat (e.g., it is a Western nation with Eastern influences) animates both a concern with national identity in an era of increasing Europeanization and the anxiety of falling short of being "European." Such a discourse of anxiety shows not only a concern with how others perceive the nation but also contributes to the reproduction of the notion of an "us": an "us" always already in danger of being misperceived and thus also always desirous of being perceived anew. In short, it presents those who participate in such an "imagined community" as continually subject to the process of objectification. Further, an understanding of the self which stem from such an imaginary as one in lack vis-à-vis a more symbolically powerful other (e.g., "Europe," "the West") in turn solidifies the perception of the self as a "national" and "nationalized" object.

# Ambivalences of Being Finnish

I first visited Finland in 1993 during the depression following upon the collapse of the Soviet Union. I was struck immediately by a widespread preoccupation with "Finnishness." Every conversation seemed to lead to the subject. This was not just because I was foreign—at the conference I was attending this formed the subject of a number of academic papers

intended as much for a Finnish as a non-Finnish audience. I had traveled fairly widely in western Europe over the years, and whilst national
characters and traits flitted in and out of conversations ("typical French,"
"part of the German mentality," "how very British") I had never encountered such a sustained concern with a seemingly palpable national
essence. Indeed, I thought it naïve, even quaint. Here was a nation on
the edge of Europe which, with its welfare state, regulated economy and
strong sense of an ordered society, seemed a strange survival of a pre-
sixties, national-service world before counter-cultures, rock 'n' roll re-
bellion and the ironic blasts of post-modernity and consumption-driven
lifestyles.

—Justin O'Connor, *Polarities*, January 2007,
http://www.lausti.com/focus/alphabetical.html

In 2006 when I began my fieldwork, I, too encountered what O'Connor calls
a "preoccupation with 'Finnishness.'" This attention to managing perceptions
of "Finns" extended to nearly every interaction: I remember once being quite
perplexed when a bank clerk asked me what I thought about Finns as she helped
me open a Finnish bank account. However, as O'Connor suggests, rather than
reify this relationship "Finns" have to the "imagined community," I build on
my arguments above to state that the idea of a nation and of the self in need of
continual reassurance and mollification comes from both the way in which
subjects perceive themselves to be part of the imagined community and also
from how that imagined community in turn is then posited vis-à-vis an ideal
Europeanness.

Indeed, the question, "What am I to you?" follows the Lacanian construction
of the hysteric's discourse in that both discourses develop from a sense of lack
which stems from an unequal relationship of power. Lacan describes the hysteric's
discourse as one that speaks to the elusive issue of the subject—more specifically,
what the subject *is* to others within the symbolic field as determined by those in
power. The hysteric "wants the other to be a master, and to know lots of things,
but at the same time she doesn't want him to know so much that he does not
believe she is the supreme price of all his knowledge. In other words, she wants
a master she can reign over. She reigns, he does not govern" (Lacan 2007, 129).
In this configuration, or what Lacan calls the hysteric's discourse, the subject
sets up a powerful Other from whom she demands to be told of her true value.[7]
Lacan argues that this discourse provides knowledge, as it is the only discourse
that reveals the limits within the master discourse.

For example, I found that answering such a question (e.g., "What do you
think about Finns?") often met with a direct contradiction. For an answer that

was positive (e.g., "I think they are very nice!") the response came in the negative (e.g., "No, we are not!") and vice versa. Such contradicting actions, asking a question only to counter the answer, parallels the hysteric's discourse in that it demands that the other know the value of the subject (or its incarnation in the nation) only to show the other that he or she in fact does not have such a knowledge. Lacan's figure of the hysteric, then, mirrors a condition of lack. A condition that could be said of Finland or of any nation that comes into existence as "latecomers" to embodying a European ideal. This condition of lack manifests in the need to provide constant reflections on one's Europeanness or to provide caveats at every turn. This lack, or this desire, for becoming and acceptance repeats as assurance for one's "European" or whatever status falls short. The Other fails to stand in for the authority figure that would once and for all provide the proof demanded by the figure of the hysteric. This shortfall of those presumably in the know (or those we construct as "knowledgeable" of an ideal) contributes to a re-reckoning of national ideals and the repetition of this concern over Finnishness.

Besides asking foreigners about their perceptions about Finland, I found that people often provided a disclaimer about themselves for not being "a typical" Finn. Anita (mentioned in chapter 1, as the mother of the Anne to whom I taught English) commented when I told her I had to cancel class next week as I was going to Tallin, Estonia, that

> Oh, I am sure you will see so many drunk Finns on the boat going over there! Did you know that Finns behaved so badly that our minister of culture, or was it tourism, I forget, and it doesn't matter, but one of them wrote in the newspaper telling Finnish citizens to 'Behave!' and to 'Dress more nicely!' You see, Finns would go in hordes to buy cheap alcohol[8] in the duty-free stores wearing sweatpants and waist pouches.... Something had to be done before other tourists start snubbing their noses at us! Of course, when I travel with my family, we are not like that; we are really not *typical Finns*!

Like Anita, I found that my Finnish friends often provided a caveat on their own stereotypes of the nation by stating that they themselves are not "typical Finns" but that they know of others who fit this label. Thus, although for instance, Anita knows that the stereotype does not apply to herself, she confirms the notion of "typicality" as a social reality through her presumption that it be embodied in some *others*. The "typical," as an expectation that finds social resonance enables a particular form of subtle violence. For Anita, it becomes a reason for her and her family to "dress more nicely" and to not buy cheap duty-free alcohol by the box. This in no way translates as "violence" proper, but in the sense of informal injunctions within the everyday, these subtle imperatives operate in the most intimate ways to demand obeisance to its laws.

Riina, a graduate student at the University of Helsinki I had met at a party, was one who strongly believed herself not to be a "typical Finn." She explained to me what she meant through how she felt about coming back to Helsinki after a year in Argentina as an exchange student. "Buenos Aires felt so free," said Riina.

> There, people were more physical with each other, they hugged each other more, they told each other that they loved them, and families talked a lot more about everything over dinner. When I came back to Finland and I turned on the news, I fell down laughing because Finnish people make Finnish, an already monotonous language, more monotonous and flat sounding. I mean, OK, it was the news, but people [in general] are not very expressive. They think that if you get angry and you lose control, then, you embarrass the person you are angry at as well as yourself. Typical Finns think that if you blow up, it becomes your problem because it means that you can't control yourself. Women are allowed to have more outbursts, but men are absolutely not. If men blow up, they are seen to be rather feminine.

Feeling "free" when outside of a familiar milieu seems to be a common enough phenomenon. What makes Riina's statement here more significant and supportive of the links between a notion of "typicality" and expectance to what I see as the subtlety of social violence comes from what Riina said immediately afterward: "In Buenos Aires, I didn't care about blowing up because no one expected you to hold it in. But here [in Helsinki], I just feel that I shouldn't. I would just appear as the weak one." Riina's belief of a "typical" or expected form of address frames how she feels she can express anger.

As we sat drinking for a while and the crowd got louder, she jokingly explained that drinking is a "free ticket to get angry and shout." This freedom from social injunctions parallels the freedom expected in the forest. As Tapio said, "You can run around like a madman" in the forest: similarly, when quite obviously under the influence of spirits, you can act as if "mad" and not suffer the social consequences. Although Riina denies that she herself manifests any of these "typical" traits to any great extent and she provides a judgment that she felt "freer" in Buenos Aires, she nonetheless reproduces the very injunctions from which she desires to be freed by observing these rules she thinks apply to the "typical" Finn. Even though she might want to "blow up" in public, the imagined presence of "typical Finns" and the unspoken pressure of their social judgment causes her to censor her own behavior—the very "subtle" form of violence I mentioned above. One can argue that the desire for a space against the social then comes from this unrequited desire—for example, to "blow up" in public without appearing "weak" or unable to live up to an imagined ideal. These perceived injunctions, then, contribute to the sense of sacrifice one must make for the sake of the social and thus make spaces such as the forest and drunkenness all the more full of jouissance and unbridled authenticity (e.g., the space for the "real" self). The forest and/or acting drunk gains more significance as these spaces (and conditions) manifest the extent of one's participation in the social.

Anita's and Riina's responses to notions of typicality and expectation cannot be simply framed under obeisance or acquiescence to social expectations. Rather, they show how certain imaginaries of what count as "Finnishness" circulate and through its circulation engenders a response. "Typical Finnishness" here, however, cannot be made synonymous with reified notions of cultural stereotypes. The rather pejorative term *typical* becomes most relevant when in the case of Anita, individuals happen to see themselves in a less-than-pleasant light based on unexpected criticisms received from outsiders (e.g., Finnish tourists in Estonia and their fanny packs). For Riina, she "fell down laughing" when she heard the newscaster in Finland after a year away in Buenos Aires precisely because she had forgotten what to expect when she turned on the evening news. These encounters with the unexpected, much like in gift exchange, where one feels the weight of the gift even more when receiving something from the least expected donor, engenders a response. Thus, although Anita and Riina (and most individuals in general) do not see themselves as being particularly "typical" and may also laugh at clumsy depictions of "Finns" by the foreign media, their encounters with unexpectedness within their so-called own society upholds the notion of a particularism that must be embodied by others within the imagined community, if not by themselves. Thus, although they may opt out of such typicalities, encounters with unexpectedness that cohere around the notion of "Finnishness" upholds the fantasy of its existence and thus creates a response: Anita feels a need to dress up when traveling abroad, and Riina feels she must hold in her anger. The unfamiliarity of the familiar is domesticated through its translation into the "kernel" of what makes Finns different.

As in Marcel Mauss's logic on the circulation of gifts, individuals do not reciprocate in gift giving merely through acquiescing to the injunctions of gifting. Rather, the spirit of the gift engenders an affective response—it gives birth to affect such as guilt, obligation, and pleasure. As the gift comes from somewhere, so do these affective experiences. Similar to the impossibility of a "pure gift," as Derrida argues, "Finnishness" and the notion of "typicality" act as the pure symbol for what is never fully embodied in any one person but comes to stand for the subject. In terms of the gift, a gift becomes an impossible object inasmuch as it obligates a return gift (for such a return would contradict the very definition of gift giving), but like this notion of "typicality," it comes to symbolize that which it cannot put into social play. Anita and Riina may not have felt anything particularly "Finnish" about the way Finnish tourists dress or how Finnish newscasters speak. However, in both cases, noticing something unexpected (e.g., criticism in the case of Anita and seeing the news in Finland after a considerable amount of time for Riina) amounted to their categorizing of this accidental recognition under the symbolic framework of "Finnishness." Further, as typicality always resides somewhere beyond the self and in an anonymous other, the term *typical Finn* comes to stand in as a pure symbol of a characteristic that is immediately not self nor immediate other but for the fantasy of a collective that nonetheless becomes the cause of one's affective experience.

If, on the one hand, Finland's nobility's self-categorization and mystification as "the forest people" referenced a noncosmopolitan, simple, and peripheralized country vis-à-vis the rest of Europe, on the other hand, being a "forest people" also signified for a sense of moral superiority reserved only by those without artifice, different from those at the center of power. For Terhi, my friend who attended hotel school in Helsinki, what typified "Finnishness" manifested in not "putting on airs." Once, Terhi, her two friends, and I met at an up-and-coming bar in Helsinki. The place was immaculately decorated, and when one of her friends produced a camera, I offered to take a picture of them under a huge chandelier made of reindeer antlers bound by leather thongs. They stood tall and smiled but kept their hands to their sides, keeping a tight profile. I jokingly demanded that they relaxed and posed for the camera a little. "Just take the picture. We're not Russians!" Terhi said. Later on that night, she brought up the topic again and explained, "Finns don't act like that!" As more people joined the scene, Terhi ran up to our table from the bar and pulled me to the side. Peering from behind a pillar, she pointed to two girls standing under the same chandelier getting their pictures taken. In each shot, they took several different poses. "See?" Terhi said, pointing to one of the girls who careened dangerously on silver heels as she arched her back to highlight her long shiny hair. "They're Russians! They don't care. They'll do anything!"

I refer to this anecdote as something representative of a common stereotype of "Russians" that people often used as a way to define "Finnishness." "Russians," according to many of my informants, were loud, wasteful, self-involved, and into physical appearances. As such, they obligated those near them to deal with their excesses. Such stereotypes played out on an international stage as well. For instance, in 2006, smoke from wild forest fires across the border in Russia caused alarm in Helsinki. Around the coffee table, several comments were made among friends about how "they," meaning Russians, did not know how to take care of "their" forest and how "we Finns" must suffer from living next to such a big but irresponsible neighbor. "It's just infuriating they [Russians] think they can get away with everything! They'll say anything to cover up what they are doing," said one of Terhi's friends as we sat around the coffee table on a separate occasion. Terhi commented that Finns lose out in dealing with "the Russians" because Finns "are too honest." This sentiment also came up against big players within the EU.[9]

In the next section, I turn to how people often blended the trope of having no "artifice" into the imaginary of being a "forest people" during my field research.

# Marking Space

At the beginning of my fieldwork, I spent several weeks without appointments and without friends. It was summer and most of my key contacts had left Helsinki to enjoy their cottages (*mökki*) tucked away in the forest, ideally, by a lake in their parents' hometown. "You can't come around this time of year and expect Finns to stick around," said Anne, one of my few correspondents who had decided to remain in Helsinki. "Around this time of year, the city is left for people with no place to go and no one except for Japanese tourists with their cameras!"[10] She advised me to seek out "the Finns" in their "natural" dwellings. She directed me to Nuuksio, a national park located not too far from Helsinki, where she guaranteed that even a foreigner and a city person like myself would come to understand the call of "the Finnish forest."

After a bus ride of less than an hour, I made it to Nuuksio and clambered about on the rocky terrain. Having walked for several hours into the woods, I sat down on a patch of soft reindeer moss having seen virtually no one on my trip. However, to my surprise, I found that I was in fact not alone. Behind a rounded gray mound of rock (Nuuksio was famous for these rocks) peeped a pair of legs. I immediately felt conscious of having made several loud sighs when I had believed myself to be alone. Becoming more aware of my surroundings, I noticed that people sat quietly in groups or alone in discreet shadows of the forest. Compared to hiking trails I knew in the United States (mostly Ithaca, New York and Oahu, Hawaii), the trails in Nuuksio were not exactly trails but suggested paths. People sat off the "trail" and beyond it, often even in big trees. I also got off the path to find a better place to sit. Once ensconced in a dark glade away from the afternoon sun, I heard teenagers laughing somewhere off in the distance and someone singing. I sat there just listening to the sounds and voices of the invisible people surrounding me and thought of what Anne said before I left on my excursion: "You will see that Finland is a place where you can enjoy yourself without having much money! It's not like in the US, where you have planned activities, $100 for scuba diving, another $50 for snowboarding. . . . Here, you just go to the forest alone or with your friends, with food or with just wine, you just go and you enjoy yourself." I sat there until I had to catch my bus back to my district in Helsinki, but as a final prize, I came across a patch of blueberries, where a group had already gathered to pick the fruit.[11] "Go ahead! Try them! They won't kill you!" joked one college-aged man. I rode the bus back with fingers stained blue and a quiet satisfaction.

Once my friends came back from their respective *mökki*, I had plenty of time to ask them what they did. Although they chided me for not telling them of my field-work schedule, many modestly claimed that "we did nothing. All we did was the typical Finnish thing—drink beer and grill sausages [*makkara*]." While they played on the national stereotype of the "typical" Finnish thing, with more prob-ing, Terhi confessed that her summer was so "crazy that after a while you feel numbed by it!" A group of her and her boyfriend's friends gathered at someone's family *mökki* to drink and swim in the lake. "Doing nothing" involved getting together with intimate friends, usually from childhood, to drink, to eat, and to enjoy the sauna. "I was getting annoyed because the boys were getting so drunk, they started taking their clothes off and running around the forest naked! One guy got his penis stuck in a beer bottle and the other guy went to steal some more booze from another *mökki* not too far away!"

Kalle, another friend who had spent time at his *mökki* was less forthcoming on information, but he, too, explained that a lot of drinking was involved, as was swimming, fishing, going into the sauna with his childhood friends and grilling a lot of *makkaraa* out in the open. These examples of summer life among the small group I came to call my friends exemplify a common thread that ran through many excursions into the forest: many involved going to the forest with only intimate others and engaging in "doing nothing" while eating and drinking by the lakeside.

The importance of having only "childhood friends" (*ystävä*) for "doing noth-ing" became clearer to me after I made the blunder of calling someone I had just known for less than a week or so "a friend." "Americans are so quick to call anyone a friend!" chided one researcher to whom I was introduced through this "friend" of mine. "Here, in Finland, we make a big difference between acquaintances [*tut-tava*] and friends. Friendship here is not as opportunistic as it is in the United States.[12] When we call someone a friend, we mean that we will do anything for that person. Americans call friends they think will get them somewhere and for that they are always worried about keeping them interested." Thus, the forest not only provides refuge for those who wish to "scream," as Tapio says, but also to be among the select circle of "real" friends, friends one does not need to worry about "entertaining." "Doing nothing," then, implies the degree of personal intimacy and the mutual nature of exchange. Intimate friends demand more sacrifices (e.g., per the researcher, "we will do anything for [a friend]"), but the exchange between "intimate friends" (*ystävä*) does not end when these individuals no longer provide what made them desirable in the first place as in the case of the "Americans." "Americans" in this researcher's formulation must "do something" (e.g., "constantly entertain and make small talk") if they are to get what made the "friend" appealing in the first place. The "friend," here, has a utilitarian function. As this researcher charged, I "used" my friend of very young maturation to get him to notice my request for an appointment. Such a friendship based on self-interest, he argues, creates a need to entertain the other to keep the other interested enough to provide the utility in question. In contrast, when one considers only intimate others as friends (*ystävä*), such a need to entertain and to keep the other interested becomes irrelevant. Something other than self-interest brings the friends together.

According to the researcher, one sacrifices "all" for an intimate friend, but paralleling Mauss's (1990) logic of the gift, as each member of this intimate relationship obligates the other to a mutual "contest of honor," the return gift is just as bountiful. Unlike in the case of utilitarian exchange where a specific function creates the need to entertain the other, and thus once this exchange ends, no bond exists between the two to outlast this exchange, the sacrifice made between intimate friends further increases the social bond. Among mutually engaged others, mutual trust and an extended timeline of such a bond makes "having to entertain" the other on an everyday level irrelevant. And as implied in the formulation "to not *have* to," this kind of engagement creates a mask of authenticity. Individuals do not engage in anything that stems from a force they "*have* to" recognize. This sense of authenticity comes from the perception that as they do not "*have* to" perform, then what they do must be what comes "naturally."

This notion that among intimate others one can do what one wants echoes Aino and Tapio's explanation of nature as a space where "you can . . . run around like a madman . . . [and] do what you want and not be seen." Like in the forest, the space between intimate others represents one where individuals feel they can step out of certain expected rules of society. Moreover, this distinction between intimate others from the public (including acquaintances) points to a specific relationship the subject *imagines* it has with the social. Pauli Kettunen (2000) argues that a "Nordic" relationship to society stands in contrast to Margaret Thatcher's claim that "there's no such thing as society. There are individual men and women and there are families. And no government can do anything except through people, and people must look after themselves first. It is our duty to look after ourselves and then, also, to look after our neighbours" (1987).

Kettunen claims that in the case of Nordic, or social democratic countries (and especially in the case of Sweden), "'society' . . . has to carry the responsibilities for social security instead of private and voluntary actors" (2000, 162), or rather individuals are expected to feel responsible for the provision of universal guarantees of basic security for all. In other words, unlike Thatcher's formulation where the individual imagines himself caring for himself, in a social democracy, individuals look after themselves via looking after their neighbors. The tenets of universalism and equality pushed by social democratic ideology posit that what your neighbor gets, you will also, but all must hold off hoarding wealth for himself.

Such a difference in the imaginary of the social also affects the meaning of individualism. Viivi put it most succinctly when she complained to me one day of her experience as an exchange student in Stamford, Connecticut. "I felt so dependent and embarrassed," she said. She explained to me how she had to ask her host family for a ride in their car whenever she needed to run errands. "I couldn't even go to the supermarket by myself!" she said. "In Finland, we are all ensured our independence. Our country makes sure that each of us has access to great public transportation." Independence, according to Viivi, comes not from private property ownership (e.g., your own car) but from a public concern for all citizens to go where they want without having to enter into a commercial contract.

This ideal of universal access to resources and the injunction against hoarding put toward the subject also affects his relationship not only to "himself" but also to his neighbor. As the subject must watch himself from overstepping his boundaries, he also watches the other. Åke Daun (1991) links the valuation of this form of individualism in Sweden to everyday rules of interaction between neighbors. He claims that "many Swedes hesitate to ask neighbors for assistance, since they do not want to get into a dependency relationship outside their private sphere" (166). In this formulation, "dependence" is excused within the "private" sphere of close friends and family but not in the public sphere unless through the anonymous arms of the state bureaucracy. Superficially, it echoes Thatcher's claims about the primacy of individuals and families over society; yet, on second reading, it appears to be quite the opposite. Avoiding dependence on one's neighbor parallels the relegation of relations between acquaintances in pejorative terms: relations with non-intimate others involve an obligation to perform. In the lack of a mutual bond of trust that characterizes intimate relationships, relations with neighbors and other public figures require that one entertain and make "small talk"—another common complaint many of my friends had about the "encroachment of American" ways of doing business that forced people to talk about "nothing."

In a conversation with Viivi during one of our frequent midweek coffee chats, she claimed she believed Finland to be a nation made of a people bent on the principle of *pärjään itse* (manage by myself), an equivalent of the "do it yourself (DIY)" ethic: a society of individuals who "don't need help and who don't want to bother others for anything small like building a house! Of course," she added, "if a childhood friend asked me for help, I will do anything to help her. But it's because when a Finn asks for help, it means they really need it." The subtext here can be read that "Finns" only make demands on others when the need surmounts individual abilities to cope: also that one should only demand from another in times of great need.[13] This comment came about during a low point in my fieldwork when I made slip that I found it hard to get around sometimes in Helsinki. Especially during the first few months of living in Finland, I held up the line getting onto the tram, the train or getting food at cafés. It took me some figuring out to see where the line began for the food or to buy tickets for the tram. I often found myself bumbling around searching for things for a lack of signs. "People will think you are managing by yourself and will not offer help unless you ask for it," Viivi said. "Finns think it's rude to think less of you, and it's also considered rude to approach strangers."

Although this sense of noninterference differs depending on how well one knows the other person, Viivi interpreted my situation as an effect of the belief that it is rude to interfere in someone else's business. Similarly, I came across this concept of social decorum via noninterference again in my Finnish conversation class. The conversation topic of the week happened to be "making small talk." The teacher started with her dislike of making small talk and how this concept came to Finland with the new need for Finnish businesspeople to participate in joint projects with their cohorts in the English-speaking world. "Why talk about the weather? What's the point?" she joked. "In Finland, it is polite to not come out of your house or your apartment when your neighbor is also coming out or waiting for the elevator. You don't want to force people to have to make small talk!" We all laughed, but we each had similar stories of never having shared the elevator with neighbors from the same floor. In fact, on several instances when I waited for the elevator, I thought I heard my neighbor clicking open the locks on the front door as if to come out but then closing the front door shut again.

This idea of noninterference also extended to casual greetings on the street. Once I happened to be walking down my street with Salli, a daughter of a friend of mine, and I bumped into a woman I knew who lived next to me. I said, "Hello!" (*Terve!*), and she most politely lifted her hand. Salli looked at me and asked, laughing, "Where do you think you are!" I had no idea what she meant, but although it was common to say hello to strangers in Helsinki, she told me to think better of it outside of the capital. "It's a good thing you look like such a foreigner," she joked. "If I said it, she's going to wonder if she had another granddaughter she's forgotten about!" For Salli, greetings are not casual. Greeting and making someone on the street acknowledge you, in her formulation, forces yourself into their thoughts—you thus "bother" them. Yet, I recalled Salli's characterization once during my first visit to the rehabilitation center in Ilomantsi. As I walked from the room I had rented to the city center, I passed by a man in his late fifties who seemed to be on an afternoon stroll. Much determined to make an affable impression in a new town, I gave him a very cheerful "*Moi!*" (an informal "Hello"). He appeared not to hear me and walked on, but after I had passed him, I heard him stop and ask, "What?" (*Mitä?*). Much encouraged, I turned around and repeated "*Moi!*" He seemed very taken aback. "*Moi?*" he said as if asking me to confirm whether what he had heard addressed to him was correct, and then he repeated in succession, "*Moi . . . moi!*" and then looked me in the eye the third time and said, "*Moi!*" He then laughed. Then he waved his hand and left.

Putting these events together made me rethink my own taken-for-granted notion of personal space. It was obvious the old man had no malicious intentions. He had merely not expected that someone unknown to him would address him on his late-afternoon stroll. Thus, he moved on until it struck him that someone *did* address him. The first *moi?* he voiced as a question addressed to himself, repeating and confirming that he had indeed heard someone saying "*Moi!*" The second utterance confirmed that I had indeed addressed it to *him* and the third *moi* he addressed to me. The *moi* he returned to me, however, seemed to be more of a triumph at having recognized the intentions behind my address to him. It then appears that my greeting obligated him to acknowledge my presence, since if I had not addressed him, he would not have been forced to think through what I had wanted of him. In a way, then, I had forced him into an exchange he was not initially obligated to enter. In greeting the elderly man on the street, I had forced an impression on him: forced, seem an appropriate term here, as he had to take several steps to come to terms with recognizing what I had demanded of him.

Lars Trägårdh (1997) argues that the Nordic conceptualizations of "society" protect men from the "specter of personal servitude" and that resistance exists in Sweden to the idea of getting "maid" service—that is, showing obvious class differentiation. For instance, an article in the Finnish newspaper *Helsingin Sanomat* raised a related issue on the problem of table service in Finland. The article framed reluctance for table service in Finland not only as an issue of expense but also one of social "awkwardness": if you are able-bodied, why not get the coffee yourself?

> Finns are burdened by history. In the postwar period there were no services, nor did people have the money to pay for them. Appreciation for doing things one's self and instinctive penny-pinching became imbedded in the subconscious of a prudent nation.
>
> Those who are more affluent do not like to show it. In addition, many find the idea of hiring a domestic servant to be awkward, even if cleaning help is bought from a company that seeks to make a profit.
>
> Good public services have made Finns used to the idea that it is not necessary to pay for everything. In addition, buying services has been, and still is, expensive.

This lack of familiarity with services is apparent. Finns continue to be the ones who will jealously hold on to their suitcases while abroad, defending their luggage against a hotel porter offering to help carry them.

—Eeva Eronen, *Helsingin Sanomat International Edition*, August 13, 2006

As the article claims, few cafés and restaurants (if of a smaller caliber) offer table service and café entrances would often display a note that simply says "self-service" (*itsepalvelu*). Besides the abhorrence involved in the "specter of personal servitude" as mentioned by Trägårdh (1997), the specter of elitism haunts the idea of table service as well. It is not simply that this "penny-pinching" is so "instinctive" that personal service is rare. The *Helsingin Sanomat* article clarifies this initial characterization by explaining that table service does indeed exist but that "those who are more affluent do not like to show it." Similar to the case mentioned before in chapter 1 of Kirsti's parents who covered up their window with a carpet, the "burden of history," then, is the imagined egalitarian relationship with one's neighbors that makes one hesitant of a move that sets oneself above the other. For in addition to revealing the truth of economic differentiation, one could potentially prove oneself as a hoarder and therefore incur the envy and wrath of one's neighbors.

## The Social Fantasy and Its Effect on the Ethics of Exchange

I met Terhi for a cup of coffee at her workplace after her classes at the city's hotel school and before her night shift at the club started. As we sank into the soft white couches of the club, she said in English, "I am burning to the end."

I instinctively asked her whether she wondered if she had *työuupumus*, the official category for burnout. "Your problem is that you keep asking people about *työuupumus*," she laughed. "People don't say in an ordinary context '*olen työuupunut!*' [literally, I am work exhausted]; instead, they say '*olen loppuun palamassa*' [I will burn to the end]." She explained that this metaphor commonly expressed a feeling of being overwhelmed by "pressure" and that the use of the metaphor had nothing to do with *työuupumus*—something requiring medical intervention. "It's more about expressing suffering, normal suffering that you get through having to deal with people. It's about dealing with something beyond your control," she said. And as an example of one such social force, she pointed to a coworker of hers who visibly grimaced as she walked past us with a tray of new glasses. Terhi explained, "She has a bad cold, but it's Friday here; it means we will be very busy. If she took off today, she knows that we will all feel her absence. It's a matter of honesty." And she added as an afterthought, "There is a lot of pressure to be honest in Finland."

Coming into work despite having a bad cold becomes a matter of "honesty," as Terhi articulates: the more pressure there is for her coworker to be present at work, the more there would be a need for the sick worker to provide evidence that she really is sick. According to Terhi, "normally" people would not doubt her, but with a high turnover rate and no supportive friends at work, in her formulation the sick coworker lacked the social network necessary to legitimize her condition—she lacked friends who would vouch for her "honesty." According to Terhi's analysis, her coworker came into work, as "people would much rather just show up to work rather than have to worry about what others might think. It's competitive nowadays, and there's just that much more pressure," she said.

Thus, with high turnover rates and the "competitive" nature of the present, one's moral standing as an "honest" worker falls under constant scrutiny. Terhi's referral to "dealing with something beyond your control" and the pressures associated with such an experience, then, can be seen as the pressure of having to continually build up one's moral credit in the face of a constantly changing workforce. With so many new faces turning up to work, Terhi, nor her sick coworker, Sara, has no time to build a relationship with others in a way that allows mutual trust. The negativity implicit in the metaphor "burning to the end" (*loppuun palaminen*) then speaks to a sense of limit that appears from responding actively to this social pressure.

Moreover, as the example of her coworker showed, it is not necessarily the case that it is "work" per se that adds to the sense of "pressure" incurred by the subject: rather, it is the experience of being under observation of others (and not even just the supervisor's) that contributes to the guilt and obligation to respond. The term *burning to the end* (*loppuun palaminen*) speaks to the trauma of an impression made on the subject by the social valuation of "honesty."

Moreover, seeing Sara struggle at work prompted Terhi to note, "There is a lot of pressure to be honest in Finland" (*Suomessa on paljon paineita olla rehellinen*). It seems thus "honesty" or how such a category gains social relevance must be through Sara's struggle and the impression it made on Terhi. More specifically, the translation of Sara's struggle as one that should be framed under national terms (that of the myth of a "Finnish" valuation for honesty), speaks not only to the specific relationship between Terhi and Sara but also to the force of the laws of exchange at large.

I turn now to my conversations with writer and business consultant Seppo Tamminen who broke down this notion of exchange in terms of a differential understanding of trust. He explained to me the biggest challenges facing American companies that operate in Finland as follows: "American supervisors like to chitchat with workers and follow up on their progress. Finns find these practices intrusive and off-putting because it feels like the supervisor doesn't think the worker is up to do the job. Finnish supervisors let workers do their work until it's done. It's like a challenge: Can he do it or not? But the sense here is that there is trust. The worker said he will do it and so you trust that he will do it!"

As I have suggested in the case of Sara, Seppo also points to a buildup of credit: that is, of moral credit. Unlike in the case of "American" supervisors, "Finnish" supervisors give credit to individuals in that they already believe or "trust" that the employee will live up to the challenge. Seppo historicized this trust as stemming from Finland's agricultural past in which parishioners had to depend on each other's labor for survival.

> It's a matter of *honesty*. Everyone must do the same amount of work, and if you are given a task, you must do it. In a small country, others depend on you and trust that you do it. It's honest to do what you said you will do. We are a really small country! Our success is built on this trust. There are no free-riders here; and if there is one, we'll make them suffer!

Indeed, agricultural cooperative work or *talkoot* work, as it is called, has a long history in Finland and is the system through which individuals in a village contributed their labor for communal projects. In the past, *talkoot* labor made possible the construction of public buildings: today in rural areas where *talkoot* still refers to community-based projects, it brings individuals together to solve common issues such as keeping public areas clean (Haddad 2007, 151). As Mary Alice Haddad (2007) who did a study on the notion of voluntarism and *talkoot* in Finland notes, shirkers are accused on both moral and social grounds for not contributing to the community, and thus while not paid or made mandatory by law, most everyone from the community participates in *talkoot* activities. The question of honesty in cooperative work revolves around putting in *enough* of one's labor and becoming a part of the social through working together. When one member of a "team" holds back from pulling their weight in this system, others must put in more effort to compensate for this lack. The idiom of "honesty" (*rehellisyyttä*) matters in this way, as your lack of efforts translates as more work for others.

Sara's dilemma to come to work or not despite her obvious malaise must be considered within the notion of moral exchange particular to the history and myths that uphold the social moral exchange system. Defending one's honesty occurs at a cost as *not* coming into work—the "honest" thing to do in the case of Sara does not count as acting honestly. "Honesty" is upheld via engaging with the social in the way that it dictates in a "mutual contest of honor." I use these terms that

Mauss (1990) used to describe the potlatch to refer also to the demand to be "honest" as in the case I describe here, as both cases point to a display of destruction that nonetheless constructs the social ideal. If in societies engaged in the potlatch, social hierarchy that build on notions of "honor" take shape through the frame of the potlatch, in the case of Sara (and in Terhi's understanding of Sara's actions), the symbolic ideal of "honesty" come alive precisely because of and through the "destructive" act of coming into work despite suffering from a bad cold.

Mauss says of the potlatch and of gift exchange in general that such forms of exchange take place "in a form that is both disinterested and obligatory. Moreover, this obligation is expressed in a mythical and imaginary way or, one might say, symbolic and collective" (1990, 33). Even as Mary Douglas argues against Mauss that he should not apply the logic of the gift to social democratic mechanisms of redistribution because individuals in such a society fail to obligate the state in a "mutual contest of honor," I argue that although individuals may not have the power to obligate the "state" as such, they nonetheless succeed in obligating neighbors, coworkers, and community members to comply. This notion of honesty thus refers back to discussions on shame and guilt made in the introduction, without which, the political and redistributive mechanisms of the social democratic state fail to gain social resonance.

The value of social democracy or of the fantasy of the "Nordic good society" comes from the merging of the discourse of a highly nostalgic agricultural past through the fetishization of a national sense of honesty as well as from the annual commemoration of those who died during Finland's wars against the USSR. These symbolic edifices not only serve to bridge the political idealisms of social democracy with everyday imaginaries of citizenship and what one owes each other but also undergirds the notion that the present state of affairs come as a gift from those who died saving the nation and from the sacrifices of those who struggle at work in the present. The field of meaning that surrounds the notion of social welfare, then, obligates members to reciprocate.

In comparison to the language of social democratic law and the laws of exchange characteristic of business that makes explicit the value of that to be exchanged, the value of a gift remains hidden. The gift circulates based on this very fact that one can never fully give back enough. And as the value of the gift remains unknown, one never fully satisfies the obligation to respond. This unknown value cloaks the obligation to reciprocate in mythical terms. The repetition of the references made to Finland's Winter War against the Soviet Union and the nobility of the Finnish farmers as they work in communal harmony feed into the present condition of wealth and economic prosperity as stemming from the ingenuity of the *Volk* and of the sacrifices of "our" forefathers to ensure that "our" land does not fall behind the Iron Curtain.

Moreover, James Siegel argues that calling an act or an object as "gift" amounts to the "domestication of the pure gift" (2006, 8). Following Jacques Derrida's logic that no "true" gifts exist, in that a gift by definition should not incur a counter-gift as such an exchange would negate the gift as gift. However, Siegel argues that a gift that comes to us as a surprise approximates the quality of a true gift. If nothing about us obligated another to give a gift, that gift appears to us as proving "previously unknown attributes" about ourselves (5). In this way, the gift contributes to the emergence and confirmation of something within us that we did not know existed before. This value symbolized by the gift, however, remains a mystery until it gains social value as "honor" or "honesty." The conversion of this mysterious element into social meaning as "honesty" then amounts to the domestication of the pure gift and its potential for the propagation of "more honesty."

For, as Siegel argues, the circulation of the gift does not involve the volition of the participants. The gift given to me that confirms some value in me does not result from the immediate volition of the donor himself. Instead, the donor only circulates the spirit of the gift that transcends the relationship between him and me. He merely mirrors a societal value placed on what is in me that I do not yet know. The gift, then, communicates this value. The naming of which frames the sentiments and affective experience such as guilt, shame, and fear that stem from a failure to respond to its dictates.

## The Forest as Symptom

Through the use of several vignettes, I attempted in this chapter to examine why certain social spaces stand out in everyday discourse as desirable. I began with the genealogy of the "Finns" as the "forest people" through an examination of Finland's national beginnings and its relationship to idealized European others. In light of Finland's "lack" of Europeanness, which, as I argue above, is something compulsively denied but anxiously admitted, such positings of a judging social other contribute to the reproduction of the discourse of "Finnishness" and of the social reality of the national *Volk*. As Michael Herzfeld (1996) argues in *Cultural Intimacy*, national elements that gain international derision or are found to be embarrassing or undesirable are often paradoxically made the very things that invoke and inspire a sense of national unity. Alternatively, the experience of embarrassment in itself transforms the imagined nation into a tangible social reality. Individual experiences of embarrassment speak to how the concern with "Finnishness" manifested by the short excerpts in this chapter blends into a concern about the subject.

The point is not, as Timothy Mitchell warns, to see people as a "'self-contained totality'—a 'them' against an 'us'" (1988, 17). Edward Said argues that an encounter with difference runs the danger of confirming for the anthropologist what the anthropologist already knows—that "they" are different as a whole and that the reason for difference lies within the particularities of the people rather than in the particularities of class, political circumstances, and/or economic factors (1979, 107). Naoki Sakai adds further that such a perpetuation of difference—for instance, the idea of "the Finn" or "the Japanese" or the "values of the Japanese" (a common category during World War II in the Allied nations)—comes from "a desire that is made possible by the positing of 'Japanese thought' as its ultimate objective" (1997, 42–43).

Here, following John Pemberton (1994), I treat these "differences" as "effects" of history and of the particular ways in which the symbols that came to signify for "Finnishness" blended with notions of self, subjectivity, and laws of social exchange. Discursive and affective manifestations of guilt and fear of dishonesty, per Terhi and her interpretations of "Finnish society" and its demand for honesty, reproduces as affective experience, the force of the social within the subject. The circulation of symbols that spell out what it means to be part of the imagined community brings about these effects as affects. These experiences manifest as an effect of entering into an exchange with others and through the belief that "I am part of this imagined community."

Thus, the desires and self-identifications of the individuals mentioned here do not speak to "Finns" but to the construction of self that is always formed within a dialectic with the Other (the symbolic order—for example, the discourse of the state, national myth, political ideology, etc.). As Riina shows, her fascination with Buenos Aires or her experiences there stem from the injunctions and demands she grew up with in Finland. Although her fascinations, her desires have nothing to do with the "nation," Finland itself, her affective experiences stem from her imagined relationship with the symbolic order of which she believes herself a part. The "freedom" she felt while in Buenos Aires, then, does not depend on whether Buenos Aires itself provides more freedom than Helsinki but rather depends on Riina's own perceptions about being "freed" from the "typical" expectations that she believed bound her at home.

By focusing on the imaginary of "society" via the specific manner in which interlocutors spoke about spaces created as against the social, I teased apart the desires and fears of individuals based on the laws that regulate social exchange. Although one does indeed *imagine* the larger society, per Benedict Anderson (1991), the community takes on the quality of social reality through the affective experiences of subjects that stem from the particular history of religious, moral, ethical, and juridical registers that give rise to feelings of obligation, guilt, embarrassment, and a desire for freedom. How one imagines social exchange within a community, for instance, what one can expect from one's neighbors, and how one can be expected to be treated from others all profoundly make tangible the violence of the imagined community on the subject. Sara's fear of appearing "dishonest" and Terhi's to not pose in front of the camera—a practice she made synonymous with "putting on airs"—both point to the rules that apply to the individual as well as to those others the subject believes should adhere to the same rules as themselves. These fears of failure speak to the force of the social, which obliges individuals to respond. The obligation to contribute one's labor, the obligation to be honest, the obligation to participate in the redistributive mechanisms of the social democratic welfare state on the flip side point to the subject's having already been credited with trust, having already received benefits gained through the sweat of one's neighbor's labor, and so forth.

In contrast to Louis Althusser's (2001) notion of interpellation, where the subject always already appears to *be* the object of the call, examining the demand for honesty through the logic of the gift highlights the fact that ambivalence accompanies responding to such a call. Just as in the potlatch, a notion of "credit, of time limit placed on it, and also the notion of honor" (Mauss 1990, 35) compels each clan to maintain prestige chiefs do not enter into this competition of honor out of volition and agency but by the force of the gift. A chief at a potlatch can only prove "he is haunted and favoured both by the spirits and by good fortune, that he is possessed, and also possesses it" (39) via sharing and destroying in the most extravagant manner possible his possessions. A chief does not merely respond to a call, per Althusser, as a subject who already sees himself as in need of such display. Rather, something other than his own agency animates and drives him to respond. Thus, the logic of the gift reveals a certain dehiscence. The subject engages in the social as a split entity: something possesses the subject to engage. Without the conscious knowledge of the subject, the subject nonetheless participates in the mutual competition of honesty. Even if Sara may not necessarily edify herself as an "honest" person, a force despite herself possessed her to respond. In the eyes of the observer such as Terhi, such an act of sacrifice takes on the significance of a "gift"—here symbolized by the term *honesty*.

The fantasy of universalism of law within the particular history of social democracy in Finland, then, produces "the forest," "real friends," and the "real self" as symptoms. However, these "symptoms" paradoxically reinstate the social ideal. These symptoms do not alter the hegemonic ideal; they in fact "recharge" the subject so that he can better observe the social rules. As Lacan argues, even something as subjective as desire paradoxically manifests the desire of the Other.

The desire for solitude or for the forest, then, stem not from the subject but from the injunctions placed by the social. The imaginary of the forest as a space for authenticity helps reproduce the very ideals against which they come into being.

Although the "Day in Nature" and "relegation" of individuals diagnosed with burnout to rehabilitation centers located far from their homes help distance these individuals from everyday expectations, the course itself, with its emphasis on "energizing" the self as a way to combat workplace stress, reminds participants of their own failures. Although the rehabilitation course helps reconstitute the clients' ego by focusing on self-objectification, it also shores up traces of the original violence. The use of the forest as a symbolic cue for participants to talk about themselves further reinstates the notion of a particularized demand placed on citizen workers within the culturalized framework of "Finnishness."

# CONCLUSION

The Baltic Sea remains frozen into late spring.[1] Wind carries the sound of crunching ice as cruise ferries that connect Helsinki harbor to Stockholm to the west and Tallinn to the east carry their passengers across the water. Yet, the sun rises a little higher making the days a little longer. Light bounces off snow and ice. It tempts denizens of Helsinki out of their warm apartments.

Finnish has a wonderful word for atmospheric temperatures below zero—*pakkanen.* People from areas with real winters, winters where the sun remains mostly below the horizon, winters where the temperature drops so much it makes the wooden beams in houses pop, winters where your tears freeze instantly on your face, winters where the cold grips you by the bone—people with real winters like these, truly appreciate the coming of spring.

The coming of spring marked the end of dark sunless days. It opened closed doors and peeled back thick curtains. Even dive bars cracked open their doors allowing a glimpse of the bleary-eyed patrons within. Cafés push chairs out onto the snow-covered streets, and people pour out to enjoy their cups of coffee in the minus-degree weather. Orchids, amaryllis, and daffodils sit on apartment windowsills, waiting their turn to bloom. The city throws fresh gravel onto the snow, and people walk with straighter backs when two or three months ago, they walked hunched over against the force of the blizzards.

Energized by the sun, I, too, felt drawn outside, despite the snow that still clung onto the sidewalks. One late afternoon, as I headed back to my apartment in Puna-vuori from a walk through the city, I ran into a group of young men who had blocked off the street that led up to it. Instinctively, I flattened myself against the wall in an effort to slide past them. They saw me, however, and one of them came right up to my face. As I braced myself for the unexpected, he shouted, "Sun! Sun!" (*Aurinko! Aurinko!*) and pointed behind me in the direction of the setting sun. As he did so, the others bowed to the sun in mock worship. Turning west with them, I saw the gentle rays of orange, red, and magenta in the horizon. I finally caught onto what this was all about. I, too, pointed and shouted, "Sun!" [*Aurinko!*].

I sensed this spring elation among my friends as well. Lena, one of my closest friends in Helsinki, invited me to go cut a hole in the ice. I balked. She explained to me a tradition called *avantouinti* which literally means to "cut a hole in the ice and swim."

It surprised me that Lena, someone who saw herself as a counterpart to people who took national traditions seriously—those she dubbed the "real Finns"—to invite me to such an event. "It's special," she explained. "I have never tried it before, and I want to try it with you. Come on! It will be fun."

Having a foreigner as a friend, she explained, allowed her to participate in her national traditions she might not have otherwise. I saw her move as paralleling that of a host who might show a part of the house to the guest that he or she does not necessarily use but would showcase it as part of the official introduction of the house by a host to a guest. I thanked her, but I declined.

Lena never invited me to *avantouinti* again. Her look of disappointment took me aback somewhat, but I was adamant I did not want any part of it. When several other friends invited me to take a dip in the ice with them, I was to disappoint them as well. Having turned everyone down, however, I was filled with a sense of anxiety.

Lena's almost pleading tone when she asked me to take part in what was "special" to her burned uncomfortably in my head. Concerning also was my having turned down an activity friends and interlocutors considered a national tradition, a tradition of some import to the field. Thoughts of "missing out" on an event necessary to the fieldwork experience kept rushing through my head.

When conducting ethnographic work, a tension emerges between time *saved* for the project and time *spent* with no project in mind. When lucky, they coincide. Most often, however, the latter form of expenditure falls into a gray zone of productivity. It goes down in field notes as time spent without direct usefulness to the project. But these moments remind us of the importance of time we do not sacrifice to utilitarian ends.

It is, moreover, the core lesson we learn from ethnographic fieldwork. We spend time in situ of "the field" precisely to experience "it" in full and in excess of time devoted to the project. It is this time in excess that gives the project its authenticity, its fire. Moreover, I would argue that it is time spent outside of project time that allows field notes to carry the potency to words capable of contagion.

But what is ethnographic data? In rethinking this artificial divide between productive and unproductive time in the field, I came to realize data to include that which reveals itself retrospectively. Data are not always immediately visible as data. There is a certain given-ness (*datum*) to data that, as it blends into what we take for granted, hides itself from direct view as data. Thus, even as there may be social exchange, what exactly is exchanged remains to be seen (Fernando 2015). It is thus necessary that we give ourselves over to chance—to the accident—that we could touch on something that could count.

Living life under the regime of projects could thus paradoxically run counter to what becomes meaningful as project. In managing time through the telos of the project, one faces the danger of foreclosing what is necessary to it. Fieldwork thus necessitates a certain "non-knowledge" (Bataille 1988) of the "work" that we do, a nonrecognition that we work, that we collect data, and that we produce that awful thing in the academy we call deliverables.

It is through such contemplations provoked by my own inadequacies that in this conclusive chapter I revisit the question with which I began this book: How can we rethink the energetic economy that moves us to do what we do? In short, "What moves us?"

According to George Bataille (Hollier 1995), it is that part of life that "burns," that part that refuses to leave us alone that ignites us into action. It is, moreover, he would claim, what makes us human.

What burns in us is that part of consciousness in excess of calculation; it is that part that burns with love, that burns with excitement, that burns with guilt. This burning, this combustive energetic expenditure, however, finds no place in an economy structured around production and the logic of the ledger. A work of art, for example, though a "product" of sorts, comes from the yearning to create. What drives work, here, is the experience of being on fire that demands an outlet. Creations such as art, then, according to Bataille, in an economy centered on combustion and expenditure is not something in excess, something extra to the economic infrastructure, or "superstructure," as Karl Marx puts it. According to Bataille, art, if we rethink economy as one centered on energetic expenditure, is economic praxis in itself.

Bataille places the concept of economy on its head by putting forward a theory of economy in which what drives exchange is consumption, rather than the production of wealth (Bataille 1985). In what he calls the "principle of loss" (118), he argues that what moves us to give, to receive, and to reciprocate resides not in what an economy based on production tells us—namely, wealth accumulation—but in spectacular forms of waste and consumption.

He explores this principle of loss through examining the building of pyramids, our continued enchantment by jewels, as well as our fascination with "violent pleasure" (116). Through a look at examples of sumptuary expenditure, he reveals how what counts as exchange is more than what can be calculable on the balance sheets.

Contra the part of life, that "share of life" (Bataille 1985), that is put to use toward productive activity, there is another share of life, the "accursed share" (Bataille 1989). It is a share that resists the bourgeois ascetic impulse to scrounge and save. The accursed share is the part of existence that escapes timely constraints that dictate how one is to manage one's share of life according to the dictates of today's workplace. It is that timeless and unruly aspect of humanity that haunts political and economic concerns over how to give order to the social field. It is thus, as Bataille puts it, a share that condemns us to "destruction" (1989, 11) and against which administrative impulses arise. The concept of economy as one driven by wealth accumulation and its attendant projects to manage wealth, thus appears secondary to the primacy of this principle of loss.

In Bataille's varied texts on this subject, however, he does not necessarily pit the economy bent on production against the economy bent on loss. Rather, he highlights how there will always be a remainder, the accursed share, a part of energetic discharge that resists the calculus and techniques of productive management. The accursed share thus marks a limit to what it is we can articulate and enumerate as part of the social field under control. Thinking economy through this notion of negativity, the share that refuses to be counted, forces a rethinking on the current science around well-being and self-management.

Although my story of *avantouinti* may appear as an insignificant challenge between friends, it revealed to me how what one dares or dares not do on an everyday basis carries the potential to ineffably shape how you come to socially count and want to count. How I counted to Lena as a "good" friend gnawed on my conscience after I turned down what she said was "special" to her. It affected me most since I had no reason to decline the invitation other than my sheer lack of guts to withstand the icy-cold water. It made me quick to accept her other invitations, and although I attended all the events she hosted thereafter, somehow I felt that nothing I did was enough and that nothing I did counted. There was much to make up for, and yet I knew not what balance there was that counted.

The act of counting here concerns not itemization and numeration—for instance, many were the things I tried to do for Lena after the fact—but the experience of what matters. What moved me thus resides not in the logic of the ledger. If what we do for someone else fails to translate into an experience of significance, it counts for very little.

But how do we account for that which supposedly slips through the accounting books? Moreover, how does an exchange count without its proper management?

Bataille drew much from Marcel Mauss's work on the potlatch, and it is to his piece that I now turn. In this discussion of the potlatch, Mauss describes how it is not enough that a chief participates in what he calls the game of gifts, or the potlatch, to maintain his authority and status. Mere participation fails to count. There is no set limit or standard number of gifts to be expended. To make himself count as a chief, a chief must ignite a sense of awe among his enemies and his community.

A chief maintains his authority, Mauss says, "if he can prove he is haunted and favored both by the spirits and by good fortune, that *he is possessed, and also possesses it*" (1990, 39; italics added). To prove that he is so possessed, a chief must cast precious woven rugs, copper objects, and other valuables into the sea or into the roaring fire (16). And he must do so until it counts, until the destruction of valuables gives rise to awe.

Awe does not arise when the goal of ostentatious waste becomes apparent—the production of awe. Awe emerges rather when the chief can "prove he is haunted and favored by the spirits and by good fortune."

There is nothing extraordinary in the attempt to make others take one as their chief. A chief gains authority when he shows that what moves him to destroy or give away his wealth comes from somewhere beyond him—beyond his own profane interests.

Here, Mauss shows us that one cannot *make oneself* count. Authority must be *given* by another. Authority, like charisma (*kharisma*), is a divine gift (cf. Fernando 2015), proof that one is "possessed and possesses" good fortune. A chief makes himself count via giving himself to the spirits, through being powered by something beyond himself. What moves him, then, comes from an origin that remains veiled. What moves him is the very enigmatic force Bataille speaks of, the accursed force that drives extreme sacrifices.

It is with this detour that I now return to spaces of care centered on occupational burnout and to the narratives of those who gave me their time. Each of the following sections depicts individual struggles with a force that remains out of control and yet drives action.

# Pekka

Asking someone to talk about a mental health condition he or she feels ashamed of is never easy. However, I found that people either jumped on the opportunity to talk about a topic that is harder to talk about outside of a rehabilitative context or refused to talk. Thus, my first self-introduction at rehabilitation centers always came with a lot of trepidation. Will people talk to me?

Complicating the issue was that those with occupational burnout often suffered from depression. In clinical discourse, depression and suicide ideation are considered part of the many symptoms of occupational burnout.[2] In fact, many of the clients were on antidepressants and, together with having to get used to the new drugs they were prescribed, had a harder time opening up to a complete stranger.

Given these hardships, Pääskynpesä offered me a small office to use for more privacy. Pekka was one of the first to volunteer for interviews. Even so, he agreed to do so almost midway through the program. On our first meeting, he came ready with answers to questions I had handed out to the group of clients on the day I introduced myself. I wanted everyone to know what questions drove my project and thus had made copies of my interview questions for all to take. I had hoped that this question-based approach would provoke conversation, but only Pekka came by to make an appointment.

Only later did others start addressing the specific questions I had when we "knew" each other. They never consented to a one-on-one interview, but they responded to my questions on an organic basis through sharing meals together, through sitting through a particularly sleepless night together in the lobby, and/ or during breaks in the exercise routine at the rehabilitation center. In comparison, Pekka and others who responded positively to my request for a one-on-one interview did so with the urgency of something to tell.

As we sat down in a small office with bright white walls, Pekka's eyes appeared even more bloodshot than they appeared to be outside. "Did you sleep well last night?" I asked, going off-script. Pekka, too, pushed the piece of paper with the list of questions aside on the table and began.

"My employer didn't tell me what I *should* or *shouldn't* have to do. So it was *again* a kind of a mess," said Pekka. The stress he placed on the word *again* turns the latest workplace from which he got sick as repeating the failures of his previous place of employment. He said with some degree of exaggeration that in his previous position at an information technology (IT) company, he worked with his other four colleagues doing what a hundred worker should do. At the height of Finland's IT revolution led by Nokia in the early 2000s, it was such a position of prestige that he felt he was lucky to be working in that industry, let alone have a job. However, despite his pride in his position, he quit after four years of working for the IT company and moved on to work at a local ice rink—an idea he said at the time had given him much pleasure. He explained that even though his knowledge of IT would be ill-used at the ice rink, that there he would at least have the satisfaction of completing what filled his task list—something that he claimed was impossible in his previous position.

However, it was at the ice rink that his struggle with insomnia began, and his health deteriorated. Going back to his earlier statement: the mess—or in his words, not knowing "what I should or shouldn't have to do," burned inside him and kept him up at nights. Pekka explained that not being given exact limits on what to do made it impossible for him to "complete" anything at work and that this frustration between not being able to count his work as being "finished" and feeling guilty because of his supervisor's poor management skills disabled his ability to sleep. His latest job at the ice rink thus repeats the problems of the previous IT workplace in that in both cases his work had no limits—no sense of "completion" was allowed. Nothing seemed to count. Nights interrupted by anger, frustration, and guilt also resulted in days of torpor, irritation, and more guilt.

Once, he said that he decided to confront his supervisor at the ice rink about the confusing demands made on him, but his supervisor only told him that he could either "take it or leave it."

"He was so inspiring, my boss," said Pekka with a wry smile. It was soon after this confrontation with his supervisor that Pekka went to see his occupational health professional for the second time. The first time, Pekka said, he left the occupational health professional's office in anger. "I couldn't accept that I had something wrong with my mind!" he said. The second time, however, he said, "I felt I could not cope with myself alone. I felt hopeless."

He told me that he really wanted to be sent to Pääskynpesä because he felt too ashamed to be seen at a rehabilitation center close to home. However, he confessed he felt less ashamed of himself after taking this course. "Before I came to the rehabilitation center, I thought I was a bad person, someone who couldn't do what he was supposed to do," he said. But he claimed that through attending the program and getting to know other people who suffered from similar conditions as himself, he came to "see" that the problem lies not with him per se but with his relationship not only with his supervisor but also with a transformed society. He was not, as he put it, a "bad person." The "mess" stemmed from something beyond himself. Through the rehabilitative program, he saw what needed to change. He needed to expend himself in a manner that made timely sense. He needed to shift the expectations he had of his supervisor and of himself.

His change in perspective came from the diagnosis of occupational burnout itself. "I want to thank the people here for giving me the tools to talk about what happened," he said. In giving Pekka's condition a name, health experts helped him make sense of his "mess" through the lens of occupational burnout. Pekka also expressed appreciation to the center by providing a space where he could develop a sense of community with the other participants of the rehabilitation program. He explained that forging a sense of belonging with individuals who had similar narratives contributed much to bringing about his change in perspective.

Yet, as we got closer to the end of the rehabilitation program, Pekka still complained of sleeplessness, irritability, and depression. Despite this, he was often highly energetic at group sessions, physical exercise, and relaxation training sessions. He was quick to act on the commands of physical therapists to grab a mat, pick a partner, and so on. When I commented on his enthusiasm, he told me that he merely dreaded going back home.

Thus, even though Pekka changed his perspective to see the "mess" as a problem that extends from changes in the Finnish workplace, he nonetheless feels dread when it comes to going home. There is thus a disconnect between what rehabilitation gives Pekka—for example, the "tools to talk about what happened"—and what Pekka takes as what counts in terms of what would ensure a safe return, the rehabitation of one's place in the world. As we see, occupational burnout, although opening a space for social critique among the unsick, does not propel those who suffer from it into the limelight of social and political movements against the trends of contemporary capital.

James Siegel speaks of repetition and of trauma as "the person who suffers from trauma repeats the traumatic event in his dreams or in his speech precisely because he cannot believe it. He cannot understand what happened to him, even though he can say what it is that occurred" (2006, 48). Pekka's ability to "say what it is that occurred" in no way shows that he embodies what he says.

Some while after the end of the rehabilitation program, I received a nice message from Pekka along with a picture of his hunting dog in a dense forest. We have had several pleasant conversations about dogs and how we love them, and so it seemed fitting that he sent me this picture. I was grateful for his having remembered our conversations. In the message, he told me that he had decided to take extended time away from home and work by spending time at his summer cottage (mökki) alone with his dog.

Although Pekka appreciates the "tools" rehabilitative experts gave him to make sense of his condition as a part of unfolding history, it does not inspire the "return" from the center per the larger goals of rehabilitation—a return to work. Thinking oneself through the discourse of burnout as a product of history, for instance, a "martyr worker," a worker of another era, does not lead then to its correction; rather, they transform perspectives. It is a shift in perspective that is definitely a goal of rehabilitation. Yet, for Pekka, the "mess" remains unresolved, and this feeling that one is in a mess appears to be chronic. What, then, explains this disjuncture between the tools given by rehabilitative experts and what Pekka takes from it?

The tools of rehabilitation help understand their "mess" as an issue of untimeliness. Individuals are thus encouraged to realign their workplace expectations in accordance with the limits and rewards of today's workplace. But in pushing for the need for timely exchange, we unintentionally reveal the horrific contingency of existence in which nothing lasts, nothing remains beyond what is now, nothing is sacred, not even a worker's desire to complete his task. I asked Pekka whether he would return to seek the services of mental health experts. I never got a response.

But neither his choice not to seek the services of other mental health experts like many others nor his decision not to return home are acts of mere refusal. Pekka's choice reflects his position that is neither dismissive of rehabilitative efforts nor one of ownership, one in which he has made these techniques his own. In this state in between, he complicates not only the very idea of what counts as rehabilitation but also the idea of "sickness."

Taking his position in the forest, Pekka expands the conceptualization of what "timely self-awareness" could signify. Occupational burnout marks the untimely, those whose efforts fail to effectively count in the present. It is a disorder, then, that names as "disordered" those who fail to mediate between subjectivity and history. Yet, Pekka, from his position from the forest, shows us what form being timely could take outside of time articulated and managed as part of the labor of timeliness.

# Päivi

Satu, a psychologist at a rehabilitation center, explained how creative exercises were vital for individuals with burnout. She characterized her clients as individuals overly concerned with the wishes and needs of others. Such individuals fell short of giving themselves enough attention, "especially, today, when there is an intensification of workplace demand," she said. Satu strongly recommended me to join a session that she claimed pushed clients to visualize their goals. I happily agreed.

On the day of this exercise, I followed the activities leader as she assembled us participants in a room with a table laden with scissors, glue, magazines and a stack of construction paper. She directed us to make a "treasure map" (aarrekartta), a map that makes visible the professional or life goals of the individual and to imagine what steps we could take to ensure this passage. She parceled out big batches of magazines to each participant and told us to cut out images that we like from the magazines and glue them onto the construction paper. "The key is to think about how you are now and where you might like to be," she said. "Use this map as a way to think about how and whether your present actions lead to the realization of your goal." With no further questions from the clients, she told us where she could be found and left us to the task.

After she left, many grumbled about the task as being something "for children," but the room was quiet for the hour that clients took to leaf through magazines, cut, and paste. I sat with Päivi, a schoolteacher who was one of the first to be-friend me in the rehabilitation center lobby. She sat hunched over a stack of maga-zines, cutting slowly, deliberately, and silently. She had pasted an image of a blue sky onto construction paper. She had chosen the abstract "joy" (*ilo*) as her goal and was going to assemble a large ILO out of tiny individual *i*'s, *l*'s, and *o*'s. As the hour passed, she was still finding and cutting out the small individual letters from the magazine pages. Each tiny letter was laborious to cut out of the maga-zine, and she needed many to assemble her larger word. I moved in to help her to cut out more letters, as did other clients who had already finished. Silently, Päivi began to cry but continued cutting letters. After she had finally pasted "ilo" onto the paper, she looked over at the mounting pile of leftover letters *i*, *l*, and *o* strewn across the table and remarked to me, "I wonder how my life started to fall apart."

As Satu intended, the demand to make a "treasure map" provoked Päivi into self-analysis. But it is not the sort of self-analysis that Satu had intended. It is not a concrete path to a "dream" or a successful path back to the workplace. Rather, her quixotic quest to assemble the word *ilo* from piles of tiny letters ends with tears, frustration, and a feeling of obligation to her fellow rehabilitation clients who joined her in cutting letters or sat politely waiting for her to finish so that they may all leave the room together. Päivi's breakdown reveals not a sense of new becoming as it is propped up by the "treasure map" as a conceptual map of transformation but a slippage between rehabilitative intent and outcome.

It is a slippage that not only grounds potential for self-authorized action (e.g., there are those who come out as "role models" for self-help groups) but one that also provokes participants to question their own ontological status as individuals trapped within temporally contingent demands to "be" a certain way.

In his discussion on anomic suicide, Émile Durkheim points to society as playing a vital role in limiting individual excesses. Society, according to Dur-kheim, is an "external regulative force" (1951, 247) that keeps individual drives in check. It is society that draws a line between what is reasonable and what is un-reasonable to do. Needs, according to the individual, Durkheim argues, are "un-limited" (247). It is thus that cases of anomic suicide increase during moments of social, economic, and political transformation, not just because of an increase in poverty but also because of the crisis in "collective order" (246) that arises.

Anomie, Meštrović, and Brown (1985) remind us, is not mere "normlessness." Durkheim uses *dérèglement* as a synonym to anomie. It is a term connoting madness, derangement, and disorder. It is a state of loss that comes when "the limits are unknown between the possible and the impossible, what is just and what is unjust, legitimate claims and hopes and those which are immoderate" (Durkheim 1951, 253). According to Durkheim, without a common collective sense of limits, individuals suffer from an "insatiable will" (253). With no limits, there is also no sense of what counts as closure. Being on fire to do "right" in such a situation brings about a certain hopelessness. Thoughts of suicide ensues.

Where for anomic suicide the antidote appears to reside in the social, it is not the case with burnout. The restoration of a collective sense of what the present demands does not renew the balance between what is "normal" from what is not. Instead, here, the *dérèglement* stems from what I call the horror of the social. It is a horror that comes from taking a step away from what was self-evident and a part of the fabric of everyday life to see "it" as a specific space-time in history, as an idea of what is. Losing the status of what goes without saying, what was done without thinking emerges as an act estranged from oneself. Giving voice to that which ought to remain silent gives rise to an uncanny element. Moreover, rendering visible the divisions between this time and that time, and through it, how one is to belong *in time* has the effect of illuminating that which is horrific to regard.

## Sanni

I came to know Sanni, a woman in her late twenties, from a nongovernmental organization (NGO) that offered programs for occupational burnout. Most of these NGOs worked closely with the Finnish Insurance Institution (KELA) and sponsored self-help groups (*itseapuryhmä*) for burnout. Moreover, these NGOs sold rehabilitation packages to KELA and were thus fluent in the language and framework through which people came out from the public health programs.

Since the economic crisis of the 1990s, the role of NGOs grew in terms of supplementing already existing state health programs as municipalities faced broad budget cuts on all public programs. However, compared to in-patient-oriented rehabilitation centers, NGO programs provided the final bridge between rehabilitative centers and everyday life for those seeking further assistance after attending public programs for burnout.

Moreover, NGOs had an informality about them that made them different from programs at rehabilitation centers. NGOs often relied on volunteers to assist them run their programs, and people like Tarja, who had once attended these programs as a participant but had since recovered, became key assets as role models. Knowing Tarja, a volunteer and a group leader for self-help groups for people with burnout, I had easy access to members and group leaders I could talk to. Through meeting Tarja and other group leaders like her, I was allowed access to five groups who met once a week in a small conference room in an annex wing of an office complex.

Although I leave out personal characteristics of the individual members to protect their identity, most members' ages ranged from their late twenties to their late fifties. According to Tarja, who had led groups like this for almost five years, most members turned out to be women even though men often called her on the hotline.

Even though women came to these meetings more than men, Tarja and others at the NGO explained that this did not mean that men did not find the services offered by the NGO beneficial. "I think women find it easier to talk about their symptoms with others more than men," said Tarja. "Men find outlets elsewhere." Among the "other outlets," Tarja pointed to hobbies, summer cottages, and fishing.

Although Tarja has no professional clinical background, as a "survivor" of depression and burnout symptoms herself, members of her group looked up to her as a "spiritual guru." Group leaders who volunteered their time played key roles in mediating between the public rehabilitative sessions as they themselves went under the same treatments as former clients of the Finnish public health-care system. In fact, group members often made explicit the value of the group leaders as providing what clinicians fail to offer.

At the meetings, many spoke dismissively of doctors who failed to understand their suffering from their perspective. "It's not that they don't care," one female member explained to me after one long meeting in which the group came together to complain about their treatment at the local health centers. "It's just that many of them [doctors] don't see burnout in the same way we do here." As examples, she pointed to the time when her doctor prescribed her antidepressants and told her not to work so hard. She said that her doctor kept emphasizing the need for her to balance both work and life. However, as she exclaimed, "it's not the work."

Another female member complained of feeling "hopeless" when it came to explaining how she felt beyond the patient-physician relationship. "My family and friends will never understand what I am going through, but here, with the [self-help] group, I feel that words just come [*sanat vain tulivat*]."

Sanni, however, spoke of a different kind of hopelessness, one in which she claims to have lost "the will to go on." Sanni was diagnosed with occupational burnout about a year ago. She used to work as a secretary at an office.

She complained that no matter how much she worked, she received bad reviews at her monthly evaluations (*kehityskeskustelut*). "I kept telling myself I shouldn't care about this so much," she said. But she did. Hopelessness set in, she said, as no matter how much work she took home, her efforts went unrecognized in her monthly work assessment.

"I don't know what a normal amount of work means anymore," she said. If Saija described her condition as being "wrapped in plastic," Sanni told me how an inability to sleep and sudden crying fits followed by severe depression forced her to seek medical help.

One afternoon when we got together for coffee, she told me how she could not get any sleep at all the night before. I asked her what kept her up at nights. Instead of answering my question directly, she replied by comparing the workplace today to her "mother's time."

"In my mother's time people were more appreciated as workers and were more prone to be loyal to the company," she said. "But today," she continued, "you could be fired at any time, and the feeling is more like 'why put all your heart into it?'" Paradoxically, she explained how she did just that: "put all her heart" into work.

Under the slogan of her department, loosely translated as "Cooperation makes things go smoothly" (*Yhteispelillä se sujuu*), Sanni explained how she felt she needed to put in that extra time if she were not to appear "dishonest" (*epäre-hellinen*) to others in her team who were presumably also putting in that extra time. Sanni explained that she *had* to hide the fact that she took work home if she did not want to confirm her supervisor's suspicion of herself as the slow inefficient worker. Moreover, she worried about not "letting everyone down." According to Sanni, it would be "dishonest" not to do as much work as her coworkers as she assumed that each relied on the other to "do their part." Most of all, she feared that she would "let the office down" by not finishing her part of the job and thus having others make up for the amount of work she could not accomplish. She explained that at nights, verbal abuse and frustrations she suffered at work came back to keep her awake. She described how she started to take work home secretly so as not to appear as the weak link in her department section. It was then that she started to feel "hopeless."

Sanni said that despite the call for "cooperation," none of her coworkers gave her a straight answer as to exactly how much work they accomplished at the office. Individual attempts made by workers in her department to appear efficient and productive got in the way of Sanni's attempts to gauge how far she fell behind, if at all. No one confessed to taking their work home even though Sanni claimed that she could not have been the only one doing so. "Cooperation" at the office level translated into a perverse competition in which no one could see the productivity of the other but must still "keep up."

Sanni sees the slogan "Cooperation makes things go smoothly" as conjoining her ideals of "being honest" with being efficient in the workplace. Yet, frustration mounts as her efforts to fit herself into the ideal worker image fail to gain social response. Her continuing symptoms of sleeplessness speak to the gap in what she expects from responding to her supervisor's demands and social resonance of her actions. Sanni expresses this dissonance by comparing the present with what she imagines as her "mother's time." If in her "mother's time" social pressure to "volunteer" one's labor nonetheless begot participants of this exchange recognition, today the parameters of this exchange duplicate the premise of the competitive economy.

Volunteering one's labor, or rather responding to a paradoxical obligation to give labor *voluntarily*, fails to beget a response from management or from co-workers as the competitive logic of the labor market frames this moral obligation not as a "gift" (e.g., "voluntary" labor given to the group) but as a way to boost the value of the donor. Keeping up with others, then, in the language of the competitive economy translates into keeping up one's competitive edge. In such an equation, Sanni will not receive the kind of social and moral approval she seeks.

Andrea Muehlebach (2012), for instance, reveals in her monograph on the place of morality under capitalist states of competition that the spirit of voluntarism and voluntary labor are indispensable to capitalist production. It is a productive morality put to use that resonates with the conditions Sanni describes, though not one enforced at the level of the state per the case in Italy as Muehlebach describes.

Sanni asks, "What's a normal amount of work and what is being normal these days?" Her question speaks to the gap between what she expects and what she gets as a response from her supervisor. Despite her efforts to work as much as the others, she feels herself falling short of their expectations. She complained that as she had always managed to complete her tasks on time, she could not understand how she could become the worker who would "let everyone down." Her symptoms recur, as she cannot control how others should come to recognize her efforts. She falls dependent on their approval, as she dares not "let everyone down."

In this struggle for recognition and self-objectification, she loses a sense of who she thinks she is. Neither her conviction to be "honest" nor her ideal image of herself no longer resonate with the social, and in this moment of doubt, she asks, "What is being normal these days?" Wrapped in doubt as to the legitimacy of herself as how she imagined herself to be, she finds it hard to communicate her demands. Moreover, not knowing how far behind she fell in terms of her work and not knowing how others fair in terms of the monthly evaluations, she cannot make demands to the management in the way expected by the Occupational Health Act.

Her question of normalcy also exposes how burnout not only speaks to stress and overwork per the public health community but also to the historically and ideologically contingent nature in which a "normal amount of work" gets defined. If working enough as to not let "anyone down" as Sanni says in her "mother's time" consisted of offering labor in ways publicly visible and thus demanding of recognition, then Sanni faces a demand for labor that differs from what she thought she knew. In a context where the amount of work accomplished is revealed only to the supervisor, Sanni has no way of knowing how much work should be considered socially reasonable, moral, and ethical per her contribution to the group effort. She has no way to distinguish "reasonable" stress due to "work overload" from that of her distress as her own failure to cope with the new demands. What comprises "overload" in an era with limitless demands for surplus production? Moreover, the opacity of productivity per worker at Sanni's workplace stands in stark contrast over the demand of economic policymakers and health officials that the workforce be transparent to themselves in order to know their limits.

Paralleling the history in which conditions of fatigue and stress have been dealt by clinicians (see the introduction), Finnish researchers of burnout often pointed to "extreme" individual character and orientation to work such as idealism (e.g., seeking work that goes beyond one's skill level or seeking impossibly utopic aspirations at work) and "workaholism" as factors contributive to burnout (Salmela-Aro and Nurmi 2004). Some occupational health professionals I interviewed complained of those who suffer from burnout as suffering from "unrealistic" motivations.

According to one such professional who worked for a large IT firm in Helsinki, people with burnout "are not sick. They only suffer from their own lack of self-knowledge. They take on tasks and positions that they are actually not qualified to take and because they don't know their own limits, they get stressed and then they complain about getting sick." This professional recommended that in her professional opinion, workers with burnout are often highly ambitious and motivated individuals but that once they start to see how they do not measure up to the demands at work, they should get to know themselves better and possibly look for a new position elsewhere.

Although linking individual "character" to an illness has the universalizing function of allowing clinicians to recognize the "same" tendency in individuals across societies and contexts, at the same time it makes irrelevant local cosmologies of why and for what moral and ethical ideals individuals catch "on fire." It further disregards how what matters and what is at stake at work gain different articulation through time and space. I turn now to Saija.

# Saija

I met Saija through a mutual friend. We met by a lakeside café in Lahti, not far from Helsinki. She was just released from hospital from complications she said stemmed from stress. Saija told me that although she initially refused to see a mental health expert, she is now comfortable about self-identifying as being "burnt out" (*Olen palamassa loppuun*).

We sat for a minute watching seagulls fight over scraps from empty tables nearby until Saija asked me how I would like her to begin. I asked her to begin where she wanted.

"I felt like I was wrapped in plastic [*muovikäärössä*]," Saija began. She explained the days leading up to this condition as something typical—typical in that she felt that her coworkers assumed that she would "be the reliable one" and help. She, however, described how despite the typicality and everyday banality of the injustices she experienced those days right before this condition, she nonetheless felt that she had reached the limits of her tolerance. "I felt those several days before this happened that I could take no more," she said. She explains the context in detail as follows:

> I had a very bad day a few days before it happened. My other colleague came late and as the only other dispatchers were on sick leave or on holiday, I was alone on the phones for three hours. For three hours, I tolerated it, but then afterward I walked up to my ball-less boss [*muna-ton mies*] and told him that I wanted to quit, that I wanted to go away, that this is *enough*! I started yelling and screaming and crying a lot. He didn't know what to do. He called in this woman, his own boss—and the only woman in management—well, he called her in. When this lady came into the room, I stopped shouting and I just cried. I became quite quiet. She asked me what they could do so that I could continue my work.

Saija then described how she went quietly back to her desk without responding to the female supervisor's question. That whole week she worked as if nothing had happened, but then she said, "One day, I *found myself* unable to leave the couch [*Eräänä päivänä huomasin etten kykene nousemaan sohvalta*]." The idiom of being "wrapped in plastic" (*muovikäärössä*) she explained referred to this condition, a condition in which she said she "found herself" no longer the agent of her own body. She said she sat on her couch, immobile, looking at the ceiling. But from the way she described this condition as "finding herself" thus, her idiom also points to observing herself observing the ceiling. Her idiom refers, then, not to a mere state of fatigue but to a condition of disembodiment in which she finds herself estranged from herself.

To rouse herself out of this condition, she confessed that she took to drinking. She said that some nights she would drink so much that she would fall asleep in the hallway of her apartment building. I asked Saija why she could not answer her supervisors when they asked her directly what she wanted changed. Why did she go back to her desk without replying when she was so ready to quit—when she had nothing to lose? To this, Saija replied, "When she asked the question, 'What can we do for you to continue your work?' it was the worst because I realized it was hopeless [*pahinta oli että tajusin sen olevan toivotonta*]."

Instead of seeing the direct inquiry made by her supervisor as a chance to speak her mind, Saija felt hopeless. Why does Saija feel *hopeless* the moment she has the chance to speak? Why could she only "yell, scream, and cry a lot" and return to her desk? Why did speech fail to take shape vis-à-vis her supervisor, when to me, Saija has no problems explaining her demands?

Echoing other clients of rehabilitative programs for occupational burnout, Saija said that she rose to the challenge whenever instances of voluntarism arose as it depended on her feelings of "honesty." She "dared not appear dishonest."

For instance, Saija recalled a time when her supervisor asked for a favor, and despite already helping a new coworker set up in the office, Saija volunteered to offer more of her time. She spent several evenings showing two upper-level managers from the company headquarters in Amsterdam around Helsinki, and as the host, she lost much needed rest and sleep as she stayed out late and could not come home until three in the morning.

"I can't let things be. If I know that someone is having a hard time doing something and I have the ability to do it, I feel it's dishonest to not offer my help," she said. But by doing so, she had expected a sense of reciprocity from her supervisor so that it came as a shock when she requested to come in thirty minutes late for work and was flatly told that "[they were] trying to run a business here" and that he could not accommodate for individual demands.

These experiences of dissonance, as exemplified here by Saija and Pekka, manifest an encounter with the "present" as a state in which assumptions about the moral economy of exchange and sociality no longer holds. A direct question such as the one addressed to Saija by her supervisor (e.g., "What can they do to change?") thus fails to address this fundamental schism.

In essence, Saija's desire would be nullified by making a request outright. The moral economy of reciprocity is implicit: if she were to make explicit her desire, it would only reinforce the fact that what moves and inspires her supervisors to act the way they do does not animate her in the same way. Saija, like Mauss's chief, would fall short of inspiring awe among her peers or among those in upper management. Rather than expending herself for the lofty goals of honesty, she would only appear to be doing these extra tasks for the sake of her own advancement up the corporate ladder.

If her supervisor participated in what Saija takes for granted as a just exchange, he should have been able to anticipate what Saija would find offensive and would have been able to respond to her without having to ask her. Saija faces the dilemma of one having given a gift and repeatedly not receiving anything in return: expressing this anxiety through asking "Where is my gift?" would only further increase this anxiety. Making such a demand explicit already negates the possibility of an expected return. In the spirit of Mauss (1990), one can never openly demand a gift, as a gift must be given voluntarily and must circulate based on the total ethical, moral, just, and religious facts of a given society.

Saija's statement that "it was the worst" when her supervisor asked her the question and why in that moment Saija felt "hopeless" and she could only "yell, scream, and cry" further support this analysis that Saija's demand represent something that cannot be voiced.

Although the Finnish Occupational Health-care Act (No. 1383) of 2001 made specific references to the importance of face-to-face discussions (*kehityskeskuste-lut*) between supervisors and workers to take workers' opinions into consideration when setting an appropriate workload for the department, Saija's inability to state her case exposes the limit of such legal mandates.[3] Where law opens the space necessary to speak out, here we see that the mere opportunity to speak does not mean that speech can cut through the silence. Just as silence cannot be produced at will (Picard 2002, 15), nor can speech.

Saija falls speechless and yet there is something in excess of it that demands a release. What finds no place in language opens like a wound from which spill out yells, screams, and cries.

Taking seriously Saija's idiom of being "wrapped in plastic," we see the transformation of Saija from an agent to a spectator of her own self. Quite notably, she describes the day she felt "wrapped in plastic" as the day she "[found] herself unable to get out of bed." In the next section, I continue this discussion on what is revealed by "finding oneself."


# Taru

I met Taru through accompanying Tarja as she manned the hotline for inquiries concerning depression, burnout, and suicide at the NGO headquarters. On these days, when Tarja sat at her desk by the phone, I had plenty of opportunities to meet and talk with other self-help group leaders and other group participants who came by Tarja's office. One afternoon, when the phones were unusually quiet, Taru asked me to explain my project. As we sat at a round table in the middle of the office, I ended my project summary with my concern over asking people to relive frustrating points in their lives by retelling their stories to me. Taru politely stepped in and assured me that "it is also good for us to keep retelling our story." She seemed to know exactly where she wanted to begin her narrative of how "it" happened.

Taru was diagnosed with burnout in 1999, and by the time she allowed herself to be taken to the hospital by her family, she said she already had lost "all reason to live." She said she wanted to kill herself, but the thought of leaving her two children behind kept her from doing so. She used to work as a chef at the symposium center (*Messutkeskus*) organizing and cooking meals for thousands of conference goers. She said that although she loved her job, she felt "tired" and she "felt nothing inside." I introduce her story below:

> I had too much work. I was too kind. I never said no to work that came my way. I was a "yes-person." I couldn't sleep. I never had a holiday and I never thought of myself. But one day, I was in bed all day and *I found myself unable to get up.* I got six months off. The doctors (at the municipal health center), especially the older doctors had difficulty understanding that people with burnout need holidays. But now, these past five to seven years, they know better, and if they can't help, they will refer you to someone who can. But the problem was that I didn't want any holidays. I already knew about burnout, but I didn't understand that it was happening to me. I didn't know and of course my family didn't know. Nobody knew. But taking the rehabilitation class, I realized that I wasn't the only one and that it's not just my own fault. I realized that I had a right to feel what I feel but that I had to accept all the sadness: that I had to give something up to get better. Things were in pieces, and I learned to put things together. It really helped me to know that there were others like myself. The people in the group are still my friends. We are family. We have the same blood. We understand each other.
>
> The bosses were not so understanding, however. Nobody asked me how I felt. I also had problems with finances with my coworkers. The executive chef and my company were all money- and profit-oriented. My boss said that she was a "chef for money and not for people." They only cared about being efficient and cutting costs. It was very busy, and cooking meant being efficient.
>
> I am now fifty, and for twenty years I have worked as a chef in hospital kitchens and restaurants. It was hard, but chefs were like a big family. It is sad that since the economic recession the board of kitchen owners only thinks of money. If the restaurant is not efficient, they just sell it without telling the employees why!

Taru echoes the sentiments of many who attend self-help groups for burnout and continue to keep in touch with former classmates from the rehabilitation course for burnout. She also exemplifies, along with Saija, another common idiom of burnout in which she describes how she "*found*" (*huomasin etten*) herself unable to get out of bed.

Franz Kafka examines this condition of "finding oneself" changed in his short story *The Metamorphosis* (1948). In it, Kafka describes how his hero, Gregor Samsa, woke up one morning and "found himself transformed in his bed into a gigantic insect" (67). Even though Gregor is conscious of everything around him, none of what he experiences, the food, the diurnal activities of the household appear familiar. Instead, he finds comfort in tastes that previously would not have agreed with him. In finding himself thus, however, he sees more clearly. He sees how his family treats him and how he is treated at work. In Kafka's tale, the moment Gregor finds himself transformed is also the moment in which he sees himself from the perspective of the other and finds himself trapped in their gaze.

It is a sense of alienation that resonates with Taru who describes how she one day "find[s] herself unable to get up." Finding oneself thus, Taru cannot get up, Saija feels like she is "wrapped in plastic," and Gregor famously turns into an insect. Each of these instances point to a loss of will to project oneself, a loss evident in the fact that neither Taru nor Saija states the issue using the first-person pronoun.

Rather than saying "*I* couldn't get out of bed" (*En voinut nousta sängystä*), they find themselves thus trapped. It is here that the rehabilitative discourse intervenes to help clients reclaim the capacity to say "I" and to rehabit this subject position.

Yet, this capacity to say "I" appears strongest in spaces of rehabilitation. According to Tarja, those who attend self-help groups rarely quit coming to the meetings even after attending regularly for two years. Even Tarja, a group leader admired by many in her group as a "spiritual guru," confessed that despite the fact that she now helped others with burnout, "you never completely heal after this illness."

In thinking through this point, I return to what Taru told me before she began sharing with me her narrative of burnout. Her assurances that it is "good for us to keep retelling our story" reveals how it is in *telling* the story that she can say "I." It is in telling and retelling the story that she can reclaim a sense of herself.

# Tarja

Every year, NGOs set up around mental health issues held an annual symposium in a large gymnasium in Helsinki. It was a huge event with rows and rows of tables and booths set up to showcase the work of different NGOs and their projects.

I joined Tarja and her group as they also set up their section. Given the size of their organization, their section was quite large. They had several long tables, a section where they sold T-shirts and cloth bags with the NGO's logo, as well as a lecture hall for speakers they had lined up. Along with the other volunteers, I helped put out pamphlets, set up chairs, and put out the items for purchase.

Two NGO members manned the booth desk while several others kept an eye on the merchandise. Two other members manned the entrance to the lecture hall which was only open to those who had paid in advance. When Tarja took over this position as door guard, she told me to go ahead and look around the conference hall.

I gladly took my leave. Free to roam, I collected pamphlets and business cards, and I also interviewed other NGO members who also organized self-help groups for burnout. To my dismay, I found on my return that Tarja looked extremely pained. As she shifted her weight from one leg to the other, she explained she had chronic knee pain.

I immediately rushed to get her a chair, but she quickly held me back. Instead, she insisted that I should not miss out on this grand opportunity for interviews and that I should continue making my rounds around the conference hall. When I insisted, she told me that she will stand by the door and keep her position until her replacement came to take her position.

When the symposium ended, I accompanied Tarja back to her home in Paloheinä. Salli, her daughter, joined us. Where we usually walked to the bus station, we could tell that Tarja was in pain, so we took the tram. Upon finally reaching her house, Salli and I forced her to roll up her pant leg to expose her knee.

Her knee felt hot to the touch and almost purple in color. Salli ran to the fridge for some ice. As we lay Tarja down on the couch and wound down for the day, Tarja volunteered an explanation: "It's not like you can just sit down and take it easy when everyone else around you is working so hard. I can't do that. I'm a reliable person."

Her plaintive explanation stuck in my mind as I took the last bus back to Helsinki with Salli. Tarja was still nursing her knee the next time I saw her with Salli. With both Salli and I continuing to ask questions about her knee, she explained her actions with much displeasure.

"*Somehow* you can't stop giving. I didn't think I really needed that chair at the time." Then she added, as if suddenly thinking of my project, "This is how people can burn out."

Ironically, Tarja has been a team leader for a rehabilitation class titled "*Kuntoutus ja Työelämä*" (rehabilitation and work life) for people with burnout. The specific focus of her class was teaching clients "How to say no!" Moreover, just last weekend, Tarja told me that she attended a course for volunteers like herself that was meant to encourage, as she put it, "heavy soul searching."

She said that they had exercises and discussions from nine o'clock in the morning until midday and then lunch and break until three in the afternoon. From three o'clock, they had group activities such as going on walks, golf, bowling, and water aerobics mixed in with "creative activities." Rehabilitative experts called these activities social rehearsals, and attendees were asked to role-play social conflicts and challenges such as might emerge in a workplace context.

Tarja described to me one such exercise that she liked that tested the limits of personal space. In this exercise, clients were to be mindful of when the proximity of another person becomes uncomfortable. The challenge rested in whether he or she could then express this discomfort to that person and not feel guilty. The exercise exposed how uncomfortable attendees felt about making personal demands.

Given Tarja's training and leadership in lessons concerning the balance of "giving" and significantly on exercising the capacity to say no, why could not Tarja sit or ask for a chair when clearly that was what she needed given her physical condition? At the critical moment when Tarja could have used a chair at the symposium, something deterred her from expressing her need.

In the face of "everyone *else*" who is working hard, Tarja dared not ask for a chair. In comparison to "everyone else" in her observation, she came up lacking. Yet, how does guarding the door to the lecture hall while sitting down constitute working any less?

Moreover, stating that she could not "*somehow* stop giving" parallels the disconnect expressed by Saija and Taru in their idiomatic usage of "finding themselves" doing something. What moves them occur as if "beyond" the will of the subject. No matter how versed Tarja was in the ideals of the rehabilitation program and to prevention of burnout, "somehow" she finds herself, again, "giving too much."

The bus ride back from Tarja's house was always pleasant. Salli lived not far from me, so we would always sit together and talk. Conversation naturally drifted toward Tarja's knee and the enigma of why she could not take a seat. Salli had her own theory, which was wrapped nicely as a joke.

"Here's a pretty common joke in Finland that I think explains what happened to my mother," she said.

> A man's car breaks down on the highway and he realizes he needs a jack. He starts walking toward a house in the distance, but along the way, he starts wondering to himself, "Why would anyone lend *him* their jack?"

The more he thinks about it, the more he feels that they would not lend it to him. By the time he gets to the house, he is so convinced that they will not lend him a jack that he is angry. And so, upon reaching the house, the man throws a rock through the window.

The joke begins with a man in need—he needs a jack. However, having to ask the people in the house to lend him a jack shores up anxiety. Why would they lend him anything? His conviction that the people would not lend him anything however turns into anger. The people *ought* to lend him a jack. It is with this righteous anger that he breaks the window.

This makes for a great joke in Finland precisely because it touches on an identifiable injunction not to bother other people who grew up being taught this would immediately recognize.[4] Here, recall Viivi's comment that Finland was a nation of the DIY ethic. The climax of the joke, of course, is the breaking of the window. It elicits laughter since it deftly challenges a cardinal rule.

The above reading of the joke is my own. Salli interprets the joke as saying "Finnish people can be very negative at times." According to Salli, what moves her mother is also what moves the man from the joke.

Tarja gave up the need to sit down without even asking for it, without anyone denying her the right to sit. For Salli, Tarja and the man both suffer from self-abnegation. Moreover, the unreason of how Tarja "somehow" ends up sacrificing her need parallels the unreason of why we dare not refuse to give up certain things.

The sacrifice here is not the mere sacrifice of the knee. The sacrifice here comes in the form of Tarja's self-erasure, of putting aside a reasonable request to rest her hurt knee to instead give credence to an invisible authority that demands that she stands.

The horror of the social manifests in such moments when it is "somehow" that we cannot stop self-expenditure. There is something horrific in the indeterminacy of what moves us, and yet we dare not resist its force. Thinking on this "somehow" fascinates. Both Salli and I could not stop asking Tarja for explanation. But those captured by what fascinates find explanation impossible.

In this search for the origins of the force that moves us, some individuals turned to ideas of personal character (e.g., "I am conscientious") and national essences (e.g., "Finnishness") as possible sources. Yet, although these codifications allowed them to name what moves them, it however falls short of "empowerment" per the goals of rehabilitation.

Knowing is not the same as being. Knowledge of the forces that may push one to engage in untimely forms of sacrifice does not necessarily translate into power over this knowledge. Paradoxically, what I found here is a case where the attempt to rehabilitate an individual on the basis of their untimely modes of exchange, rather than propel individuals into projecting themselves more fully in the present, instead revealed them as uncanny products of history. Once told they made no sense and to rethink their actions within the everyday, the automaticity characteristic of both categories evaporated.

As I have discussed, the gift of sacrifice is neither completely voluntary nor involuntary. The force that moves us to give resides somewhere in between. We fall speechless on touching on this double.

Throughout this book, I have taken moments from the field in which I was provoked into picking up my pen and scribbling into my field book. In this last chapter, I wish to end with my interactions with Helmi, a client I met at a rehabilitation center an hour away from Helsinki.

Helmi never joined early morning exercises at the rehabilitation center unless it was mandatory. Since the only sessions that were mandatory were private meetings with the resident psychologist, I never got to know her well. She ate alone, she walked alone, and she sat in the lobby café alone. Many times, I tried to approach her. Many times, she walked away.

I finally caught up with her when I spied her smoking in the designated smoking room. When I got up to the glass door, however, she violently waved her hand at me. "I'm not like the others," she said. And although it appeared that she had just lit a new cigarette, she snuffed it out as I stood at the door quite speechless.

"The others," here, could mean those others who spoke to me openly about their experiences at the rehabilitation center or others outside the center, those others who continue to build up a timely existence no matter what sacrifice it entailed.

As she glared at me from her seat on the couch I could not think of a more reasonable response. Although I later found out that Helmi was exempt from the more intense physical exercise due to her medical condition, she showed resistance to the center in other ways. In a group session I was allowed to attend, when the psychologist asked her whether she wanted to talk that day, she said no. On another occasion, when she was asked to clarify whether her long working hours at her job as a manager came from "care," she shrugged and said, "I guess so."

Every morning when I joined the other clients in the cafeteria for breakfast, I could see Helmi's solitary figure sitting in the smoking room through the glass door. Her refusal to join the group stuck in my head. Then it hit me. What was fascinating was not that Helmi, or anyone for that matter, should refuse fully taking part in the rehabilitative program. What was fascinating instead was that people who have a repeated history of expending themselves for the sake of others should again want to make themselves productive—productive in ways that make timely sense. Refusal, then, is an option missed in the political, economic, and social attempt to make sense and to make productive. Here, I learned from Helmi and all those who gave their time to talk to me of the unreason of "others" who courageously go about their business in an undoubtedly unreasonable world.

# Notes

## INTRODUCTION

1. Leading scholars of burnout, Wilmar Schaufeli and Dirk Enzmann (1998) take a broad approach to stress disorders and see burnout as an antecedent condition to death by overwork, a condition made famous in East Asian countries as *karōshi* in Japan, *guolaosi* in China, and *gwarosa* in Korea. The fact that Nordic countries place the focus not on death but on the individual *before* he or she "burns out" says much about Nordic projects of well-being developed around optimizing the productivity of the workforce. It is a point I examine further in this book.

2. In the late 1990s when health experts declared occupational burnout as a new hazard, Finnish experts from FIOH found up to 47.6 percent of the general workforce with mild symptoms of burnout and 7.3 percent with severe symptoms (Kalimo and Toppinen 1997).

3. This is in no way unique to Finland. Health effects and is affected by factors outside of the purview of those in the medical profession. Whether one has access to water, to housing, to education, to economic independence, and so forth all contribute to one's well-being. The World Health Organization, for instance, has implemented a policy (e.g., Health in All Policies) to expand the role of medical experts and to allow them to examine how different policies affect health outcomes (Funahashi 2016).

4. Bears have many names in Finland given the nation's religious history in which people worshipped the animal as a forest god. For example, the bear, *karhu*, has been called the following: *tapio*, *otso*, *mesikämmen*, *kontio*, and so forth.

5. Karatani Kōjin (2005, 13) argues that Benedict Anderson has forgotten a key feature of the marriage between the nation-state: capital. Kōjin shows the imagined community is grounded on a relation of exchange, economics, and that capital-nation-state work together in "mutual complementarity" (13).

6. Andreas Glaeser (2000) explores this link between temporality and citizenship in his examination of German unification. Taking a specific look at the police force and the travails of unifying this state institution, he reveals how western officers saw any transfer of technology to the east as a way of not only providing eastern officers with "better" patrol cars and so forth but also of "saving" them from their history. According to Glaeser, German unification involved a way forward through the "spiritual" rehabilitation of the east and its rehabitation in the future as set by the west.

7. I wish to thank Danilyn Rutherford for this crucial point.

8. For example, Selye referred to the negative impacts of stress as general adaptation syndrome (Jackson 2013) in order to keep the focus on its generality and not its manifestation as a particular disorder.

9. William Lovitt translated *Gestell* as "enframe" in *The Question Concerning Technology* (Heidegger 1977). Others have translated *Gestell* as "to install" and or as "positionality" (cf. translation by Andrew Mitchell).

## 1. EMERGENCE

1. This advert by SAK to encourage citizens to vote met with heavy criticism from the more conservative parties and was pulled off the air quite rapidly. In it, the actor, Lohtander,

plays the role of a greedy capitalist eating from a table laden with roast meat, fruit, and other choice delicacies. It was intended to show what happens if one voted for the right or did not vote at all. People complained that the SAK went too far by offending the Kokoomus (NCP). Some commented that the advert's "unfair" depiction of the right gave parties like the Kokoomus more votes by pushing voters to feel sympathetic to their cause.

2. Kojin Karatani (2005) argues that had Benedict Anderson specified the position of capital in his notion of the nation-state, he could have expanded his take on the imagined status of national communities through the added lens of the exchange and how the imaginary of national belonging is grounded on the sentiments of reciprocity, obligation, and indebtedness.

3. In contrast to the liberal model, which promotes social stratification via the equation of state dependency and poverty levels, Esping-Andersen (1990, 27) argues that in the "social democratic" regime type, the laws of universalism and decommodification operate together to ensure that all citizens benefit from similar standards of social security.

4. Andrea Muehlebach (2011) investigates a particular moral citizenship gaining currency in post-Fordist Italy. Here, one might ask how such a citizenship built on the marriage of "proper affect and action" look like through the trinity of capital-nation-state.

5. Pertti Anttonen (2005) argues that the choice of Karelia as the hunting ground for such an undertaking stems from territorial anxieties over Finland's easternmost province. Thus, mythologizing Karelian poetry via transforming it into a national epic consolidates the place of both territory and people as integral parts of Finland's body politic.

6. A Karelian string instrument in the zither family that often accompanies rune songs.

7. Nancy Scheper-Hughes (2001) famously experienced difficulties working on issues of mental health in Ireland where she faced death threats and critique for providing what her interlocutors felt were "ungenerous" views of the community.

8. Risto Heiskala (2007) argues that the rise of Nokia caused the Finnish Ministry of Trade and Industry to put more emphasis on research and design over making physical investments in factories, thus galvanizing what he calls the "third industrial revolution" that transformed Finland into a full-fledged service industry.

9. During the Cold War, Finland adopted foreign policies that appeased its neighbor to the east while not isolating itself from countries to the west. This condition of a small country acquiescing to the demands of a larger neighbor has become known as Finlandization, much to the regret of the Finns (cf. Järvenpää 1990).

10. When I pointed to the works of Juha Siltala (2004, 2007) and Risto Heiskala (2007), both famous figures in the field of Finnish labor history, that suggest the obverse, she fell silent. She retorted that I was referring to scholars who had no inside knowledge of how corporations work. She insisted that Finland "has always had an advanced modern economy" and that they were never as ideologically driven as I make them out to be.

## 2. UNTIMELY SACRIFICES

1. Transcendence here does not point to a condition that is eternal but to a state that transcends its own condition of immediacy. The untimely is thus paradoxically always timely in that it is outside of any conceptualization of time and space that is only relevant to a specific moment in history.

## 3. PÄÄSKYNPESÄ

1. For example, Confederation of Finnish Industry and Employers (*Teollisuuden ja Työnantajain Keskusliitto* or TT); the Employers' Confederation of Service Industries (*Palvelutyönantajat* or PT).

2. In 2004, for example, KELA provided rehabilitation services to "86,174 individuals (1.7% of the population) at a total cost of 286 million euros" out of which 80 percent were those of working age (Suoyrjö et al. 2007, 198).

3. Depending on the medical needs of the client, some individuals could opt out of some of the more strenuous activities based on prior approval by the medical establishment.

4. Another aspect to consider when discussing elements of shame for those getting rehabilitative care for mental illness is that there is a public perception of such individuals as "economic burdens" (cf. Rose 2019).

5. This use of juniper as a metaphor for the nation comes from the writer Juhani Aho (originally Johannes Brofeldt, 1861–1921), who coined the term *katajainen kansa* (people of the juniper).

## 4. THE QUESTION OF "FINNISHNESS"

1. Finland fell under Swedish control in the twelfth century when King Eric of Sweden led a military crusade against the Finns and brought them under his reign. Whereas Swedish and Novgorod's states were already established by the twelfth century, the territory of Finland consisted of three separate Finno-Ugric "tribes"—the Finns, Tavastians, and the Karelians—who had neither a centralized state nor a written language of their own (Singleton 1998). Historians Eino Jutikkala and Kauko Pirinen claim that this decentralized condition of these tribes can be ascribed to the sparseness of settlements and to the stretches of wilderness in between (1996, 39).

2. Finland inherited the Swedish political system of the four estates.

3. W. R. Mead (1973) describes how college students from Helsinki traveled to Finland's eastern peripheries to collect cultural artifacts and to hear the songs of rune singers.

4. Pertti Anttonen (2005) argues that nineteenth-century nationalists often exoticized Karelians via relegating them in the past and representing them as people imbued with "mythical" and "natural" knowledge, thereby "feminizing" them in the mode expounded on by Edward Said.

5. Linguistic links between Finnish and languages in Central Asia are strong enough to be unquestioned, but Finns often describe Finnish as a linguistic isolate in Europe—a flat denial of the extremely close links that Finnish language shares with Estonian.

6. Olli Alho, "Guide to Finnish Customs and Manners," *Virtual Finland*, last viewed March 20, 2006, http://virtual.finland.fi/netcomm/news/showarticle.asp?intNWSAID=25001.

7. Hysterics often take on the female pronoun after cases of hysteria made famous by Sigmund Freud (e.g., Dora).

8. ALKO, the national alcoholic beverages monopoly in Finland, levies heavy taxes, making trips to Estonia a way to buy cheap alcohol.

9. See also Susanne Ådahl's (2007) dissertation on the plight of Finnish farmers. She describes how the Finnish farmers she came know critiqued farmers from other EU countries for not being "honest" about reporting on needs for farm subsidies.

10. Here, Anne is engaging in a common tendency to categorize all Asian tourists as "Japanese."

11. Finland's law, *jokamiehenoikeus* (everyman's right), allows the gathering of flora in any part of the territory for the sake of personal consumption if it does not destroy the crop or land.

12. This statement here purposefully or inadvertently described how I came to know this researcher. My "friend" was a close friend of this researcher's, and I included her name when I asked for his time.

13. "It is like winning the lottery to be a Finn" (*On lottovoitto syntyä Suomeen*) was a phrase often said with irony but with a certain acceptance that compared to liberal states with high income gaps, Finland at least offered a "good life" to all. What threatens the system, however, according to one professor at the University of Helsinki, is the immigration into Finland of those others who do not understand what it means to be part of the *yhteiskansa*—a productive member of society who feels an obligation to return the debt incurred by access to public services. At a reception party where I met this professor, she commented that "now the force of globalization can be felt in the smallest village of Finland." As examples, she noted having seen workers from Thailand picking strawberries at a farm in her hometown northwest of Helsinki, as well as the increasing numbers of refugees from Somalia now moving into government housing in Helsinki. "They just want our *godis*," she said, using the Swedish word for "candy." The problem, according to this professor, was that "they," these immigrants, do not understand how the system works. Similarly, in an editorial section in *Töölöläinen* (2006), a free newspaper that was delivered to the doors of each resident of the neighborhood of Töölö, Martti Huhtamäki lamented that

> in the buildings built during the last fifteen years, half are in use by invited foreigners or by illegal immigrants. . . . Even though most African or Asian refugees who escaped the jungles or big city slums are accustomed to environments far from the luxury of Vuosaari or Mellunmäki, these good residential areas are now destroyed by gangs. Helsinki citizens or other Finns are last in line to get housing and are discriminated against.

## CONCLUSION

1. Portions of this chapter has been previously published with in "Wrapped in Plastic: Transformation and Alienation in the New Finnish Economy," *Cultural Anthropology* 28, no. 1 (2013): 1–21.

2. Schaufeli and Enzmann (1998) identify 132 symptoms that spans all cognitive, affective, physical, and motivational spheres of the psyche.

3. The Health and Social Care Act of 2001 emphasizes the responsibility of the employer to ensure that the workload matches the resources (e.g., job control, training, support, etc.) made available to the worker and to provide health-care services. And in turn, the act holds workers responsible to communicate their health concerns directly to the supervisor, as only the worker knows his or her own limits.

4. Michael Herzfeld (1996) has a wonderful concept that expands on this point he calls "cultural intimacy."

# References

Abbey, Susan, and Paul Garfinkel. 1991. "Neurasthenia and Chronic Fatigue Syndrome: The Role of Culture in the Making of a Diagnosis." *American Journal of Psychiatry* 148: 1638–46.

Abu-Lughod, Lila. 1996. "Writing against Culture." In *Recapturing Anthropology: Working in the Present*, edited by Richard Fox, 137–62. Santa Fe, NM: School of American Research Press.

Ådahl, Susanne. 2007. "Good Lives, Hidden Miseries: An Ethnography of Uncertainty in a Finnish Village." PhD diss., University of Helsinki.

Agamben, Giorgio. 2009. *What Is an Apparatus? and Other Essays*. Translated by David Kishnik and Stefan Pedatella. Stanford, CA: Stanford University Press.

Ahmed, Sara. 2010. *The Promise of Happiness*. Durham, NC: Duke University Press.

Ahola, Kirsi. 2007. *Occupational Burnout and Health. People and Work Research Reports 81*. Finnish Institute of Occupational Health. Tampere: Tampereen Yliopistopaino Oy-Juvenes Print.

Ahola, Kirsi, Teija Honkonen, Erkki Isometsä, Raija Kalimo, Erkki Nykyri, Arpo Aromaa, and Jouko Lönnqvist. 2005. "The Relationship between Job-Related Burnout and Depressive Disorders: Results from the Finnish Health 2000 Study." *Journal of Affective Disorders* 88: 55–62.

Ahola, Kirsi, Teija Honkonen, Erkki Isometsä, Raija Kalimo, Erkki Nykyri, Seppo Koskinen, Arpo Aromaa, and Jouko Lönnqvist. 2006. "Burnout in the General Population: Results from the Finnish Health 2000 Study." *Social Psychiatry and Psychiatric Epidemiology* 41: 11–17.

Alapuro, Risto. 1988. *State and Revolution in Finland*. Berkeley: University of California Press.

Alapuro, Risto. 1989. "The Intelligentsia, the State and the Nation." In *Finland: People, Nation, State*, edited by Max Engman and David Kirby, 147–65. Bloomington: Indiana University Press.

Allardt, Erik. 1993. "Having, Loving, Being: An Alternative to the Swedish Model of Welfare Research." In *The Quality of Life*, edited by Martha Nussbaum and Amartya Sen, 88–94. Oxford: Clarendon.

Althusser, Louis. 2001. *Lenin and Philosophy, and Other Essays*. New York: Monthly Press.

Anderson, Benedict. 1991. *Imagined Community: Reflections on the Origin and Spread of Nationalism*. London: Verso Books.

Ang, Ieng. 1998. "Eurocentric Reluctance: Notes for a Cultural Studies of 'the New Europe.'" In *Trajectories: Inter-Asia Cultural Studies*, edited by Kuan-Hsing Chen, 98–108. London: Routledge.

Anttonen, Pertti. 2005. *Tradition through Modernity: Postmodernism and the Nation-State in Folklore Scholarship*. Helsinki: Finnish Literature Society.

Araki, Shunichi, and Kenji Iwasaki. 2005. "Death due to Overwork (Karoshi): Causation, Health Service, and Life Expectancy of Japanese Males." *Journal of the Japan Medical Association* 128 (6): 889–94.

Arter, David. 2006. *Democracy in Scandinavia: Consensual, Majoritarian or Mixed?* Manchester, UK: Manchester University Press.

Aslama, Minna, Anu Kantola, Ullamaija Kivikuru, and Sanna Valtonen. 2001. "Politics Displaced, Politics Replaces: Elites' and Citizens' Talk on the Economic Crisis." In *Down from the Heavens, Up from the Ashes: The Finnish Economic Crisis of the 1990s in the Light of Economic and Social Research*, edited by Jorma Kalela, Jaakko Kiander, Ullamaija Kivikuru, Heikki Loikkanena, and Jussi Simpura, 168–88. Helsinki: Gummerus Kirjapaino Oy.

Baer, Drake. 2014. "Here's What Google Teaches Employees in Its 'Search inside Yourself' Course." Business Insider, August 5.

Bakhtin, Mikhail. 1981. *The Dialogic Imagination*. Austin: University of Texas Press.

Baraitser, Lisa. 2017. *Enduring Time*. London: Bloomsbury.

Bataille, George. 1985. *Visions of Excess: Selected Writings, 1927–1939*. Edited by Allan Stoekl. Minneapolis: University of Minnesota Press.

Bataille, George. 1988. *Inner Experience*. Translated by Leslie Anne Boldt. Albany: State University of New York Press.

Bataille, George. 1989. *The Accursed Share, vol. 1*. Translated by Robert Hurley. New York: Zone Books.

Bataille, George. 1992. *Theory of Religion*. New York: Zone Books.

Bataille, George, and Annette Michelson. 1986. "Sacrifice." *October* 36: 61–74.

BBC. 2005. "'Playboy' Berlusconi Irks Finland." June 23, 2005, https://news.bbc.co.uk/2/hi/europe/4122596.stm.

Bear, Laura. 2014. "Doubt, Conflict, Mediation: The Anthropology of Modern Time." *Journal of the Royal Anthropological Institute* 20 (1): 3–30.

Beard, George. 1881. *American Nervousness: Its Causes and Consequences*. New York: GP Putnam's Sons.

Bhabba, Homi. 1994. *The Location of Culture*. London: Routledge.

Blanchot, Maurice. 1982. *The Space of Literature*. Translated by Ann Smock. Lincoln: University of Nebraska Press.

Blanchot, Maurice. 1993. *The Infinite Conversation*. Translated Susan Hanson. Minneapolis: University of Minnesota Press.

Bratton, Benjamin. 2006. "Introduction: Logistics of Habitable Circulation." In *Speed and Politics*, edited by Paul Virilio, 7–26. South Pasadena, CA: Semiotext(e).

Breazeale, Daniel. 1997. Introduction to *Untimely Meditations* by Friedrich Nietzsche, vii–xxxiii. Cambridge: Cambridge University Press.

Brown, William. 1845. *New Zealand and Its Aborigines: Being an Account of the Aborigines, Trade and Resources of the Colony; and the Advantages It Now Presents as a Field for Emigration and the Investment of Capital*. London: Smith Elder.

Cannon, Walter B. 1942. "'Voodoo' Death." *American Anthropologist* 44 (2): 169–81.

Caputo, John. 1997. *The Prayer and Tears of Jacques Derrida: Religion without Religion*. Bloomington: Indiana University Press.

Case, Anne, and Angus Deaton. 2017. "Mortality and Morbidity in the 21st Century." *Brookings Papers on Economic Activity* (Spring): 397–476.

Castells, Manuel, and Pekka Himanen. 2002. *The Information Society and the Welfare State: The Finnish Model*. Oxford: Oxford University Press.

Cathébras, Pascal. 1991. Du "burn out" au "syndromes yuppies": Deux avatars modernes de la fatigue. *Sciences sociales et santé* 9: 65–94.

Cathébras, Pascal. 1994. "Neurasthenia, Spasmophilia and Chronic Fatigue Syndromes in France." *Transcultural Psychiatry* 31: 259–70.

Cederström, Carl, and André Spicer. 2015. *The Wellness Syndrome*. Cambridge, UK: Polity Press.

Chakrabarty, Dipesh. 2000. *Provincializing Europe: Postcolonial Thought and Historical Difference*. Princeton, NJ: Princeton University Press.

Copjec, Joan. 2006. "The Object-Gaze: Shame, Hijab, Cinema." *Filozofski Vestnik* 2: 11–29.

Daun, Åke. 1991. "Individualism and Collectivity among Swedes." *Ethnos* 3 (14): 165–72.

Davidson, Deanna. 2007. "East Spaces in West Times: Deictic Reference and Political Self-Positioning in a Post-Socialist East German Chronotope." *Language and Communication* 27 (3): 212–26.

Davies, William. 2011. "The Political Economy of Unhappiness." *New Left Review* 71:65–80.

Davies, William. 2015. *The Happiness Industry: How the Government and Big Business Sold Us Well-Being*. London: Verso.

Deleuze, Gilles. 1991. *Empiricism and Subjectivity: An Essay on Hume's Theory of Human Nature*. Translated by Constantin V. Boundas. New York: Columbia University Press.

Deleuze, Gilles. 1992. "What Is a Dispositif?" In *Michel Foucault Philosopher*, edited by T. J. Armstrong, 159–68. Hempstead, UK: Harvester Wheatsheaf.

Derrida, Jacques. 1986. *Glas*. Translated by John Leavey Jr. and Richard Rand. Lincoln: University of Nebraska Press.

Derrida, Jacques. 1995. *Archive Fever: A Freudian Impression*. Translated by Eric Prenowitz. Chicago: University of Chicago Press.

Douglas, Mary. 1990. "Foreword." In *The Gift: The Form and Reason for Exchange in Archaic Societies*. Marcel Mauss. Translated by W.D. Halls, vii–xviii. New York and London: W. W. Norton

Durkheim, Émile. 1951. *Suicide: A Study in Sociology*. New York: Free Press.

Durkheim, Émile. 1995. *The Elementary Forms of Religious Life*. Translated by Karen E. Fields. New York: Free Press.

Eagleton, Terry. 2018. *Radical Sacrifice*. New Haven, CT: Yale University Press.

Erber, Pedro. 2013. "Contemporaneity and Its Discontents." *Diacritics* 41 (1): 28–48.

Esping-Andersen, Gøsta. 1990. *The Three Worlds of Welfare Capitalism*. Princeton, NJ: Princeton University Press.

Fassin, Didier. 2014. "True Life, Real Lives: Revisiting the Boundaries between Ethnography and Fiction." *American Ethnologist* 41 (1): 40–55.

Ferguson, James. 1994. *The Anti-politics Machine: "Development," Depoliticization, and Bureaucratic Power in Lesotho*. Minneapolis: University of Minnesota Press.

Fernando, Jeremy. 2015. *On Thinking With—Scientists, Sciences, and Isabelle Stengers*. Singapore: Delere Press.

Ffrench, Patrick. 2007. *After Bataille: Sacrifice, Exposure, Community*. New York: Modern Humanities Research Association and Routledge, Legenda.

Foucault, Michel. 1972. *The Archaeology of Knowledge and The Discourse on Language*. Translated by A. M. Sheridan Smith. New York: Pantheon.

Foucault, Michel. 2014. *On the Government of the Living: Lectures at the Collège de France 1979–1980*. Translated by Graham Burchell. Edited by Arnold I. Davidson. New York: Picador.

Freud, Sigmund. 1991. "A Note upon the 'Mystic Writing Pad.'" In *Freud, General Psychological Theory: Papers on Metapsychology*, edited by Philip Rieff, 207–12. New York: Simon & Schuster.

Freudenberger, Herbert. 1974. "Staff Burn-Out." *Journal of Social Issues* 39 (1): 159–65.

Friberg, Torbjörn. 2009. "Burnout: From Popular Culture to Psychiatric Diagnosis in Sweden." *Culture, Medicine, and Psychiatry* 33: 538–58.

Funahashi, Daena Aki. 2016. "Rule by Good People Health Governance and the Violence of Moral Authority in Thailand." *Cultural Anthropology* 31 (1): 107–30.

Glaeser, Andreas. 2000. *Divided in Unity: Identity, Germany, and the Berlin Police*. Chicago: University of Chicago Press.

Hacking, Ian. 1998. *Mad Travelers: Reflections on the Reality of Transient Mental Illnesses*. Cambridge, MA: Harvard University Press.

Haddad, Mary Alice. 2007. *Politics of Volunteering in Japan: A Global Perspective*. Cambridge: Cambridge University Press.

Haimekoski, Tuija. 2007. "Ole Kiltti, Mutta Älä Liian Kiltti." *Anna*, January 18.

Hamacher, Werner. 1997. "Ou, séance, touche de Nancy, ici." In *On Jean-Luc Nancy: The Sense of Philosophy*, edited by Darren Sheppard, Simon Sparks, and Colin Thomas, 38–62. London: Routledge.

Han, Byung-Chul. 2017. *Psycho-politics: Neoliberalism and New Technologies of Power*. London: Verso.

Hannerz, Ulf. 1997. "Scenarios for Peripheral Cultures." In *Culture, Globalization and the World-System: Contemporary Conditions for the Representation of Identity*, edited by Anthony King, 107–28. Minneapolis: University of Minnesota Press.

Harding, Susan, and Kathleen Stewart. 2003. "Anxieties of Influence: Conspiracy Theory and Therapeutic Culture in Millennial America." In *Transparency and Conspiracy: Ethnographies of Suspicion in the New World Order*, edited by Harry G. West and Todd Sanders, 258–300. Durham, NC: Duke University Press.

Hardt, Michael, and Antonio Negri. 2004. *Multitude: War and Democracy in the Age of Empire*. New York: Penguin.

Häkli, Vesa. 2006. "Masennus vei Pepe Willbergiltä Työkyvyn. Nyt Jaksan Taas." *Oho!*, September 27–October 3, 218–31.

Hätinen, Marja. 2008. *Treating Job Burnout in Employee Rehabilitation: Changes in Symptoms, Antecedents, and Consequences*. Jyväskylä Studies in Education, Psychology and Social Research 348. Jyväskylä: Jyväskylä University Printing House.

Häyhä, Juha. 1993. "How Does the Welfare State Fit into the Finnish Legal System?" In *The Nordic Welfare State as an Idea and as a Reality*, edited by Pekka Kosonen, 26–44. Helsinki: Helsinki University Printing House.

Heidegger, Martin. 1977. *The Question Concerning Technology, and Other Essays*. Translated by William Lovitt. New York: Harper Perennial Modern Thought.

Heiskala, Risto. 2007. "Social Innovations: Structural and Power Perspectives." In *Social Innovations, Institutional Change and Economic Performance*, edited by Timo J. Hämäläinen and Risto Heiskala. Northampton, MA: Edward Elgar.

Herzfeld, Michael. 1996. *Cultural Intimacy: Social Poetics in the Nation-State*. New York: Routledge.

Hietanen, Juha. 1999. "Action Programme Launched to Promote Ability to Cope at Work." *European Foundation for the Improvement of Living and Working Conditions (Eurofound)*. https://www.eurofound.europa.eu/publications/article/1999/action-programme-launched-to-promote-ability-to-cope-at-work.

Hollier, Denis, ed. 1995. *Le collège de sociologie*. Paris: Gallimard.

Honkapohja, Seppo, Erkki Koskela, Stefan Gerlach, and Lucrezia Reichlin. 1999. "The Economic Crisis of the 1990s in Finland." *Economic Policy* 14 (29): 399–436.

Hubert, Henri, and Marcel Mauss. 1964. *Sacrifice: Its Nature and Functions*. Chicago: University of Chicago Press.

Impola, Richard. 1991. Foreword to *Seven Brothers* by Aleksis Kivi. Ann Arbor, MI: Braun-Brumfield.

Jackson, Mark. 2013. *The Age of Stress: Science and the Search for Stability*. Oxford: Oxford University Press.

Järvenpää, Pauli. 1990. "Finland: An Image of Continuity in Turbulent Europe." *Annals of the American Academy of Political and Social Science* 512: 125–39.

Johnson, Andrew Alan. 2016. "Dreaming about the Neighbors: Magic, Orientalism and Entrepreneurship in the Consumption of Thai Religious Goods in Singapore." *South East Asia Research* 24 (4): 445–61.

Jonung, Lars, Jaakko Kiander, and Pentti Vartia, eds. 2009. *The Great Financial Crisis in Finland and Sweden: The Nordic Experience of Financial Liberalization*. Cheltenham, UK: Edward Elgar.

Jutikkala, Eino, and Kauko Pirinen. 1996. *A History of Finland*. Translated by Paul Sjöblom. Porvoo, Finland: Werner Söderström Osakeyhtiö.

Kafka, Franz. 1948. *The Metamorphosis, The Penal Colony, and Other Stories*. New York: Schocken.

Kaila, Eino. 1934. *Persoonallisuus* (Personality). Helsinki, Finland: Otava.

Kalela, Jorma, Jaakko Kiander, Ullamaija Kivikuru, Heikki A. Loikkanen, and Jussi Simupura, eds. 2001. Down from the Heavens, Up from the Ashes: The Finnish Economic Crisis of the 1990s in the light of Economic and Social Research. Helsinki: Valtion Taloudellinen Tutkimuskesus.

Kalimo, Raija, and S. Toppinen. 1997. *Työuupumus Suomen Työkäisellä Väestöllä* [Prevalence of burnout in the Finnish working population]. Helsinki: Finnish Institute of Occupational Health.

Kamat, Vinay. 2008. "Reconsidering the Allure of the Culturally Distant in Therapy Seeking: A Case Study from Coastal Tanzania." *Medical Anthropology* 27 (2): 106–35.

Karatani, Kōjin. 2005. *Transcritique: On Kant and Marx*. Translated by Sabu Kohso. Cambridge, MA: MIT Press.

Kaukiainen, Yrjö. 2006. "Foreign Trade and Transport." In *Road to Prosperity: An Economic History of Finland*, edited by Jari Ojala, Jari Eloranta, and Jukka Jalava, 127–63. Helsinki: Suomalaisen Kirjallisuuden Seura.

Kemiläinen, Aira. 1998. *Finns in the Shadow of the "Aryans": Race Theories and Racism*. Helsinki: Suomen Historiallinen Seura.

Kemppainen, Jouni, Tarmo Vienonen, and Tarmo Koivisto. 2007. "*Pääkaupunki* (The Capital)". *Kuukausiliite*. Helsingin Sanomat, 103.

Kettunen, Pauli. 1998. "Globalization and the Criteria of 'Us': A Historical Perspective on the Discussion of the Nordic Model and New Challenges." In *Global Redefining of Working Life: A New Nordic Agenda for Competence and Participation?* edited by Daniel Fleming, Pauli Kettunen, Henrik Søborg, and Christopher Thörnqvist, 33–80. Copenhagen: Nordic Council of Ministers.

Kettunen, Pauli. 2000. "*Yhteiskunta*: 'Society' in Finnish." *Finnish Yearbook of Political Thought* 4:159–97.

Kierkegaard, Søren. 2003. *Fear and Trembling*. London: Penguin.

Kitanaka, Junko. 2011. *Depression in Japan: Psychiatric Cures for a Society in Distress*. Princeton, NJ: Princeton University Press.

Kivi, Alexis. 1991. *The Seven Brothers* [*Seitsemän Veljestä*]. Translated by Richard Impola. Ann Arbor, MI: Braun-Brumfield.

Kleinman, Arthur. 1980. *Patients and Healers in the Context of Culture: An Exploration of the Borderland between Anthropology, Medicine, and Psychiatry*. Berkeley: University of California Press.

Klinge, Matti. 2003. *Finland in Europe*. Helsinki: Otava Publishing.

Korkeila, Jyrki, Saara Töyry, Kirsti Kumpulainen, Juha-Matti Toivola, Kimmo Räsänen, and Raija Kalimo. 2003. "Burnout and Self-perceived Health among Finnish Psychiatrists and Child Psychiatrists: A National Survey." *Scandinavian Journal of Public Health* 31: 85–91.

Koselleck, Reinhart. 2002. *The Practice of Conceptual History: Timing History, Spacing Concepts*. Stanford, CA: Stanford University Press.

Kurenmaa, Pekka, and Riitta Lentilä. 2005. "Sodan Tappiot" [Casualties of war]. In *Jatkosodan Pikkujättiläinen* [The little giant of the continuation war], edited by Jari Leskinen and Antti Juutilainen, 1150–62. Helsinki: WSOY.

Kuusi, Pekka. 1964. *Social Policy for the Sixties: A Plan for Finland*. Helsinki: Finnish Social Policy Association Publications.

Lacan, Jacques. 1992. *The Ethics of Psychoanalysis 1959–1960: The Seminar of Jacques Lacan, Book VII*. Translated by Dennis Porter. New York: Norton.

Lacan, Jacques. 2007. *The Other Side of Psychoanalysis: The Seminar of Jacques Lacan Book XVII*. Translated by Russell Grigg. Edited by Jacques-Alain Miller. New York: Norton.

Lane, Edwin. 2017. "The Young Japanese Working Themselves to Death." BBC World Service, Japan, June 2. https://www.bbc.com/business-39981997.

Lazzarato, Maurizio. 1996. "Immaterial Labor." In *Radical Thought in Italy: A Potential Politics*, edited by Paolo Virno and Michael Hardt, 133–46. Minneapolis: University of Minnesota Press.

Lehto, Anna-Maija. 2008. "Tackling Occupational Burnout at the Workplace." *Statistics Finland (SVT)*, September 24.

Lehto, Anna-Maija, and Hanna Sutela. 1999. *Efficient, More Efficient, Exhausted: Findings of Finnish Quality of Work Life Surveys 1977–1997*. Helsinki: Statistics Finland (SVT).

Lévi-Strauss, Claude. 1987. *Introduction to the Work of Marcel Mauss*. Translated by Felicity Baker. London: Routledge & Kegan Paul.

Li, Jian, Frank Pega, Yuka Ujita, Chantal Brisson, Els Clays, Alexis Descatha, Marco M. Ferrario, et al. 2020. "The Effect of Exposure to Long Working Hours on Ischaemic Heart Disease: A Systemic Review and Meta-analysis from the WHO/ILO Joint Estimates of the Work-Related Burden of Disease and Injury." *Environment International* 142 (105739): 1–38.

Lingis, Alphonso. 2009. "Contact and Communication." In *The Obsessions of Georges Bataille: Community and Communication*, edited by Andrew J. Mitchell and Jason Kemp Winfree, 119–32. New York: State University of New York Press.

Lönnrot, Elias. 1989. *The Kalevala: Epic of the Finnish People*. Champaign: University of Illinois Press.

Luo, Fei, and Jim Ruiz. 2012. "Comparing Police Overwork in China and the USA: An Exploratory Study of Overwork ('Karoshi') in Policing." *International Journal of Police Science Management* 14 (2): 177–98.

Mannila, Simo, Hanna Kaipainen, and Veijo Notkola. 2005. "Disability, Labour Participation and Needs of Rehabilitation in Finland." In *Disability and Working Life*, edited by Simo Mannila and Aila Järvikoski, 26–44. Helsinki: Helsinki University Press.

Marmot, M. G., Geoffrey Rose, M. Shipley, and P. J. S. Hamilton. 1978. "Employment Grade and Coronary Heart Disease in British Civil Servants." *Journal of Epidemiology and Community Health* 32: 244–49.

Maslach, Christina. 2001. "What Have We Learned about Burnout and Health?" *Psychology and Health* 16: 607–11.

Maslach, Christina, Susan Jackson, and Michael Leiter. 2001. "Job Burnout." *Annual Review of Psychology* 52: 397–422.

Mauss, Marcel. 1990. *The Gift: The Form and Reason for Exchange in Archaic Societies*. New York: Norton.

Mead, W. R. 1968. *Finland*. New York: Praeger.

Mead, W. R. 1973. "The Natural Provinces." In *Finland: An Introduction*, edited by Sylvie Nickels, Hillar Kallas, and Philippa Friedman, 92–123. New York: Praeger.

Mead, W. R. 1989. "Perceptions of Finland." In *Finland: People, Nation, State*, edited by Max Engman and David Kirby, 1–15. Bloomington: Indiana University Press.

Meštrović, Stjepan and Hélène M. Brown. 1985. "Durkheim's Concept of Anomie as Dérèglement." *Social Problems* 33(2): 81-99.

Miller, Jacques-Alain. 2006. "On Shame." In *Jacques Lacan and the Other Side of Psychoanalysis. Reflections on Seminar XVII*, edited by Justin Clemens and Russell Grigg, 11–28. Durham, NC: Duke University Press.

Milne-Smith, Amy. 2016. "Shattered Minds: Madmen on the Railways, 1860–80." *Journal of Victorian Culture* 21 (1): 21–39.

Ministry of Social Affairs and Health. 2006. *Health in Finland*. Hyvinkää, Finland: Suoman Printman Oy.

Mitchell, Timothy. 1988. *Colonizing Egypt*. Cambridge: Cambridge University Press.

Muehlebach, Andrea. 2011. "On Affective Labor in Post-Fordist Italy." *Cultural Anthropology* 26 (1): 59–82.

Muehlebach, Andrea. 2012. *The Moral Neoliberal: Welfare and Citizenship in Italy*. Chicago: University of Chicago Press.

Myllyoja, Essi. 2012. "Kiltti Vai Ihan Vaan Marttyyri?" *Me Naiset*, September 18–September 22.

Nancy, Jean-Luc. 1991. *The Inoperative Community*. Minneapolis: University of Minnesota Press.

Nancy, Jean-Luc. 1993. *The Birth to Presence*. Translated by Brian Holmes. Stanford, CA: Stanford University Press.

Nelson, Robert H. 2017. *Lutheranism and the Nordic Spirit of Social Democracy: A Different Protestant Ethic*. Aarhus, Denmark: Aarhus University Press.

Nielsen, Morten. 2014. "A Wedge of Time: Futures in the Present and Presents without Futures in Maputo, Mozambique." *Journal of the Royal Anthropological Institute* 20 (1): 166–82.

Niemelä, Heikki, and Kari Salminen. 2006. *Social Security in Finland*. Helsinki: Vammalan Kirjapaino Oy.

Nietzsche, Friedrich. 1997. *Untimely Meditations*. Edited by Daniel Breazeale. London: Cambridge University Press.

Noys, Benjamin. 2012. *The Persistence of the Negative: A Critique of Contemporary Continental Theory*. Edinburgh: Edinburgh University Press.

Nykänen, Riitta. 2006. "Tanja Saarela Toipumassa: Masennus Katoaa Metsässä." *Apu*, September 29, 2006.

Nyman, Jopi. 2000. *Under English Eyes: Construction of Europe in Early 20th Century British Fiction*. Boston: Brill.

Ojanen, Maarit. 2006. "Remarkable Features of Finland Plus Some Common Misconceptions." In *Virtual Finland*, http://virtual.finland.fi/netcomm/news/showarticle.asp?intNWSAID=25001. Last viewed March 20, 2006.

Peltomäki, Päivi, and Kaj Husman. 2002. "Occupational Health Services and Maintenance of Work Ability at Workplaces." *Archives of Industrial Hygiene and Toxicology* 53: 263–74.

Pemberton, John. 1994. *On the Subject of "Java."* Ithaca, NY: Cornell University Press.

Petryna, Adriana. 2002. *Life Exposed: Biological Citizens after Chernobyl*. Princeton, NJ: Princeton University Press.

Picard, Max. 2002. *The World of Silence*. Wichita, KS: Eighth Day Press.

Pine, Jason. 2007. "Economy of Speed: The New Narco-capitalism." *Public Culture* 19 (2): 357–66.

Pines, Ayala. 1993. "Burnout: An Existential Perspective." In *Professional Burnout: Recent Developments in Theory and Research*, edited by Wilmar Schaufeli and Christina Maslach, 33–51. Philadelphia: Taylor & Francis.

Rantanen, Jorma. 1999. "Research Challenges Arising from Changes in Worklife." *Scandinavian Journal of Work Environment and Health* 25 (6): 473–83.

Raunio, Tapio, and Teija Tiilikainen. 2003. *Finland in the European Union*. London: Frank Cass.

Rose, Nikolas. 2019. *Our Psychiatric Future: The Politics of Mental Health*. Cambridge, UK: Polity Press.

Said, Edward. 1979. *Orientalism*. New York: Vintage.

Sakai, Naoki. 1997. *Translation and Subjectivity. On "Japan" and Cultural Nationalism*. Minnesota: University of Minnesota Press.

Salmela-Aro, Katariina, and Jari-Erik Nurmi. 2004. "Employees' Motivational Orientation and Well-Being at Work: A Person-Oriented Approach." *Journal of Organizational Change Management* 17 (5): 471–89.

Salovaara-Moring, Inka. 2004. *Media Geographies: Regional Newspaper Discourses in Finland in the 1990s*. Helsinki: Publication of the Department of Communication, University of Helsinki.

Sannemann, Ritva-Liisa. 2006. "Kontrolli Hiipi Työpaikoille." *Motiivi*. 13.

Sartre, Jean-Paul. 1992. *Being and Nothingness*. New York: Washington Square Press.

Schaffner, Anna Katharina. 2016. *Exhaustion: A History*. New York: Columbia University Press.

Schaufeli, Wilmar, and Dirk Enzmann. 1998. *The Burnout Companion to Study and Practice: A Critical Analysis*. Philadelphia: Taylor & Francis.

Scheper-Hughes, Nancy. 2001. *Saints, Scholars, and Schizophrenics: Mental Illness in Rural Ireland*. Berkeley: University of California Press.

Selye, Hans. 1956. *The Stress of Life*. New York: McGraw Hill.

Selye, Hans. 1974. *Stress without Distress*. New York: Harper & Row.

Shirom, Ari. 2003. "Job-Related Burnout." In *Handbook of Occupational Health Psychology*, edited by J. C. Quick and L. E. Tetrick, 245–65. Washington, DC: American Psychological Association.

Siegel, James. 2006. *Naming the Witch*. Stanford, CA: Stanford University Press.

Sihvo, Hannes. 1989. "Karelia: Battlefield, Bridge, Myth." In *Finland: People, Nation, State*, edited by Max Engman and David Kirby, 57–72. Bloomington: Indiana University Press.

Siltala, Juha. 2004. "Aggression at Work: From Structured Labour Market Conflict to Inter- and Intra-personal Tension." *Organisational & Social Dynamics* 4 (1): 46–66.

Siltala, Juha. 2007. *Työelämän Huonontumisen Lyhyt Historia: Muutokset Hyvinvointivaltion Ajasta Globaaliin Hyperkilpailuun*. Helsinki: Otava.

Singleton, Fred. 1998. *A Short History of Finland*. Cambridge: Cambridge University Press.

Smith, Anthony. 1999. *Myths and Memories of the Nation*. New York: Oxford University Press.

Smith, Vicki. 1996. "Employee Involvement, Involved Employees: Participative Work Arrangements in a White-Collar Service Occupation." *Social Problems* 43 (2): 166–79.

Snellman, Saska. 2001. "What If Nokia Comes Tumbling Down?" *Helsingin Sanomat. Business & Finance*, April 1.

Stenius, Henrik. 1997. "The Good Life Is a Life of Conformity: The Impact of the Lutheran Tradition on Nordic Political Culture." In *The Cultural Construction of Norden*, edited by Øystein Sørensen and Bo Stråth, 161–71. Oslo: Scandinavian University Press.

Suoyrjö, Heikki, Katariina Hinkka, Mika Kivimäki, Timo Klaukka, Jaana Pentti, and Jussi Vahtera. 2007. "Allocation of Rehabilitation Measures Provided by the Social Insurance Institution in Finland: A Register Linkage Study." *Journal of Rehabilitative Medicine* 39: 198–204.

Tarkka-Tierala, Hannele. 2004. "Ants of Our Lord." *Helsingin Sanomat*. www.helsing insanomat.fi/english.

Tervo, Mervi. 2002. "Sports, 'Race' and the Finnish National Identity in Helsingin Sanomat in the Early Twentieth Century." *Nations and Nationalism* 8 (3): 335–56.

Thatcher, Margaret. 1987. Interview for *Woman's Own*. Journalist Douglas Keay. September 23. Margaret Thatcher Foundation. http://www.margaretthatcher.org/document /106689.

Thompson, E. P. 1967. "Time, Work-Discipline, and Industrial Capitalism." *Past and Present* 38: 56–97.

Trägårdh, Lars. 1997. "Statist Individualism: On the Culturality of the Nordic Welfare State." In *The Cultural Construction of Norden*, edited by Øystein Sørensen and Bo Stråth, 253–85. Oslo: Scandinavian University Press.

Tweedie, Alec. 1898. *Through Finland in Carts*. New York: Macmillan.

Uusitalo, Hannu. 1996. *Economic Crisis and Social Policy in Finland in the 1990s*. Kensington, Australia: Social Policy Research Centre.

Valtiovaara, Ilkka. 1987. *Burnout. Henkin Pahovointi*. Helsinki: WSOY.

Verdery, Katherine. 1991. *National Ideology under Socialism: Identity and Cultural Politics in Ceausescu's Romania*. Berkeley: University of California Press.

Verdery, Katherine. 1999. *The Political Lives of Dead Bodies: Reburial and Postsocialist Change*. New Yok: Columbia University Press.

Viner, Russell. 1999. "Putting Stress in Life: Hans Selye and the Making of Stress Theory." *Social Studies of Science* 29: 391–410.

Virilio, Paul. 2006. *Speed and Politics*. Translated by Mark Polizzotti. Cambridge, MA: MIT Press.

Walicki, Andrzej. 1999. "Intellectual Elites and the Vicissitudes of 'Imagined Nation' in Poland." In *Intellectuals and the Articulation of the Nation*, edited by Ronald Suny and Michael Kennedy, 259–87. Ann Arbor: University of Michigan Press.

Wessely, Simon. 1990. "Old Wine in New Bottles: Neurasthenia and 'ME.'" *Psychological Medicine* 20: 35–53.

Whyte, Susan Reynolds. 2009. "Health Identities and Subjectivities: The Ethnographic Challenge." *Medical Anthropology Quarterly* 23 (1): 6–15.

Wilson, William A. 1976. *Folklore and Nationalism in Modern Finland*. Bloomington: Indiana University Press.

YLE Uutiset. 2004. "Conscientious Workers Burn Out." March 10, 2004, https://yle.fi /uutiset/3-5155338.

Young, Allan. 1980. "The Discourse on Stress and the Reproduction of Conventional Knowledge." *Social Science and Medicine* 14: 133–46.

Žižek, Slavoj. 1989. *The Sublime Object of Ideology*. London: Verso.

# Index

www.ingramcontent.com/pod-product-compliance
Lightning Source LLC
Chambersburg PA
CBHW030329270326
41926CB00010B/1553